PARTY AND FACTION
IN
AMERICAN POLITICS

RECENT TITLES IN
CONTRIBUTIONS IN AMERICAN HISTORY

PARTY AND FACTION
IN
AMERICAN POLITICS

The House of Representatives
1789-1801

Rudolph M. Bell

Contributions in American History

Number 32

Greenwood Press

Westport, Connecticut ● London, England

242908

Library of Congress Cataloging in Publication Data

Bell, Rudolph M
    Party and faction in American politics.

    (Contributions in American history, no. 32)
    Bibliography: p.
    1. United States. Congress. House—History
2. Political parties—United States—History.
3. United States—Politics and government—1789-1797.
4. United States—Politics and government—1797-1801.
I. Title.
JK1323 1789.B4   328.73'07'2   72-782
ISBN 0-8371-6356-0

Library of Congress Catalog Card Number: 72-782

ISBN: 0-8371-6356-0

First published in 1973

Greenwood Press, a division of Williamhouse-Regency Inc.
51 Riverside Avenue, Westport, Connecticut 06880

Manufactured in the United States of America

To Laura

CONTENTS

LIST OF TABLES

ACKNOWLEDGMENTS

I am pleased to acknowledge the many institutions and people who assisted me in producing this book. The City University of New York, the Rutgers University Research Council, and the New York Society of Colonial Dames provided generous financial aid. My intellectual debt is particularly great to Professor E. James Ferguson, who guided the study in its beginnings as a doctoral dissertation, and to Professors Richard H. Kohn, Richard P. McCormick, and Jackson T. Main. Paul Gilvary and Roy Vella probed with me the statistical methods used in the study. The staffs of the computer centers at City College, Metropolitan Life Insurance Company, and Rutgers University made as pleasant as possible the relationship between man and machine. Richard Mautner assisted greatly in converting programs to IBM-360 format. President Clifford Lord of Hofstra University allowed me to use the unpublished material of the Congressional Vote Analysis Project he directed, and Professor Jerome Clubb and his staff eased my use of the material at a time when it was not available on tape.

PARTY AND FACTION
IN
AMERICAN POLITICS

1

INTRODUCTION

James Madison believed that when "men exercise their reason coolly and freely on a variety of distinct questions, they inevitably fall into different opinions on some of them." Highly disciplined legislative behavior, he wrote, with the same names consistently appearing together on the calling of the roll, indicated a "party" ruled by *"passion* not *reason*."[1] The new Constitution, Madison hoped, would eradicate the party spirit that had characterized Congress under the Articles of Confederation. At another point, the Virginian argued that factionalism was as great a threat to republican government as blind party attachment, but he did not use the two terms, party and faction, interchangeably. Conspicuously absent from the well-known discussion of faction in Number 10 of *The Federalist* is any emphasis on cohesive voting on "a variety of distinct questions." Stemming primarily from "the various and unequal distribution of property," a factious spirit was part of man's nature; not even the Constitution could eradicate it. However, wrote Madison, the extensive array of interests, particularly economic interests, coexisting in a complex and geographically dispersed society would promote factions so lacking in duration and numerical strength as to render them unable to permanently endanger the greater good of society as a whole.[2] Whatever the shortcomings of Madison's predictions concerning patterns of legislative behavior, his analysis of party and faction serves as a useful starting point for a study of politics in the 1790s.

Historians agree that during the decade, at about the time of the Jay Treaty and President Washington's retirement, temporary political alliances gave way to highly disciplined, organized parties. There is much less agreement, however, concerning the details of this process, and a number of important questions remain unresolved. What factors motivated the alliances of the early 1790s? Did distinct, cohesive, consistent voting behavior occur even in the absence of party discipline? What role did sectional, regional, and local attachments play in the formulation of national policy? What was the relationship between the Federalists and Republicans of 1800 and the legislative alliances of 1790?[3] The answers to these and other questions have been less than satisfactory in part because of an unfortunate lack of clarity in definition and use of the term "party." Madison's emphasis on legislative discipline addresses only one of the many facets of a political party.

Political scientist and historian William Nisbet Chambers, taking a very different approach, analyzes party in terms of structure, functions, nature of support, and in-group perspectives. Each of these four aspects of party requires some amplification. Structure involves a durable, relatively fixed linkage between political leaders and their followers. Clearly, structural parties began to develop during the 1790s. Although such significant phenomena as the convention and the primary election were unknown in the first party system, the essence of American party structure—geographically defined local units maintaining their independence—was firmly established by 1800.[4]

Chambers' functional analysis emphasizes six major roles of a party: nominating candidates for office, working for the election of these candidates, shaping opinion on political issues, mediating conflicts among groups within the party, providing effective government when in office, and coordinating activity within different branches and units of government. Parties had no monopoly on the performance of these tasks in the 1790s, but the successes and failures of Federalists and Republicans can be understood, at least in part, in terms of these functions.

An analysis of the support bases of early national parties is as essential as it is elusive. Simplistic assertions that all the well-to-do were Federalists and all the hard-working yeomen were Republicans have been shattered by a host of regional and state studies. Chambers notes that a party "may be built in Hamiltonian style, by joining parallel interests behind advocacy of a bold policy," but historians are far from agreement in isolating the interests that were in parallel. The rapid expansion of the support base of the Republican party, from its minority position early in the 1790s to a place of dominance unsurpassed by any other party in American history, is not yet adequately understood.

Finally, Chambers calls attention to in-group perspectives or, more precisely, to "a distinguishable set of perspectives, or ideology, with emotional overtones." The charismatic qualities of Thomas Jefferson and Alexander Hamilton contributed to the emotion-charged atmosphere in which parties developed, as did the explosive nature of issues such as the Whiskey Rebellion, the Jay Treaty, and the XYZ Affair. Yet the ideological differences between Federalists and Republicans remained somewhat amorphous and intangible, especially when applied below the level of a handful of leaders.

In-group perspective and a common ideology did not provide a durable, meaningful bond between North Carolina's Presbyterian backcountry and New York City's wealthy merchants.

Chambers concludes, then, by defining party as an organization seeking a regular, predictable, and successful means of achieving elective office and of using that office to promote the general welfare by responding to interest-group pressures on government.[5]

His analytic model appears to be far removed from James Madison's attack on party as the rule of *"passion* not *reason"* resulting in dangerously polarized voting on a variety of issues. And yet both views contribute to a workable definition of party. Chambers analyzes parties primarily in "constituent" terms—that is, he sees the function of American political parties as the providing of a peaceful, stable means of deciding which individuals and groups shall control the regime. Madison, on the other hand, placed primary emphasis on the policy outputs of a party. He saw office-holding not simply as power for the sake of power but as an opportunity to legislate and enforce policy decisions. To use Theodore Lowi's phrase, Madison feared "responsible" parties that would combine electoral success with a meaningful program of action to the potential detriment of society as a whole.[6] History inverted Madison's fears and produced parties that, as Chambers and Lowi note, do not implement policy positions. The final irony, however, is that the very strength of America's constituent party system often paralyzes government in its function of promoting general welfare through the taking of positive policy steps and, in the end, the function of promoting general welfare is what Madison had in mind in advocating adoption of the Constitution.

Parties play a dominant role in American government; the role of government is to "promote the general welfare." Fulfillment of this role requires the advocacy and implementation of policy decisions. Whenever parties do not offer meaningful policy alternatives, one of three situations exists: general welfare is a reality; general welfare is not being promoted; government is promoting general welfare through some vehicle other than party. During the 1790s, shifting combinations of interest blocs (Madison might have termed them factions had he not been so actively involved in leading certain of these interest blocs) dominated the legislative process and offered significant policies intended to provide for the general welfare. These factions were highly successful in establishing the framework within which America expanded, economically and geographically, throughout the next century.

The relationship between party and faction in American politics is complex and unstable. Although each has its own goals, leaders and followers, strategy and tactics, the two are seldom totally independent. Many of those individuals involved in the factional disputes of the early 1790s turned to party as a means of pursuing policy goals. On the other hand, even the most unprincipled party men of the late 1790s, John Beckley and Aaron Burr, were not devoid of interest in policy. However, lasting confluence between the party goal of achieving power and the factional goal of implementing a particular policy is rare. America's two-party system has usually been strongest when contesting for power, weakest when engaging in ideological dispute. Factionalism has been most pronounced among those individuals and groups who are least concerned with attaining power through the elective process. Lack of concern with the elective process occurs in areas dominated by a single party, in lame duck office-holders, in deferential political systems, and among groups with no meaningful chance of controlling the regime. Primary concern with the elective process and, therefore, avoidance of factious policy positions, occurs in areas of keen and close party competition, in office-holders facing an election fight, and in mass-based, democratic, egalitarian political systems.

Before entering upon a detailed examination of this generalization, several caveats may be noted. The definitions of party and faction set forth above may not be acceptable to some readers. Party is used to refer to a durable organization that engages in the electoral process for the purpose of attaining control of the regime. Once in power, it must promote the legitimacy and continuation of the regime, but it need not necessarily pursue particular policy positions. Faction is used to refer to groups, of varying duration, strength, and motivation, that form within the political system in order to advocate and implement policy positions.

A more important objection to the pages that follow may be the absence of any treatment of party and faction at the state and local level. The objection has merit; studies of the relationship between party and faction at local levels will surely yield significant results. However, national politics is not the sum of a series of local political situations; the Republican party of 1800, for example, was not simply the sum of sixteen state Republican organizations. There is even less relationship between the national factions that formed during the 1790s in response to national issues and the local factions that existed for very different reasons. A variety of factors make it unlikely that findings at the national level can be applied to local circumstances or vice versa. The major factor is that the tendency toward deferential politics increases radically from the local to the national level. The physical remoteness of the federal government, the complexity and universality of national issues, the high ratio between electors and elected, and the inaccessibility of national office-holders combine to instill a pervasive attitude of deference on the part of the same electorate that confidently makes its opinion felt on local issues. This attitude of deference in the electorate promotes factionalism by assuring the elected that the policy positions they take are not strongly related to their chances of re-election.

Also notable for its absence in this study is any systematic attempt to analyze the views of the general electorate. Efforts to determine the attitudes of the common man toward major historical events and trends are underway; fruitful results are likely in such unexplored territory. Obviously one wishes to know the attitude of the people toward Hamilton's economic plans, the threats of war with England and France, and the election of Thomas Jefferson. However, such information is not essential for an understanding of the relationship between party and faction at the national level. A political system operates within, and usually reflects, the society of which it is a part. Legislators reach policy decisions in terms of the way they perceive society, and such decisions do have a measurable impact on the society. But the society as a whole does not formulate alternatives and reach decisions except at so general a level as to blur any possible distinction between party and faction. Rather, an office-holder responds to his individual view of society, one that is often distorted and incomplete, by adopting one policy alternative rather than another. The power to determine what policies, if any, shall be devised and implemented within the national political system effectively resides within the office-holders, who move freely so long as they support the legitimacy of the system. They are bound less by the sovereignty of the people than by their own perceptions of society.

That national legislators in the 1790s stayed within the bounds of acceptable levels of policy difference is demonstrated by the data in Tables 1 and 2. The absence of consistent change over time is the most noteworthy conclusion to be drawn from Table 1. In 1790 effective party machinery did not operate in most states and, in any event, none of the existing mechanisms were aimed at control of an ongoing national government. By the end of the decade virtually every state had developed an apparatus for contesting national elections, and national parties—Republicans and Federalists—played a major role in filling political offices. Despite the rise of this new, and in some quarters unwanted, phenomenon of party, nearly two-thirds of all incumbents were consistently returned to office. Since non-returnees include those who resigned voluntarily, moved on to other posts, and so forth, the figures indicate that the electorate did not generally oppose strongly the actions of its representatives.

Table 1. **Rates of Return of Incumbent Congressmen, 1790–1798**

			Percent Returned			
State	*1790*	*1792*	*1794*	*1796*	*1798*	*Average*
Connecticut	60	80	57	86	86	74
Massachusetts	75	75	43	71	71	71
New Hampshire	67	67	75	50	75	67
Rhode Island	100	100	100	50	50	75
Vermont	–	100	50	0	100	63
Delaware	100	0	100	0	100	60
New Jersey	25	100	40	40	20	43
New York	50	33	50	60	50	50
Pennsylvania	50	88	46	77	69	65
Georgia	33	33	50	100	0	42
Kentucky	–	100	100	0	100	75
Maryland	17	50	88	63	63	58
North Carolina	60	40	50	70	50	55
South Carolina	80	20	67	50	67	56
Tennessee	–	–	–	0	100	50
Virginia	90	89	79	53	57	70
HOUSE TOTAL	60	66	63	60	62	62

Consistency over time occurred despite large differences in rate-of-return among the various states. Election laws had only a marginal and temporary effect on the ability of an incumbent to retain office. Both Georgia and New Jersey had extremely low rates-of-return and both states elected their congressmen at large rather than by district. Changes in election laws—from at large to district in Pennsylvania for the 1796 election, from four districts to fourteen districts for Massachusetts in the same year, and from at large to districts in New Jersey for the 1798 election—were accompanied by sharp drops in rates-of-return. However, Kentucky, Connecticut, and Rhode Island also employed statewide general tickets and their tendencies to re-elect incumbents were well above average. The evidence indicates, then, that election laws were not critical in determining rates-of-return over extended periods of time.

Strength of party machinery is also inadequate as an explanation of the substantial variance in rates-of-return among congressmen from different states. Assessments of party strength in particular states are difficult to make with certainty, but it is widely agreed that New York and Pennsylvania developed effective party mechanisms earlier than any other states. Yet exhaustive studies by Alfred Young on New York and Harry Tinkcom on Pennsylvania do not correlate party activity with the widely differing rates-of-return in the two states. Georgia, New Jersey, North Carolina, South

Carolina, and Maryland had lower than average tendencies to re-elect congressmen, but generalizations cannot be made about their party systems that
do not apply also to states with high rates-of-return.

The best explanation for variance in rates-of-return lies in close study of
the degree of pluralism within particular states and districts. Legislation
governing the election process and the development of party apparatus modified the exterior form of political campaigns, but they did not alter the essence of the legislative function as envisioned by Madison in *The Federalist.*
Socio-economic interests vied for control of the regime through the process
of electing representatives. In areas where conflicting interests were in close
balance, rates-of-return were low. In areas dominated by a single interest,
incumbents were relatively assured of re-election, even though seniority did
not carry with it the extra-constitutional power currently exercised by
congressmen of long standing.

Analysis of elections during the decade reveals the extent to which they
modified policy outputs, and focuses on differences, if any, in the ability of
the various voting blocs that existed during the period to achieve re-election.
In Table 2 the votes of first-term congressmen are compared with those of
returning delegates. A cohesion difference of more than 34 percent occurred

Table 2. Cohesion Differences: Freshmen Against Returnees, 1791–1801

Congress	0–14%	Range of Cohesion Differences 15–24%	25–34%	35–100%
		Number of Roll Calls in Each Range		
Second	62	27	8	5
Third	50	14	5	0
Fourth	73	9	1	0
Fifth	128	24	1	0
Sixth	88	7	1	0
TOTAL	401	81	16	5

only five times out of a total of 503 roll calls recorded by the House. This
absence of polarized voting by freshmen against returnees leads to the conclusion that the infusion of new members did not modify polity outputs
and that particular voting blocs did not achieve overwhelming victories in
any of the five elections under consideration. Despite an occasional hotly
contested district race, the electorate did not control the direction of
national policy in the 1790s. Explanation of the shift from faction to
party lies elsewhere.

Finally, the chapters that follow rely heavily on numbers, on the counting of votes. The reduction of ideas to a numerical formula, no matter how

complex the mathematics employed, tends to blunt the fine points of discussion. A computer cannot read between the lines of a letter or capture the emotions of heated debate. Added to the limitations of the computer are those natural to the historian; he must be content with the data that exist. No roll calls were recorded on the tariff bill of 1789, funding in 1790, or taxing stock transfers in 1793. These are only several of the many gaps that exist, and while they do not make conclusions impossible, they do create special problems. Computers can also be used to provide a thin veneer of scientific jargon for purely subjective ruminations. Errors in basic assumptions can invalidate an otherwise well-formulated analysis. Notwithstanding these shortcomings, however, the quantitative approach can add a degree of objectivity to the historian's quest for answers that is not possible using the more traditional methods. The success of quantification is directly related to two factors—the degree to which the subject matter can be reduced to numbers while maintaining its full meaning, and the care with which assumptions are made, controlled, and compensated for.

The laboratory for the present effort to identify national political blocs is the House of Representatives. The data put under the microscope are the votes of each member of the House on every roll call recorded in the years 1789 through 1801, or the First Congress, first session, through the Sixth Congress, second session. The House of Representatives was chosen primarily because it was the largest national institution, subject to local interests, that operated throughout the period. The district represented by a particular delegate can be identified and, with some reservations, votes can be taken to represent the position of the district. The smaller size of the Senate and the lesser availability of detailed proceedings and roll calls in that body make it less useful as a vehicle for quantitative analysis. Study of the House is also more revealing than analysis of other national institutions because its entire membership was subject to change every two years, and in this election process the "will of the people" was more clearly visible than in other contests for federal office. It provided, more accurately than any other body, the common arena necessary for party development.

The problem of assumptions is especially critical in quantitative analysis because ultimate results are so heavily determined by the initial method used. The assumptions made in the present effort are justified by the nature of the data and have been rigidly controlled.

The first methodological axiom is that all roll calls are given equal quantitative importance. This assumption need not, however, dissuade the investigator from casting aside certain votes on the basis that they are insignificant or redundant. In the normal course of parliamentary maneuver the same basic issue may arise several times, though often with interesting minor variations. In the First Congress, for example, the choosing of temporary and permanent sites for the federal government resulted in thirty-seven roll calls, or more than one-third of all those recorded. Therefore, any purely quantitative summary of votes will be dominated by this issue whereas, while these roll calls show an important sectional alignment, there are other questions, voted upon only once, that are of at least equal significance.

Although the initial raw data included all votes, the narrative that follows does not devote equal space to each roll call. The possibility of error in interpreting voting behavior cannot be eliminated completely, but it is rigidly controlled by the presence of the raw data. Let us return to the case of locating the capital. If all thirty-seven roll calls reveal identical patterns of divisiveness, the votes are redundant. However, if patterns change on one or more of the thirty-seven roll calls, then location of the capital cannot be considered a single issue; its component parts must be dealt with individually. In fact, there is a break in these thirty-seven roll calls. It occurred as a result of vote trading on assumption and shows Pennsylvania delegates voting, against their geographic interest, in favor of establishing the capital on the Potomac River.

Another major assumption made in this study, related to the first, is that all representatives are of equal importance. It is neither impossible nor undesirable, after letting the numbers project their cold and impersonal results, to look for conclusions about key men—James Madison, Albert Gallatin, Fisher Ames, Edward Livingston—but the votes of such giants must not be given excess quantitative weight, for they, like their colleagues, were representing one district, and all congressional districts were of equal size and voting power in the House. Earlier monographs have concentrated upon the influence of key men. Using voting patterns developed from selected roll calls, they contend that they have isolated groups such as Madison's followers, Randolph's Quids, and Clay's War Hawks. The difficulties with such an approach are that it may fail to determine whether the group existed before its leader came along, it may exclude roll calls where the group fell apart, and it may not continue to look for the group after the leader is gone. The group's association with the leader, in fact, may be temporary and incidental. In the maze of congressional votes, it is always possible to find the followers of anyone who is not in a minority of one. The problem is whether groups vote together primarily because of one man's leadership or because they adhere to the same principles. The principles upheld may have a notable spokesman, but this does not make him the *raison d'être* of the group. In this study the intent is, as far as possible, to neutralize the significance of the individual and instead to view events in socio-economic terms by emphasizing regional characteristics, economic backgrounds, and the district represented rather than the representative.

The third important assumption concerns the significance assigned to a vote. The present study avoids assignment of weights to particular roll calls or to the positions of individuals on ranges of issues. The immediate objection to such a procedure, and one that has some validity, is that not all opposition is of equal strength of conviction, that supporters range from lukewarm to avid, and that abstention can mean almost anything. Political science and sociology have provided several tools to assist in determining the degree of support for a particular question. One such tool is cluster bloc analysis, which involves relating roll calls to a broad question. For example, votes on separate parts of a tariff bill are clustered together and delegates are assigned positions relative to the entire cluster rather than separately considered in terms of their votes on each particular of the question. Cluster bloc analysis is sometimes modified by Guttman scaling, which arranges specific roll calls according to the degree of commitment reflected in voting upon them. Another technique, used in most of the quantitative work done on the period 1789–1801, is to select key roll calls, choose which side is Federalist or Republican, and then establish a level of consistency that will indicate party solidarity. Being on the same side 67 percent of the time has satisfied some historians; others argue for a figure as high as 80 percent. All these analytic tools have serious shortcomings.[7]

The method used in this study is designed to execute two basic principles. The first is that since no two roll calls involve exactly the same circumstances, roll calls should not be clustered or scaled before counting the votes. After all the results are in, separate votes can be related; the component parts, however, are always visible. The second principle is that the level of cohesion necessary to assert bloc voting varies from roll call to roll call. A party or faction does not exist unless it is more cohesive than the body of which it is a part. Since the cohesiveness (percent voting in the same way) of the House of Representatives was different on nearly every roll call, any blocs within the House must be defined relative to a fluctuating scale. No fixed number, be it 67 percent or 80 percent, can be justified on objective grounds. In the present effort, voting blocs are always defined in terms of their relationship to other combinations that vary from issue to issue. This definition of one bloc relative to another involves only simple arithmetic: calculate the percentage of affirmative vote for each of two groups and use the difference between the two percentages as an indicator of factional solidarity. A useful rule-of-thumb for categorizing these cohesion differences is that a difference of less than 35 percent, equal to less than two-thirds affirmative against two-thirds negative, indicates low factional activity; a difference of more than 34 percent indicates a significant degree of cohesive polarized voting.

The following chapters attempt to demonstrate several aspects of policy formulation by the national legislature of the United States during its formative years. Chapter 2 focuses on the extent of congruence between policy positions and regional attachments. The stress of sectionalism in antebellum America, of course, influenced the course of national government from its very inception. In the 1790s legislative blocs consistently drew disproportionate numbers of supporters from a single region. Yet sectional attachment does not adequately explain the shift from faction to party that took place during the decade. Moreover, the forging of innovative policy outputs often occurred only because delegates set aside parochial considerations.

The next four chapters deal with legislative behavior on those critical problems facing the new nation that commanded major attention in the House. These needs were: (1) to establish central government authority sufficiently powerful to shape the nation's destiny without infringing on personal liberty; (2) to transform the vast lands beyond the Appalachians from potential to actual wealth; (3) to reconcile and harmonize divergent financial interests into an integrated, expansive economic force; and (4) to secure a peaceful and profitable place in the world community. In 1789 each of these problems remained dangerously unresolved despite a decade of effort. But the next ten years saw such giant strides in all four areas that by 1800 the innovative, factional spirit of the Federalist era gave way gracefully to a period of consolidation under the Jeffersonians. Each of these four major issues interacted with the others, and roll calls invariably involved complicating factors. Nevertheless, these basic issues were clear and distinct sources of division.

A central theme of American politics between 1776 and 1800 was the effort to strike a proper balance between government authority and personal liberty. Anti-statism, buttressed by geographic isolation, enlightened emphasis on individual perfectibility, and a selective reading of English radical political thought, vied against an equally powerful persuasion rooted in the pragmatic necessities of the Revolution, the Puritan emphases on community and depravity, and the Lockian-Whig tradition. Those for whom the past was a struggle against tyrannical government found solace in local authority, states rights, and legislative primacy. Those for whom the future was threatened by mobocracy and anarchy argued for strong central government and executive supremacy. The effort to steer a course between anarchy and tyranny was a central source of congressional divisiveness in the 1790s.

Another critical dilemma facing Congress in 1789 was the nation's inability to translate the West from potential to actual wealth. A host of conflicting interests were involved: speculators clashed with settlers, farmers with trappers, slaveholders with yeomen, the national government with the states. The quest for immediate revenue, in part to help pay the national debt, conflicted with a longer range view of the West as a continuing source of wealth arising out of the productivity of its inhabitants. Proponents of law and order on the frontier opposed those who favored a vigorous and highly personal answer to the Indian menace. The traditional view that the problem of western lands had been solved during the Confederation period places too much emphasis on form of government and not enough on price per acre. Congress faced two basic frontier issues: one involved claims to the potential wealth of the West; the other centered upon the proper degree of federal control over remote settlers. Frontier representatives, behaving as an issue-oriented faction, united in support of low land prices, small minimum acreage requirements, liberal credit terms, and maximum control by westerners of defense efforts in their behalf. Throughout the 1790s, however, eastern delegates voted inconsistently, randomly, and incohesively. The result was a stalemate situation that held both speculators and settlers at bay, provided the government with revenue but not with a financial panacea, and retarded the rise of parties.

Still another source of divisiveness in the 1790s involved the reconciling of conflicting economic interests. The most immediate questions in 1789 were the securing of revenue for the new government and the handling of prior debts dating back to the Revolution. The country's credit had to be established, at home and abroad, without totally alienating any segment of the population. Since the debt to be paid rested in the hands of the few, and the payment of it would come from the many, this was no easy task. Even after the debt problem was resolved, deeper conflicts remained between large and small farmers, producers and transporters, sellers and buyers. Permanent balancing of these interests, of course, could not be achieved. Nevertheless, by 1795 the country's economic outlook improved substantially, and sharply polarized factionalism gave way to parties that had little economic basis and that avoided serious division over such issues. The final and most lasting source of divisiveness in the 1790s was the need to establish the new nation as a credible member of the world community. A major part of the issue was whether to adhere to the side of France or England. Many roll calls fell into this pattern, at least partially, ranging from a proposal to double duties on British tonnage in 1790 to an embargo on French shipping in 1799. However, in the years before 1795 events did not provide the substantial issues that cohesive factions thrive upon. Temporary alliances and suggestive divisions occurred but, for the most part, domestic concerns were paramount. From the time of the Jay Treaty until at least after the War of 1812, however, Europe played a dominant role in American politics. The question of England or France co-existed with another significant aspect of foreign policy divisions.

Voting blocs coalesced not only on the basis of being pro-French or pro-British but also on the issue of how to achieve both security in the New World and the expansion of market opportunities. The quest for security and markets led in turn to divisions over whether to sacrifice one to achieve the other, whether to ally with power, and whether to become more fully involved in European affairs.

The concluding chapter deals with the increasing impact, and ultimate triumph, of party needs over policy considerations during the 1790s, a decade that provides clues to the workings of America's political system at other times as well. From conflicts among issue-oriented factions, there resulted innovative and meaningful action on limits of government power, on balancing of economic interests, and on foreign policy. Motivated by a powerful need to fulfill the promise of a revolutionary vision, these factions fought with great intensity and offered real solutions for real problems. By the middle of the decade, the critical issues of 1789 were settled. That the solutions were still criticized must not obscure the more important fact that they were left intact. A period of consolidation and inaction followed, during which a two-party system developed. Constitutional frameworks, the expansion of the electorate, the decline of elitism, the increasing appeal of personalities, and the stress of sectionalism all contributed to the rise of a two-party system, but it was the resolution of issues by polarized interest blocs that permitted other factors to become operative and that allowed parties to function. Two-party systems thrive in the ideological vacuum that follows periods of intense factional conflict over issues.

Perhaps Morton Grodzins' conclusion that American parties are really anti-parties is overstated. Nevertheless, Walter Dean Burnham is correct in noting the "under development" of American parties in carrying out two essential political functions: one is nation-building through integration and priority ordering of conflicting interests; the other is policy making.[8] During the critical first years under the Constitution, cohesive, polarized, issue-oriented factions carried out these two functions (with considerable success if time is a proper test), and only when their task was completed and the revolutionary vision was apparently secured did parties rise to vie for power.

2

POLITICS AND SECTIONALISM

The policy outputs of the federal government of the United States have always reflected the stresses of sectionalism. Cultural and economic groups circumscribed, coincidentally or otherwise, within politically recognized geographic units have exercised considerable influence within the legislative process. Part of the source of this influence is the Constitution itself; that is, the Constitution failed to provide for legislative delegates to represent potential constituencies transcending state boundaries and, consequently, denied power over policy to those interests that failed to achieve majority or at least "balance of power" status within a state or district, even if such interests constituted a substantial portion of the total population. For example, a careful reading of all debate in the House of Representatives for the 1790s fails to reveal any spokesman for the large number of property-less, unskilled workers that existed in every community but dominated none. On the other hand, protection of fishermen, a matter of great concern in two or three districts but a relatively minor problem on a national scale, received extensive consideration and generated positive legislation. Such an apparent imbalance in policy outputs is no surprise to students of American politics, but it does add an important dimension to any analysis of the impact of sectional attachment on legislative behavior.

Although theoreticians in the 1780s advanced and refined the concepts of representation, sovereignty residing in the people, and general welfare, the Constitution failed to check the power of state and regional interests (except through the conflict of one against another) and it provided no mechanism to assure a hearing for significant but geographically dispersed groups. As a result, only those interests with great influence in a particular district were represented in policy making functions. Sovereignty of the people became sovereignty of the represented and the general welfare became the welfare of those in whom sovereignty resided. Paternalism, elitist condescension, and some genuine good will led to occasional efforts to alleviate the plight of black slaves, or to offer some assistance to penniless land squatters, or to aid indigent orphans and widows. But these efforts were short-lived and half-hearted compared with the emphasis placed on the needs of interest groups fortunate enough to dominate geographic areas. Therefore, the following analysis of the impact of sectionalism on policy outputs, which relies heavily on roll call positions, necessarily understates that impact by accepting a body of data which excludes potential policy directions that simply never received any consideration. Nevertheless, it will be demonstrated that geographically defined interests exerted a major role in policy making throughout the 1790s.

Representatives from New England—Connecticut, Massachusetts (including Maine), New Hampshire, Rhode Island, and Vermont—were far more cohesive in voting than any region of similar size. The area was one of considerable internal diversity, but the legislative behavior of its national representatives seldom reflected a variety of conflicting interests.[1] Religion, transportation facilities, and occupational patterns all influenced New England's voting.

The rule of the Congregational clergy in Connecticut had seldom been questioned and the union of religion and politics became complete after 1795, when Timothy Dwight accepted the presidency of Yale and used that position to assure the election of candidates sworn to uphold law and order and fight deism.[2] Congregationalism was less significant, but by no means unimportant, in New Hampshire and Massachusetts. Boston had a thriving Anglican community and in both states Baptist and Methodist ministers successfully converted large numbers, so many as to lead President Dwight to encourage a revival of "true" religion.[3] According to alarmed clergy throughout New England, Vermont, especially the area west of the Green Mountains, had largely abandoned religion.[4] Although Rhode Island had strayed from the Congregational fold long ago, its religion was still a matter of political consequence. Given this diversity of religious affiliations and commitments among New Englanders, spiritual factors alone cannot account for the cohesiveness of the section's representatives in Congress.

Transportation facilities offer a better explanation for New England's solidarity. The Connecticut River provided easy access to markets for central Connecticut and Massachusetts, eastern Vermont, and western New Hampshire. The needs of Boston's citizenry and the aggressiveness of its merchants produced effective transport links through most of eastern Massachusetts and southern New Hampshire. Virtually all Rhode Islanders exchanged goods freely through Providence or Newport. On local issues the back country fought bitterly to curb the influence of Providence, but on a national level the interests of the two areas were similar.[5]

Not all New Englanders engaged in production of commodities for export but few were prevented from so doing by inadequate transportation. The region's solidarity on all legislative issues related to shipping and commerce reflected the actual and potential export business of the area.

Occupational patterns in New England surely influenced legislative behavior. John Adams was not alone in placing the interests of cod fishermen on a par with those of independence itself. Similarly, the maze of debate during the 1790s over tariff schedules and embargos had as much to do with protection of New England's shipbuilding industry as with national pride or revenue. But the major occupational difference between New England and the rest of the nation was the absence in the former of an export trade in locally produced agricultural commodities. Horses from Rhode Island and molasses from Vermont were insignificant compared with the volume and value of grain from Pennsylvania, tobacco from Virginia, and rice and cotton from South Carolina. The economy of every state outside New England was heavily dependent on the export of farm commodities. In New England, on the other hand, virtually all agricultural produce was consumed locally. Policy positions on taxation, commerce, even war and peace, reflected the unique character of New England's economy. Farmers produced for local consumption and merchants made their greatest profits in the re-export trade.[6]

Table 3 summarizes the voting patterns of all delegates from the five New England states in the period 1789–1801. The most important finding shown is the high level of cohesiveness of this geographic group; at least

Table 3. Cohesion of New England's Representatives, 1789–1801

Congress	Percent of Delegates Voting in the Same Way				
	50–59%	60–69%	70–79%	80–89%	90–100%
	Percent of Roll Calls in Each Range				
First	8	25	12	18	37
Second	10	16	17	31	26
Third	6	13	22	30	29
Fourth	7	13	19	40	21
Fifth	7	11	12	47	23
Sixth	4	3	7	46	40
TOTAL	7	14	15	35	29

four-fifths of the delegates voted in the same way on nearly two-thirds of all roll calls. Cohesion levels of 80 percent or more were reached with increasing frequency throughout the decade, advancing from 55 percent of roll calls in the First Congress to 86 percent of those in the Sixth Congress.

Less than 70 percent of New England's delegates voted in the same way on only one-fifth of the roll calls of the decade, as the incidence of low cohesion decreased slowly but steadily through time. The numbers in Table 3 outline the behavior of New England's delegates but the reasons for this behavior remain to be explained. Two factors account for the increasingly high cohesion of the five northeastern states. One is the economy of the region, a matter that has previously been considered and that explains the high absolute level of cohesion of the area. The increase through time in frequency of high cohesion is due primarily to a steady change in the nature of issues under consideration in the House.

Table 4 provides a summary of the content of roll calls recorded in the House of Representatives. Caution is in order against too rigid an acceptance of the classification of votes. Another researcher might use alternate

Table 4. Classification of Roll Calls, 1789–1801

Category	1st Cong.	2d Cong.	3d Cong.	4th Cong.	5th Cong.	6th Cong.	Total
Government authority	18%	29%	9%	10%	21%	12%	17%
Foreign policy	4	4	22	13	25	6	12
Army[a]	1	10	20	12	11	9	10
Navy[b]	0	0	4	17	11	5	6
Frontier	2	3	3	8	1	8	5
Location of capital	33	0	0	0	0	0	6
Domestic economics	32	35	32	18	16	15	24
Slavery[c]	2	1	1	1	1	2	1
Partisan politicking	0	1[d]	0	5	8	37	9
Miscellaneous and personal	8	17	9	16	6	6	10

[a]Hereafter roll calls on the army are included in the category "Frontier" or "Foreign policy," depending on their context. In general, before 1796 the questions of the size of the military establishment and the scope of its functions were in reality only a part of the larger problem of control over western settlers. After 1796 the army question became an important aspect of the foreign policy debate that dominated the Adams administration. Treatment of the army issue as a separate entity would lead to the incomplete conclusion that the nature of support for expanding the military establishment changed in 1796; rather, it was the role of the army itself that changed. Throughout the period army issues also involved "government authority," and this involvement will be considered later.

[b]Hereafter roll calls on the navy are included in the category "Foreign policy" for reasons that are considered in depth in Chapter 6.

[c]Slavery was not a deeply divisive issue in the 1790s. Hence, the handful of roll calls dealing with black Americans are hereafter included in the category "Miscellaneous and personal." For example, Absolom Jones' petition for some consideration of the plight of black Americans met defeat by a vote of 87 to 1.

[d]To avoid distortion this single roll call is hereafter included under the category "Miscellaneous and personal."

categories and might occasionally assign roll calls differently. Nevertheless, the pattern for the decade is clear: in the early years delegates dealt with a variety of different issues, but after 1795 foreign policy questions dominated legislative behavior. From the time of the Jay Treaty on, roll calls dealing with the army and the navy may properly be considered as part of the larger issue of foreign policy, and the numerous votes taken on the Alien and Sedition Acts (which are classified in Table 4 under "Government authority") were in some measure treated as foreign policy questions. Thus, from the Fourth Congress on, domestic problems were debated less frequently and most positive action concerned the nation's relationship with Europe. On this issue New England's delegates were of one mind; diversity within the region was overshadowed by the need to sustain the area's economic growth through protection and expansion of commerce and shipbuilding. Naval preparedness, whether the potential enemy was Great Britain in 1794 or France after 1796, brought important economic benefits to New England, a fact that was not lost on its delegates. Beyond this, representatives from the northeast united to promote policies intended to protect American commerce, the major portion of which happened to be with the British Empire. Naval skirmishes with France were a worthwhile price to pay for the rapid expansion of business with England that flowed from the Jay Treaty and events in Europe. Because New England's commercial profits came largely from shipping charges rather than from the value of the goods being transported (which more often than not were produced elsewhere), perilous voyages proved to be extremely rewarding. Men of commerce argued for the arming of merchant vessels, knowing that such action would escalate French response. Their patriotism was reinforced by the knowledge that the resulting increased risk of loss of goods would be accompanied by higher shipping rates. Factional behavior on foreign policy questions will be considered in detail subsequently, but for the present it is sufficient to note the correlation between the rising level of cohesion of New England's delegates and the increasing frequency of roll calls dealing with commerce.

Representatives from the South were far less cohesive than New England's delegates.[7] The major slaveholding states—Georgia, South Carolina, North Carolina, Virginia, and Maryland—did not, during the 1790s, present a consistent or united position. Once the issue of location of the capital was settled, divergent interests in the South came to the foreground in the legislative arena. The contest was not simply between Federalists and Republicans, or planters and yeomen, or coastal magnates and back country dirt farmers; rather, a variety of interests interacted with each other in complex and changing ways. Complexity of interest, combined with the South's long tradition of deference in politics, produced relatively low regional cohesion throughout the decade.[8] This is not surprising. The facile association of sectionalism with the South arises from the Civil War, but it required an issue of the magnitude of slavery to obscure diversity of interest within the region, and questions still remain concerning the degree to which the coming of the Civil War actually obliterated, even temporarily, such diversity. During the 1790s slavery was not an issue of sufficient consequence to alter southern voting patterns.

Although it is beyond the scope of the present study to survey all the interests that existed in the South, a brief consideration of those that appeared in the process of national policy formulation is in order. The most salient factors in southern voting that are geographically definable include transportation facilities, land security, mode of agricultural production, and pattern of state and local government. Much has been written on the decisive influence of river transportation.[9] Delegates from districts with easy access to markets, for obvious reasons, tended to support legislation aimed at promoting commerce. As a result, as has been shown, representatives from New England, an area of minimal variance in market accessibility, voted cohesively on foreign policy questions. In the South, on the other hand, the ability to reach export centers varied widely, and delegates had correspondingly diffuse attitudes on commercial issues. The western half of North Carolina, the southern and western portions of Virginia, and the back country of South Carolina elected delegates who usually opposed extensive aid to export interests.[10] For opposite reasons delegates from Charleston, Baltimore, and Alexandria, and from districts within range of such major river systems as the Potomac, James, and York united to support protection of commerce. As will be discussed later, these interests cut across party lines.

Land security was a source of great divisiveness in the South, more so than in New England or in the Middle Atlantic states. Clashes between speculators and settlers raged throughout the western portions of Virginia, North Carolina, and Georgia and frequently surfaced at the national level. The best known of these conflicts, concerning the machinations of Georgia's state legislature and the Yazoo Land Grant Company, ultimately resulted in a severe rupture within Jefferson's party.[11] A host of less well-known incidents combined to turn many contests for congressional seats into struggles over land holdings. The careers of John Steele and Thomas Blount of North Carolina and James Jackson and Benjamin Taliaferro of Georgia reflected the pressures of their involvement in land speculation most clearly, but other southwestern delegates were also affected by such considerations. Squabbles and even court litigation over land titles, of course, were common in all areas of the country, but only in the South did conflict over land holdings affect voting on national policy.[12] The other aspect of land security that modified the legislative behavior of southern delegates was the desire of some districts for federal assistance in the battle being waged against Indians. In general, areas bordering Indian lands— Georgia, Tennessee, western North Carolina, Kentucky, and western Virginia—sought maximum aid and minimum control. Delegates from these districts voted for monetary appropriations but against the stationing of federal troops. They vehemently opposed all efforts to restrict the right of western settlers to bear arms in Indian territories and otherwise to carry out obviously provocative defensive measures. The paradoxical position of southwesterners, in favor of national power strong enough to provide protection from Indians but weak enough to allow remote settlers to attack Indians without fear of legal restraint, conflicted with the position of southeastern delegates, who favored maximum control over western settlers at minimum expense. Thus, disputes over land, between rich whites and poor whites and between whites and Indians, generated deep divisions and correspondingly low cohesion among southern delegates.

Modes of agricultural production, which were in a transitional phase during the 1790s, varied widely in the South. At the most general level, a distinction may be drawn between districts, dominated by large plantations and dependent upon slave labor, which raised crops for the export market and, on the other hand, areas populated by small farmers and employing slaves only incidentally if at all, which produced for local markets and were relatively self-sufficient. Delegates from both types of districts were likely to acknowledge membership in the Republican party, but they quickly parted on policy questions. Efforts to generate revenue through excise taxation and protection of commerce were two issues on which southern delegates divided according to dominant mode of production. Self-sufficient areas saw little need for imposing domestic taxes in order to promote someone else's export business and their delegates voted accordingly.

Local government traditions and practices also differed substantially from one part of the South to another. Recently settled areas, mostly at some distance from the coast, tended to choose delegates inclined toward a negative view of government. Long and bitter experience in struggling against colonial and state governments controlled by eastern interests made westerners wary of a new national power that also appeared to be dominated by hostile groups. And yet remote areas needed government assistance in their quest for land security and improved access to markets. The resulting dilemma produced such curious inconsistencies as passage by Kentucky's state legislature of resolutions against the Alien and Sedition Acts and, immediately thereafter, a swing throughout the South toward the Federalist party, in part because of the secession threat implied by the Kentucky Resolutions. Eastern interests had long been the chief beneficiaries of increased power for colonial and state governments; this happy experience made delegates from coastal counties receptive to expansion of federal authority. However, these same representatives, alarmed by certain federal policies, entered a process of re-evaluation that caused many to follow James Madison into opposition to the administration. The respective voting patterns of southeasterners accustomed to strong government but afraid of its practice on a national level and of southwesterners imbued with a negative attitude toward state power but enticed by the possibility of badly needed assistance were somewhat inconsistent. In combination they account for the low cohesion of southern delegates on a variety of roll calls.

Table 5 summarizes the votes of all representatives from the South for the period 1789–1801.[13] The contrast between the voting behavior outlined in Table 5 and that of New England's delegates (see Table 3) is striking. Four-fifths of the South's representatives voted in the same way on

Table 5. Cohesion of the South's Representatives, 1789–1801

Congress	Percent of Delegates Voting in the Same Way				
	50–59%	60–69%	70–79%	80–89%	90–100%
	Percent of Roll Calls in Each Range				
First	17	18	26	20	19
Second	15	27	21	16	21
Third	29	23	13	19	16
Fourth	18	18	18	32	14
Fifth	12	27	33	18	10
Sixth	33	39	16	6	6
TOTAL	21	25	21	19	14

only 33 percent of all roll calls (versus 64 percent for New England). Less than 70 percent of southern delegates voted in the same way on 46 percent of all roll calls (for New England the figure was only 21 percent). The pattern for the decade was not consistent; the South did not move steadily toward high cohesion, as did New England, nor did it drift continuously toward low cohesion. The complexity of interests that existed in the South and the variance in frequency of issues during the decade (see Table 4) combined to produce low and unpredictable levels of cohesion for the region as a whole.

Lest the emphasis on divisiveness within the South be misconstrued, it should be noted that cohesion differences between New England and the South were great throughout the first six Congresses. Table 6 portrays these differences. The primary source of substantial polarization was New England's increasingly high cohesion, but the South did not divide so sharply

Table 6. Cohesion Differences: South Against New England, 1789–1801

Congress	Range of Cohesion Differences			Mean
	0–34%	*35–64%*	*65–100%*	
	Percent of Roll Calls in Each Range			
First	41	20	39	47
Second	32	40	28	49
Third	26	52	22	47
Fourth	34	44	22	45
Fifth	21	62	17	49
Sixth	23	72	5	44
TOTAL	29	49	22	47

against itself as to give the appearance of taking no stand at all. Cohesion differences clustered around a figure of 47 percent, indicating that an average of more than three-fourths of New England's representatives voted against an average of nearly two-thirds of the South's delegates. The degree of polarity decreased over time but the frequency of significant polarity (cohesion difference in excess of 34 percent) increased. Thus, interest groups centered in New England gained some allies in the South, but at the same time they encountered more frequent opposition from that area. The result was a stalemate situation that intensified the contest for support, in elections and in the legislative arena, from the Middle Atlantic region. The quest for power over policy that took place within the House itself was occasionally less dramatic but often more consequential than the election process.

Certain reservations are in order concerning the term "Middle Atlantic region." It is necessary to delineate the area primarily because its delegates voted in such a way that their inclusion with New Englanders under the category "North" would distort an understanding of legislative behavior by obscuring the high cohesion of northeastern representatives. However, economic and social situations in the Middle Atlantic states varied greatly and use of the term here does not imply any internal regional solidarity. A close balance of interests, in the area as a whole and in many of its individual districts, existed throughout the decade. Merchants, artisans, export farmers, subsistence farmers, and western settlers all had spokesmen among the region's delegates. A brief survey of significant geographic characteristics will indicate why the area was internally divided and why it successfully exercised a critical balance of power between New England and the South.

Upper and western New York were economically underdeveloped during the 1790s. Delegates from these districts supported the expansion of federal authority when it promised land security but opposed massive aid to commercial interests. Representatives from the Hudson Valley, an area engaged in raising commodities for export, were torn between Hamiltonian arguments on the one hand and Jeffersonian faith in agriculture on the other. However, personal feuds and familial ties probably altered voting patterns more than the "rational" economic needs of the Valley. New York City was the scene of bitter party fights but its delegates consistently supported policies designed to promote commerce. Long Island, perhaps reacting against the overpowering influence of its urban neighbor, usually voted against any measure favored by New York City's delegate.[14]

New Jersey, aptly described as a barrel open at both ends, supported the Washington and Adams administrations until 1798, when Republicans fashioned a major upset and won control of the state's delegation. Although two of New Jersey's representatives—Aaron Kitchell and Abraham Clark—expressed occasional reservations, the state's delegation consistently voted for expansion of federal powers, increases in the size of the army and navy, Hamilton's economic policies, and assistance to commercial interests. Having suffered under the power of its immediate neighbors, New Jersey apparently preferred to shift the locus of authority to a larger and more distant body.[15]

Pennsylvania may properly be divided into three areas: Philadelphia and bordering counties; a tier of counties extending from York and Lancaster northeast to Northampton; and the northern and western portions of the state. The last was dominated throughout the decade by ardent opponents of virtually every policy proposed by the Washington and Adams administrations. The middle counties, on the other hand, were inclined to support programs that assisted commerce, promoted law and order in the West, and provided for energetic government. The southeastern corner of the state—Philadelphia and the counties of Chester, Montgomery, Bucks, and Delaware—was awed by the presence of the federal government in the immediate vicinity and for several years gave consistent support to administration policies. However, the area's commitment was never deep and it disappeared suddenly as the threat of war against France diminished and the inevitable transfer of the capital became a reality.[16]

In view of the complex maze of interests represented by delegates from the Middle Atlantic states, it is hardly surprising that cohesion levels for the region were low.[17] Table 7 summarizes the votes of all representatives from Delaware, New Jersey, New York, and Pennsylvania for 1789–1801.

Table 7. Cohesion of the Middle Atlantic's Representatives, 1789–1801

	Percent of Delegates Voting in the Same Way				
Congress	*50–59%*	*60–69%*	*70–79%*	*80–89%*	*90–100%*
	Percent of Roll Calls in Each Range				
First	31	19	24	13	13
Second	33	21	15	18	13
Third	36	29	20	9	6
Fourth	41	27	16	12	4
Fifth	38	38	12	8	4
Sixth	40	40	8	8	4
TOTAL	37	29	16	11	7

Except for high cohesion levels in the First Congress on the issues of locating the capital and the national bank and in the Second Congress on the question of loan offices, the region did not unite to promote any policy. However, its delegates did shift, slowly but steadily, from moderate support for positions taken by New Englanders to narrow support for positions held by a majority of southern delegates. Tables 8 and 9 give the figures that outline this trend. Except for a brief period during the Quasi-War, the

Table 8. Cohesion Differences: South Against Middle Atlantic, 1789–1801

	Range of Cohesion Differences			
Congress	*0–34%*	*35–64%*	*65–100%*	*Mean*
	Percent of Roll Calls in Each Range			
First	58	32	10	33
Second	67	26	7	29
Third	60	39	1	30
Fourth	83	17	0	23
Fifth	69	31	0	29
Sixth	100	0	0	9
TOTAL	74	23	3	25

frequency and depth of polarization of the Middle Atlantic states against the South decreased gradually until it disappeared almost completely during the Sixth Congress. At the same time, of course, New England increasingly found itself opposed by a significant portion of the delegates from the Middle Atlantic states.

Table 9. Cohesion Differences: New England Against Middle Atlantic, 1789–1801

Congress	Range of Cohesion Differences			Mean
	0–34%	35–64%	65–100%	
	Percent of Roll Calls in Each Range			
First	70	27	3	26
Second	69	26	5	27
Third	80	20	0	22
Fourth	66	33	1	27
Fifth	90	10	0	22
Sixth	23	75	2	41
TOTAL	66	32	2	28

The voting behavior of representatives from the middle states correlates closely with the policy outputs of the House of Representatives. That is, the policy supported by a majority of the delegates of Delaware, New Jersey, New York, and Pennsylvania was usually the policy adopted by the House as a whole. Table 10 proves this point by summarizing success patterns for New England, the Middle Atlantic, and the South. The general pattern for the decade was as follows: New England, exhibiting increasingly high cohesion, opposed the South, exhibiting decreasingly high cohesion, as the Middle Atlantic, shifting gradually from support of New England to support of the South, provided a narrow margin of victory for one of the two sides.

Table 10. Success Patterns: New England, Middle Atlantic, and South, 1789–1801

Section	Issue	Pattern[a]	1st	2d	3d	4th	5th	6th	Mean
						Congress			
NE	Govt. power	Successful	70	30	67	0	73	82	54
		Polarized	25	76	83	87	82	100	76
		Polarized Success	60	30	60	0	82	82	52
		Divided Success	73	29	100	0	33	–	47
	Economic	Successful	74	74	95	54	75	69	74
		Polarized	55	66	86	77	70	100	76
		Polarized Success	78	82	100	60	83	69	79
		Divided Success	69	59	64	35	57	–	57
	Foreign policy	Successful	75	50	44	72	58	80	63
		Polarized	50	75	72	68	68	85	70
		Polarized Success	100	67	31	76	74	76	71
		Divided Success	50	0	79	63	25	100	53
	ALL ROLL CALLS	Successful	63	56	68	54	65	78	64
		Polarized	58	64	70	71	73	88	71
		Polarized Success	64	59	69	61	77	81	69
		Divided Success	62	50	67	38	33	58	51

Table 10. (Continued)

Section	Issue	Pattern[a]	1st	2d	3d	4th	5th	6th	Mean
MA	Govt. power	Successful	85	64	67	100	82	27	71
		Polarized	25	34	33	0	7	9	18
		Polarized Success	100	91	100	—	100	100	98
		Divided Success	80	50	51	100	81	20	64
	Economic	Successful	83	83	77	77	83	54	76
		Polarized	43	26	18	23	12	8	22
		Polarized Success	93	100	100	100	100	100	99
		Divided Success	75	77	72	70	81	50	71
	Foreign policy	Successful	100	100	72	92	79	50	82
		Polarized	25	50	5	36	14	20	25
		Polarized Success	100	100	100	100	100	100	100
		Divided Success	100	100	70	88	75	38	79
	ALL ROLL CALLS	Successful	89	79	82	86	77	49	77
		Polarized	35	33	20	24	16	13	24
		Polarized Success	97	97	100	100	88	100	97
		Divided Success	85	70	78	81	75	41	72
S	Govt. power	Successful	75	77	67	100	37	27	64
		Polarized	35	73	83	100	38	9	56
		Polarized Success	100	92	80	100	73	100	91
		Divided Success	61	37	0	—	15	20	27
	Economic	Successful	52	54	22	85	50	54	53
		Polarized	46	29	14	23	37	23	29
		Polarized Success	69	79	64	100	68	100	80
		Divided Success	37	44	15	80	40	40	43
	Foreign policy	Successful	75	75	62	68	60	55	66
		Polarized	50	100	62	52	47	35	58
		Polarized Success	100	75	92	92	89	100	91
		Divided Success	50	—	13	41	34	46	37
	ALL ROLL CALLS	Successful	65	69	52	80	54	51	62
		Polarized	54	44	41	51	42	20	42
		Polarized Success	74	89	85	100	81	100	88
		Divided Success	54	55	29	59	34	39	45

[a]Patterns were calculated as follows:

Given that: (a) equals the percentage of roll calls on which at least three-fourths of the group voted in the same way and for the position adopted by the whole House;

(b) equals the percentage of roll calls on which less than three-fourths of the group voted in the same way and on which the majority voted for the position adopted by the whole House;

(c) equals the percentage of roll calls on which less than three-fourths of the group voted in the same way and on which the majority voted against the position adopted by the whole House;

(d) equals the percentage of roll calls on which at least three-fourths of the group voted in the same way and against the position adopted by the whole House, then: Successful = a + b   Polarized Success = $\frac{a}{a + d}$ Divided Success = $\frac{b}{b + c}$

Polarized = a + d

During the first ten years under the new government, the position of the majority of delegates from the Middle Atlantic became the majority position of the whole House as well on more than 82 percent of all recorded roll calls, a figure nearly 33 percent higher than that achieved by New England and the South. Then, during the Sixth Congress (the last two years of the Adams administration) delegates from the middle states moved sharply toward support for "southern" positions, thus incurring a dramatic but temporary decline in success that paved the way for the political alliance that brought electoral dominance to the Republican party after 1800. The high success levels of the South in the Fourth Congress and of New England in the Sixth Congress proved ephemeral in terms of policy outputs.

The figures in Table 10 allow further conclusions about the ability of the three regions to influence legislative behavior. The very fact that delegates polarized indicates geographically circumscribed interests and, as the data reveal, these existed most forcefully in New England but were present in some measure in other sections. Rates of "polarized success" refine the picture of overall success by focusing on matters that generated greatest sectional concern. The figures for the South, ranging about a mean of 88 percent from 74 percent to 100 percent, merit attention. They show that when southern delegates united, they had their way. This remained true throughout an era properly labeled "Federalist," which the South was not. One of the keys to explaining how policies were reached during this decade, then, lies in divisions among southerners, many of whom responded to issues along non-sectional lines (mean "polarized" level for the decade of only 42 percent) and thereby defeated the position taken by a majority of delegates from the region (mean "divided success" level for the decade of 45 percent). New England, on the other hand, though far less certain that unity would lead to success (mean "polarized success" level of 69 percent) expressed a sectional interest 69 percent more frequently than did the South. Delegates from the middle states coalesced infrequently and, after resolving the national bank and location of the capital issues, generally did so only on non-controversial matters. Although most often divided (mean "polarized" level of barely 24 percent), the majority of Middle Atlantic delegates nevertheless controlled policy outouts more effectively than New England or the South (mean "divided success" level of 72 percent, against 45 percent for the South and 51 percent for New England).

Figures for particular types of issues shed further light on expressions of sectional interest in the national legislature. New England polarized most frequently and was most successful on economic issues throughout the decade and on foreign policy matters, particularly commerce, after 1795. The South polarized least frequently and met defeat most often on these same economic issues. The forces that brought the two sections into open conflict three generations later may have been primarily economic; if so, data for the 1790s indicate the need for closer examination of the political economy of New England and of the balancing role of the middle states.

*   *   *   *   *

The preceding analysis demonstrates that legislative behavior in the 1790s was influenced by geographically definable groups. Policy outputs often reflected the aims of a particular section, which some believed to be to the detriment of the general population. New England was the most cohesive region of the nation; it ordered priorities and achieved its goals with greater success than did the relatively divided southern and middle states. However, no section was sufficiently powerful to inflict fundamental damage to the interests of another region nor was there any obvious desire to do so. Sectionalism was strongest in seeking a particular advantage that appeared to be of ultimate value to the whole society. Hamilton's plans to strengthen the nation's economy and Adams' effort to protect America's commerce clearly offered short-term benefits to some areas and not to others, but the immediate argument (and the eventual reality) concerned the general welfare. The most important outputs of the legislature, those that molded policy for decades to come, were not formulated solely by sectional interests. Indeed, the Middle Atlantic states, which shared virtually no common sectional interests, exercised a critical role in determining policy outputs. Four basic sources of divisiveness existed in the 1790s; these were the breadth and depth of federal authority, the West, economic policy, and foreign policy. Sectional attachment alone did not determine the decisions finally reached on any of these four issues. Rather, temporary legislative coalitions formed to forge policies that in each case reflected a compromise of regional interest. And the parties that arose later in the decade attempted, albeit with marginal success, to build on a national rather than a sectional base.[18]

THE LIMITS OF POWER

The fundamental difference between the Articles of Confederation and the Constitution was in the amount of power assigned to national government. The actual and potential authority of Congress under the Articles was limited indeed. The will of the majority could always be thwarted by a minority of one-third plus one; an innovative policy might require the unanimous consent of the states; executive and judicial functions were minimal. But under the new Constitution, a document that bristled with phrases that begged to be defined in the crucible of experience, potential power was greatly expanded. The legitimacy of the nation itself had been established before this date, and de facto existence in the world community had begun even before victory at Yorktown. Ultimate authority over western lands had been accomplished under the Confederation. By adopting the Constitution, the states had bestowed legitimacy on the new government. In summation, the continued existence of federal authority was not in doubt.[1] But the substance of that existence was a very real issue, all the more intensely debated because of widespread optimism about the government's longevity.

The problem of establishing limits upon the authority of the state was not unique to the United States in 1789. However, the past did not offer a ready solution to the dilemma; rather, it provided several alternatives, none of which appeared fully acceptable. Limits upon the power of the federal government came from four sources. First, the power of other nations in the world community circumscribed the authority of the United States. (This limitation upon power will be considered later in a discussion of foreign policy divisions.) Second, the strength of legitimate sub-states within the nation carved out areas of control and restrained federal authority. State governments were the most important of these internal units of power, but religious organizations and economic associations also exercised effective control over matters of potential concern to the national government. Third, rights and privileges reserved by tradition and law to individual members of the community constituted a major source for curtailing the state's power. Fourth, the state was limited by internal contests between its branches and among conflicting groups within each branch. Theoretical models offering a proper balance of the limiting factors upon state power, even including the Constitution, were of marginal utility in the real world of government operations. The rhetoric of the Constitution was remarkably similar to that of the Articles of Confederation, but the reality of the power assumed by national government under the two systems differed radically. Under the Articles, the ultimate determinants of limits of national power were the state governments; in addition, federal authority rarely touched upon individual rights and privileges. Although the Constitution implied similar restraints, actions taken during the 1790s brought about a fundamental change. While retaining verbal homage to restraints on power, the federal government assumed for itself the right to decide its own limits. Challenges to these limits would, in future, be met by persuasion if possible but by force if necessary. A basal shift in government authority occurred, whereby power exercised within limits set by external forces gave way to power circumscribed only by its own volition. The Constitution, implemented during the 1790s, provided the potential mechanism for this change. In the process cohesive, polarized groups formed to debate and decide this critical issue.

The earliest controversy exhibiting significant correlations that transcended purely local interests occurred over the various constitutional amendments submitted by the states. The general trend of these proposals was to limit the power of the federal government by including in the Constitution guarantees of individual rights and definitions of state powers. In the end the ten amendments constituting the Bill of Rights emerged from the debate; however, these were only a fraction of the amendments proposed by the states. A committee appointed to consider the merits of all suggested changes in the Constitution had reported only a limited number of amendments for action by the House.[2] This procedure was opposed by a small but determined group of delegates who wished to impose severe restrictions on the federal structure and who viewed the process of constitutional amendment as one means of achieving their goal.

The hard core of this group, clearly revealed on a vote to restrict the power of the federal government to levy direct taxes, consisted of nine representatives: Aedanus Burke, Thomas Sumter, and Thomas Tucker of South Carolina; Isaac Coles of Virginia; William Floyd, John Hathorn, and Jeremiah Van Rensselaer of New York; Jonathan Grout of Massachusetts; and Samuel Livermore of New Hampshire.[3] Unlike most of the Bill of Rights subsequently incorporated into the Constitution, this proposed amendment was designed to hamstring permanently the exercise of federal power. It was defeated by an overwhelming four to one margin. On other related roll calls, however, hard core supporters of curbing national government recruited enough allies to cause some consternation among their opponents.

Several roll calls reveal the dimensions of the controversy. On August 18, 1789, Elbridge Gerry suggested bringing before the whole House all proposed amendments that were not included in the committee's report.[4] The attempt was defeated by a vote of 34 to 16. Support for Gerry's motion was as follows: Connecticut two of five, Maryland one of four, Massachusetts two of seven, New Hampshire one of three, New York three of six, South Carolina three of four, and Virginia four of eight. From the vote it appears that in all regions of the country support existed for the principle of imposing further limitations on the federal structure. The same interstate pattern existed on the vital question of inserting into what became the Tenth Amendment the word *expressly*, as follows: "The powers not *expressly* delegated by the Constitution, nor prohibited to the States, are reserved to the States respectively, or to the people."[5] The greatest support for a defeated amendment came on the proposal to prohibit Congress from interfering with the times, places, or manner of holding elections of senators and representatives, and again, adherence was on the issue rather than along geographic borders.[6] The amendment specifying "speedy and public trial by jury" was opposed by many of the same delegates because of fear that it would impose limitations on state court functions.[7]

On all these roll calls, the vote indicated an interstate alignment and a corresponding lack of intrastate cohesion. The only exception was the state of Pennsylvania, whose entire delegation consistently opposed all limiting amendments. Alternative possibilities for explaining votes on these issues such as large states versus small, self-sufficient against dependent, or region opposed to region are not supported by the ballots.[8] The most logical tentative conclusion is that a minority faction interested in sharply limiting the power of the national government existed throughout the nation. This bloc was cohesive on every roll call dealing with constitutional amendments. The hard core of the group, as isolated on the tax question, was consistent throughout and included members from all areas of the country. They were joined, in varying degrees, by other representatives whose constituencies were also widely scattered. Even these additional supporters, although not as cohesive as the hard core, were not voting randomly. The same names—Elbridge Gerry of Massachusetts; John Page, Samuel Griffin, and Josiah Parker of Virginia; Michael Stone of Maryland; and James Jackson of Georgia—appeared numerous times. Table 11 shows the voting records of members favoring limiting amendments. All five roll calls dealing directly with constitutional amendments are included.

Table 11. Votes of Delegates Favoring Limiting Amendments[a]

Delegates	Consider all Amendments[b]	Expressly Delegated Power[c]	Interference in Elections[d]	Direct Taxes[e]	Trial by Jury[f]
HARD CORE:					
Aedanus Burke	Y	Y	Y	Y	Y
Thomas Sumter	Y	Y	Y	Y	Y
Thomas Tucker	Y	Y	Y	Y	Y
Isaac Coles	Y	Y	Y	Y	Y
William Floyd	Y	Y	Y	Y	Y
John Hathorn	Y	Y	Y	Y	Y
Jeremiah Van Rensselaer	Y	Y	Y	Y	Y
Jonathan Grout	Y	Y	Y	Y	Y
Samuel Livermore	Y	Y	Y	Y	Y
MODERATES:					
Elbridge Gerry	Y	Y	Y	N	Y
John Page	Y	Y	Y	N	Y
Samuel Griffin	Y	A	Y	A	N
Josiah Parker	Y	Y	Y	N	N
Michael Stone	Y	Y	Y	N	N
James Jackson	A	Y	Y	N	Y

[a]Y indicates affirmative vote, N indicates negative vote, and A indicates abstention. All delegates not listed in the table opposed limiting amendments more often than they voted for them.

[b]Additional supporters were Roger Sherman and Jonathan Sturges of Connecticut.

[c]Additional supporters were George Partridge and George Thacher of Massachusetts, and William Smith of South Carolina.

[d]Additional supporters were George Matthews of Georgia, Joshua Seney of Maryland, George Partridge and George Thacher of Massachusetts, Peter Silvester of New York, Daniel Hiester of Pennsylvania, William Smith of South Carolina, and Andrew Moore of Virginia.

[e]There were no additional supporters on this roll call.

[f]Additional supporters were George Matthews of Georgia and Theodoric Bland of Virginia.

The delegates included in Table 11, the hard core of nine plus the six who generally supported their position, were opposed by an equally cohesive and somewhat larger group of representatives who consistently favored expansion of central authority. These twenty-eight "nationalists" also drew support from all areas of the country, but they were strongest in Connecticut, New Jersey, and Pennsylvania.[9] They all voted against every defeated amendment.[10] They were, therefore, 100 percent cohesive in their opposition to limiting the power of government by constitutional amendment. The internal solidarity of each of these two blocs was extremely high—100 percent for nationalists, 100 percent for hard core anti-nationalists, and 70 percent for moderate anti-nationalists. Delegates in these blocs accounted for more than 80 percent of all votes cast on the question.

The amendment roll calls, then, clearly resulted in a sharp factional division in the House, based on the broad issue of imposing limits on the power of central government. The problem that remains is to determine whether these factions were cohesive on other issues as well. Defining the high and low points of their solidarity elucidates their *raison d'être* and tests the validity of the tentative conclusion that they were motivated primarily by attitude toward strong centralized authority.

Table 12 portrays cohesion differences between nationalists and anti-nationalists for all roll calls recorded in the three sessions of the First Congress. It is clear that the factions formed during the amendment controversy were not highly cohesive on other basic issues. To recall Madison's phrase, men were exercising their reason freely and were often coming to opposite conclusions. Cohesion differences were not significant (less than 35 percent) on nearly two of every three roll calls. However, the tendency toward polarity varied widely from issue to issue.

Only four roll calls involved foreign policy questions and of these

Table 12. Cohesion Differences: Nationalists Against Anti-Nationalists, First Congress

Issue	Range of Cohesion Difference			Mean
	0–34%	35–64%	65–100%	
	Percent of Roll Calls in Each Range			
Government power	15	40	45	58
Frontier	67	0	33	41
Location of the capital	92	8	0	16
Economic	63	34	3	28
Foreign policy	75	0	25	34
Miscellaneous and personal	55	36	9	31
ALL ROLL CALLS	63	25	12	31

only one revealed highly polarized voting by nationalists against anti-nationalists. This single occasion, a vote on final passage of the bill that established a Department of Foreign Affairs, merits closer examination. In the days preceding this vote an extensive debate took place, centering upon the question of whether officials appointed by the executive with the Senate's consent could be removed without the Senate's consent. After voting to allow the president to remove confirmed appointees without consent of the Senate, the House reversed itself and struck out the clause. But it did so on the assumption that the power to remove without consent was granted to the president by the Constitution's silence on the matter and, therefore, ought not to be a matter of legislative approval or disapproval. As Andrew Johnson found out seventy-eight years later, the legislative branch might again change its mind. But to return to the immediate situation, anti-nationalists overwhelmingly favored restricting executive authority in this case and their vote against passage of the bill reflected this position rather than any foreign policy consideration.[11]

Extremely low cohesion differences (under 35 percent on 34 of 36 roll calls) occurred on votes concerning location of the capital, an issue on which sectional attachments weighed heavily. Viewed in conjunction with the interstate composition of both nationalist and anti-nationalist blocs, this evidence confirms the conclusion that factionalism on the problem of limiting national authority was not even coincidently related to regional interests. Further support for this conclusion exists in the absence of high polarity on frontier issues.[12] Somewhat higher levels of polarization developed on economic issues as delegates increasingly set aside narrow personal or state interests and confronted the essential thrust of Hamilton's proposals which, of course, was to establish a firm base for an energetic, expansive national government. Conflict over assumption, excise taxation, and the national bank ultimately modified divisions over the related issue of restraining federal power. James Madison was only one of several delegates who moved, often reluctantly, from the nationalist camp to the side of its opponents. However, the shift was neither sudden nor total. Madison continued to support expansion of federal authority in all areas not under Hamilton's immediate jurisdiction; the Virginian thereby materially aided the administration's effort to establish a government limited in the breadth and depth of its power only by its own volition.[13]

The tentative conclusion reached earlier, that the blocs which formed during the amendment controversy were motivated primarily by their position on proper limits upon national power, is borne out by the relative lack of polarity that characterized the same groups on other issues. The substantial cohesion differences that existed between nationalists and anti-nationalists over restrictive constitutional amendments were never equalled on other matters. In future Congresses the proper extent of central authority was explicitly or implicitly voted upon many times. The groups that formed on these early votes, and the ideological commitments that caused them to polarize, continued to exert some influence.

Questions involving the assignment of responsibility within the federal government, although related to the larger issue of limits of power, generated somewhat different voting patterns. A majority in the House moved steadily to remove restraints on the breadth of national authority, but measures to limit executive power and to curb the pretensions of the Senate also received approval from more than half the representatives at the First Congress. Not quite faded memories of accumulated grievances against royal governors and George III, exacerbated by the Senate's prolonged concern with titles for addressing the president, caused some delegates to overlook the slight inconsistency involved in opposing restrictive constitutional amendments while supporting restraints on the chief executive.

The first clear test of sentiment came when the Senate amended a bill, dealing with frontier defense, to eliminate a clause specifying the number of state militia from Pennsylvania, Georgia, and Virginia that the president might call into national service. The Senate version provided for calling as many troops as necessary. Questions of states rights and even the competence of a remote national official to reach wise military decisions were raised in debate, but the crucial issue was the extent to which the House ought to share its control over the army.[14] The casting of ballots found New England backing the Senate amendment by seven to four, but the rest of the country refusing by more than a two to one ratio. The amendment met defeat by a vote of 25 to 16.[15]

The vote involved conflicting motivations. The issue of imposing law and order in the West affected some delegates and will be discussed later. Nevertheless, a pattern reflecting division over how much authority to give the president also emerged, and the interest groups formed during the amendment controversy reappeared. Of the ten voting delegates who had favored amendments limiting federal powers, nine voted against this extension of executive authority. Twelve of the sixteen votes in favor of entrusting the president with calling of necessary troops came from delegates who had opposed all limiting amendments. However, patterns on executive authority were not exactly the same as those on the larger issue of restraints on federal power. Limiting amendments were defeated, but a majority favored restrictions on the executive branch. Further investigation reveals the reason for this shift.

In the spring of 1790, during the second session of the First Congress, another measure concerning presidential power came before the House. It involved a Senate amendment to a House appropriation bill that provided for a blanket sum, to be dispensed by the president at his discretion, for the payment of all United States officers serving abroad. The original appropriation bill passed by the House contemplated the individual determination, each year, of the amount to be paid to every individual officer and member of his staff. The time that would be needed to decide such minuscule appropriations did not dissuade the House, which exerted its right to control the purse strings by a vote of 38 to 18.[16] Once again, the anti-nationalists, isolated a year earlier during the amendment controversy, sprang to the defense of the people. All nine hard core members of the group voted against the Senate proposition. The substantial total by which the House retained its version of the appropriation bill resulted from a split in the ranks of the nationalists, almost half of whom voted to fully enforce House prerogatives. Thus, two groups that were mutually exclusive and highly cohesive on the extent of central authority as a whole took different paths on the question of how to divide that authority between the executive and the legislature. Proponents of limited central authority remained cohesive but their opponents did not. This phenomenon, demonstrated early in the First Congress, was to reappear in later years on such major roll calls as the Livingston Resolution in 1795. Whenever it happened, the friends of strong government appeared weak and divided, but when more significant issues arose, their solidarity returned.

It is apparent that, far from being random or purely state oriented, voting patterns in the First Congress revealed the effective formation of interest groups on roll calls involving the power of the central government and the allocation of responsibility within it. In actions foreshadowing future developments, the House moved toward rapid elimination of external restraints on federal authority but divided more evenly and cautiously on the matter of internal checks on power.

Appearing initially during the constitutional amendment controversy in 1789, an anti-nationalist versus nationalist split dominated the early activity of the First Congress. The essence of that division was the anti-statism of proponents of limitations on the national structure. Their position had been fairly consistent throughout the 1780s; it involved an unwillingness to delegate power and a certain degree of trust in the political judgment of the people, especially those who owned some land.[17] Nationalists felt just as strongly that "mobocracy" was the greatest single danger to a free people and that constant restraints were needed to check the will of a capricious and unreliable majority. At the core of these restraints was a strong and remote central authority. Differing degrees of trust in the common man existed on both sides, but an essential difference in philosophy remained. A basic division over how much restraint to impose on the central government clearly continued into the Second Congress. The particulars of the debate changed but the factions that formed, and their reason for existence, were similar in both Congresses. However, the question of external limits on federal power did not arise in the Second Congress; rather, the House devoted extensive consideration to internal checks and balances. As noted previously, this issue attracted much wider support than could be obtained for external restraints. A majority of the delegates united on a variety of roll calls aimed at placing the House above the administration in the minds of the people and in the functions of government. The most significant of these efforts was the attempt to radically increase the size of the House itself.

The controversy over apportionment of representatives for the next ten years, based on the census of 1790, began on November 15, 1791. The Senate had proposed the allocation of one representative for each 33,000 inhabitants while the House pressed for a ratio of 1 to 30,000. The effect of the latter version would be to increase the size of the House to 120 members from the 105 planned by the Senate, with one additional delegate going to Connecticut, Delaware, Maryland, New Hampshire, New Jersey, New York, Pennsylvania, South Carolina, and Vermont. Two additional members would be assigned to Massachusetts, North Carolina, and Virginia. Georgia, Kentucky, and Rhode Island would receive the same number under either plan. On the basis of relative voting strength under the proposals, New Hampshire, Vermont, and Delaware would gain most under the House version, while New York, Georgia, Kentucky, Pennsylvania, and Rhode Island would fare better under the Senate plan.[18] Another consideration, extensively debated, was the degree of disfranchisement that would occur at differing ratios of the House and Senate plans. One might assume that this was a matter of simple arithmetic—dividing 30,000 or 33,000 into the total population of each state. The difficulty was that all suggested ratios left "fractions" of unrepresented citizens. Under the Senate version, districts would range in size from 55,539 to 33,158, while under the House plan high and low figures were 35,911 and 27,769.[19]

An important factor in the controversy, one which counted more than the maze of numbers and percentages, was the expressed desire of several members of the House to increase representation as much as possible and thereby bring the government closer to the people. Virginia's William Giles observed that, "It will only be by increasing the representation that an adequate barrier can be opposed to this moneyed interest." He reasoned, further, that "The strong Executive of this Government ought to be balanced by a full representation in this House."[20] On the opposing side, William L. Smith of South Carolina declared that he had "voted uniformly in favor of a smaller representation than that which was contemplated in the [Senate] bill, and in doing so, he had acted from principles, without any reference to the doctrine of fractions."[21]

A review of the votes cast shows that certain members were motivated by adherence to the principle of increased representation rather than its effect on their particular states. New Hampshire, Vermont, and Delaware, the states that would gain most in terms of strength of their delegations from the House plan, consistently voted for the lower Senate figure.[22] New York, Pennsylvania, and Georgia, which would have greater strength under the Senate plan, initially voted for the House version.[23] In states whose position would have been about the same under either proposal, voting patterns reinforce the significance of the principle of increased popular representation that underlay the controversy. Two groups emerged, each more than 90-percent cohesive in upholding its position on a series of eighteen roll calls. The cohesion difference between the two blocs, which together accounted for all but a handful of delegates, was 82 percent, indicating a continuation of the deeply divisive pattern of the First Congress on restrictive amendments.[24] However, the nature of the division had changed.

In the First Congress no correlation existed between sectional alignments and the split between nationalists and anti-nationalists. Voting on apportionment, on the other hand, resulted in a significant degree of regional polarization. Table 13 illustrates the cohesive positions of New England and the South. But the Middle Atlantic region, as it was to be so often during the decade, was the critical factor in determining the final resolution of this question. Pennsylvania and New York at first unanimously supported the ratio of 1 to 30,000 but when the Senate version came to a vote in the House, half the New York delegation and a majority of Pennsylvanians switched sides and nearly brought about immediate acceptance of the 1 to 33,000 ratio.[25] The result was a compromise whereby the Senate proposal was enacted along with an amendment requiring reapportionment,

Table 13. Votes by State on Apportionment, Second Congress

	Supported Virginia				Supported Massachusetts								
State	*18*	*15*	*12*	*9*	*6*	*3*	*0*	*3*	*6*	*9*	*12*	*15*	*18*
Connecticut						(3)XXXXXXXXXXXXXXX(12)							
New Hampshire						(1)XXXXXXXXXXXXXXXXX(15)							
Rhode Island						(2)XXXXXXXXXXXXXXXX(14)							
Vermont						(0)XXXXXXXXXXXXXXXXX(15)							
Delaware						(4)XXXXXXXXXXXXX(8)							
New Jersey						(0)XXXXXXXXXXXXXXXXXXXXXX(16)							
New York				(8)XXXXXXXXXXXXXXXXX(9)									
Pennsylvania				(8)XXXXXXXXXXXXXXX(7)									
Georgia	(18)XXXXXXXXXXXXXXXXXX(0)												
Maryland	(16)XXXXXXXXXXXXXXXXXX(2)												
North Carolina	(16)XXXXXXXXXXXXXXXXXX(2)												
South Carolina	(15)XXXXXXXXXXXXXXXXXX(3)												

effective March 3, 1797, in accordance with the House version. However, President Washington, who adamantly opposed the low House ratio, vetoed the bill and the compromise was lost. An attempt to override his veto failed, as numerous representatives refused to continue their earlier support for the bill in the face of its rejection by the president.[26]

The roll call taken on an amendment providing that "Presidential Electors shall be equal to the number of Representatives and Senators at the time when the President shall take office" is significant in understanding the motivation of voting blocs on apportionment.[27] There was a general belief that the strength of the existing pro-administration majority in the Second Congress would be diminished by the additional representation afforded under reapportionment. There was no question of opposing Washington, but sentiment against John Adams was widespread. The amendment was aimed clearly at the election of 1792. If there were to be 135 electors, as would result from reapportionment, instead of the existing 99, Adams might be dislodged from the vice-presidency. Although not formally organized, proponents of the amendment included the nucleus of opposition to the administration. From New England came four votes in favor of the increased number of electors—those of Elbridge Gerry of Massachusetts, Israel Smith of Vermont, and Nicholas Gilman and Jeremiah Smith of New Hampshire. Support of the amendment to the apportionment bill was only one short of unanimous in the South, the exception being William L. Smith of South Carolina. New Jersey opposed the amendment, while New York and Pennsylvania delegates split along lines of regionally defined economic interest. The increasing association between factional formation and geographic section that manifested itself on this roll call reflects the trend of the entire apportionment controversy. Two sides, one centered in New England, the other in the South, worked to gain the support of the critical Middle Atlantic region.

The voting blocs that formed during the apportionment debate also differed from the nationalist and anti-nationalist groups of 1789 in the respective degree to which they remained polarized on other issues. In a pattern that differs sharply from First Congress voting behavior, when polarity decreased as the issue shifted away from restraints on government power, Second Congress apportionment blocs continued to vote as cohesively opposed groups on a substantial variety of roll calls. Table 14 portrays cohesion differences between proponents and opponents of radically increasing the size of the House. The two groups, of thirty and twenty delegates respectively, voted against each other in significant numbers (cohesion difference above 34 percent) on two of every three roll calls. The opposing apportionment blocs failed to coalesce consistently only on frontier issues and on miscellaneous and personal matters. On foreign policy questions and on an extensive series of roll calls on economic issues, cohesion differences clustered near 50 percent, not nearly as high as the 82 percent figure reached on the apportionment controversy itself, but nonetheless a significant degree of polarity. Before formulating conclusions about changing voting patterns on the broad issue of balancing the need for strong and energetic government against the desire to protect individual liberties, it is useful to examine briefly some of the other efforts made in the Second Congress to impose restraints on federal authority.

Table 14. Cohesion Differences: Proponents Against Opponents of Radically Increasing the Size of the House, Second Congress

	Range of Cohesion Difference			
Issue	*0–34%*	*35–64%*	*65–100%*	*Mean*
	Percent of Roll Calls in Each Range			
Government power	10	26	64	67
Frontier	69	31	0	24
Economic	22	55	23	48
Foreign policy	25	50	25	47
Miscellaneous and personal	64	30	6	30
ALL ROLL CALLS	33	37	30	48

Divisiveness on the issue of how much power to allow the central government was closely related to the conflict over assignment of responsibility among the three branches. The Supreme Court had not yet assumed a major role, and so the executive branch was the chief target of those representatives who held that the national government should be limited and should express the will of the people, as extensively as possible, through its House of Representatives. Concerning George Washington himself, the only expressed differences were in degree of praise, but about his office there were sharper conflicts.

The apparent insignificance of an amendment proposed on March 22, 1792, to remove the president's name from coins and replace it with the word LIBERTY was of major symbolic importance to many members. John Page of Virginia succinctly expressed the issue:

> It had been a practice in Monarchies to exhibit the figures or heads of their kings upon their coins, either to hand down in the ignorant ages in which the practice was introduced, a kind of chronological account of their Kings, or to show to whom the coin belonged. . . Now as we have no occasion for this aid to history, nor any pretense to call the money of the United States the money of our Presidents, there can be no sort of necessity for adopting this idea of the Senate.[28]

The sectional character of votes cast on the amendment indicates that the increasing correlation between policy outputs and region was not necessarily one of cause and result. There was no possible advantage to any section in replacing G WASHINGTON with LIBERTY. All but two New Englanders, Jeremiah Smith of New Hampshire and Nathaniel Niles of Vermont, were opposed while the South voted affirmatively by 16 to 4.[29] It is of note that three of the southern exceptions, South Carolina's Robert Barnwell, Daniel Huger, and William L. Smith, opposed the remainder of their section on numerous other roll calls, as did the two New Englanders. The other southerner, John Brown, had already been elected to serve as a senator from newly admitted Kentucky at the next session of Congress; he may have wished not to offend his future colleagues. Voting patterns were becoming increasingly predictable, consistent, and interrelated. Further evidence of this trend appeared in the middle states, which split eight affirmative and six negative, along lines indicative of the interest groups that formed on apportionment and on economic issues.[30] Senate refusal of this House amendment necessitated a second roll call and again the same pattern developed except for Pennsylvania, where Thomas Fitzsimons and John Kittera, who supported the administration on a variety of other matters, switched sides and voted to put Washington back on the coins.[31]

For the moment, however, LIBERTY won and replaced Washington on the coins.

Division on the question of allowing the president to call out the militia without the express consent of the House and during its recess was similar to that over coins and also to the pattern that had occurred when the militia issue had been debated in the First Congress.[32] John Steele of North Carolina expressed western sentiment on the proposal when he attacked the possibility that one state's militia might enter another sovereign state.[33] Representatives from frontier districts—Georgia, the Yadkin Division of North Carolina, Vermont, Kentucky, and western Virginia—united against allowing this authority.[34] Once again, New York and Pennsylvania split on the issue, the coast in favor and the interior opposed.[35]

Opponents such as Elbridge Gerry warned against "vesting a dangerous power in the Supreme Executive." This argument won the support of a majority of the House as the amendment was defeated by a vote of 37 to 24.[36] Not all pro-administration delegates voted for the measure but its support did come from that group. New England, except for Vermont, favored giving the president authority to call out the militia by 11 to 3, but the other states were opposed by more than a two to one ratio.

Apportionment, coins, and calling of the militia all involved an attempt by the legislature to deal with a fundamental question, reopened but left partially unanswered by the Constitution: how extensive should federal authority be and how should its power be internally divided and checked? The labels "nationalist" and "anti-nationalist" may be applied meaningfully to First Congress factions that contested this issue. But the labels would be less appropriate if applied to Second Congress voting blocs, for several reasons. First, the questions that came before the Second Congress were not uncomplicated tests of the issue of restraints upon government power. Apportionment, for some at least, invoked jealousies of one state against another. Removing Washington's name from coins was, in part, a very personal matter in which principle played only a secondary role. The practical question of potential use of the militia superseded, especially for frontier delegates, the larger question of controls on the executive's deployment of force. Thus, no roll call raised the issue of limiting government authority in the straightforward way that the amendment controversy had done in the First Congress. Second, voting patterns became more closely correlated with sectional attachments. Even on roll calls that offered no tangible benefit to one region rather than another, New England and the South polarized. Third, the administration, strongly influenced by Hamilton, increasingly identified itself with a series of policy outputs.

Washington's veto of the apportionment compromise, executive support for expansion of the military, and Treasury-initiated plans to increase federal revenues combined to exacerbate hostility toward the administration. Its proponents and opponents, perhaps occasionally ruled by passion rather than reason, tended to polarize against each other no matter what the issue.

For all these reasons, it cannot be said that the issue-oriented, intersectional nationalist and anti-nationalist factions of the First Congress continued unchanged into the Second. However, it would be premature to ascribe voting behavior to the influence of party, even at a very early and crude stage. Delegates continued to debate the merits of proposed restraints upon government power, using many of the same arguments that had been set forth during the amendment controversy in 1789. Although consistent polarity over a wide range of issues increased from the First to the Second Congress, blocs isolated on the apportionment contest were far more highly polarized on government power issues than on other categories of roll calls. The average of cohesion differences between proponents and opponents of radically increasing the size of the House were 46 percent on foreign policy issues, 48 percent on economic issues, and 67 percent on government power issues. Thus, over the nation's first four years under the Constitution, highly cohesive blocs of delegates formed in the House of Representatives to consider policies aimed at precisely defining the limits of federal power. A consistent majority fought successfully against any attempt to restrain national authority by establishing outside limits on its power, particularly through the vehicles of states rights and restrictions on taxing privileges. However, a narrow majority did impose curbs on the executive branch and did check the supposed pretensions of the Senate. The nature of the debate, and the pattern of legislative behavior generated by the issue of balancing liberty and power, might have continued indefinitely had it not been for the restlessness of a few yeomen in western Pennsylvania.

Washington's decision to send troops to punish angry farmers who refused to pay taxes on whiskey made it clear that the federal government, particularly the executive branch, was supreme and that in the future it ultimately could and would decide the course to be steered between infringement of personal liberty and anarchy. Suppression of the Whiskey Rebellion established central authority limited only by its own volition; these limits have been challenged in the United States only occasionally, and never with permanent success. Washington's ability to see some good arising from the episode focused on a crucial point. The Whiskey Rebellion, he proclaimed,

> demonstrated that our prosperity rests on solid foundations, by furnishing an additional proof that my fellow-citizens understand the true principles of government and liberty; that they feel their inseparable union; that notwithstanding all the devices which have been used to sway them from their interest and duty, they are now as ready to maintain the authority of the laws against licentious invasions as they were to defend their rights against usurpation.[37]

With these words Washington invoked the spirit of the Revolution of 1776 but inverted that spirit into a denial of the "Right of the People to alter or to abolish it, and to institute new Government."

The "true principles of government" to which the president referred centered on the unrestricted right of the government, once legally established, to suppress any challenge to its continued existence. In order that such challenges might be nipped in the bud, Washington urged the citizens to reflect upon the causes of the insurrection. "Let them determine," he wrote, "whether it has not been fomented by combinations of men who, careless of consequences and disregarding the unerring truth that those who rouse can not always appease a civil convulsion, have disseminated, from an ignorance or perversion of facts, suspicions, jealousies, and accusations of the whole Government."[38] This was not merely a partisan tirade against Democratic Societies or an opposing party. Rather, it was an attack on all forms of meaningful opposition to an existing government. If men could not concert their efforts, if any statement might be labeled an ignorant suspicion or a jealous perversion, then the ultimate right of revolution became irrelevant and the more practical right to individual liberty became a privilege to be exercised at the forebearance of the government. The Sedition Act, passed only four years later, was not the aberration of men excessively driven by fear of foreign invasion; rather, it was an expression of Washington's vision of an effective government, that is, one unrestrained by externally determined limits. Employing the charismatic appeal of his role as father of the country, Washington sanctified the Revolution by making it a unique experience. Henceforth, revolution was insurrection, anarchy, tyranny.

An earlier rebellion had been influential in the movement for the Constitution, a document that clearly increased government power at the expense of revolutionary principles. A second rebellion, by farmers in western Pennsylvania, materially altered the balance between federal authority and individual liberty. In word, but more importantly in action, it established a government restricted in its power only by internal restraint. Subsequent challenges to federal authority—the Virginia and Kentucky Resolutions, the Hartford Convention, South Carolina's nullification, the South's secession, the International Workers of the World, the Communist party—were met with responses that ranged from laughter and indifference to jails and bullets, but on no occasion did the government entertain serious debate about its duty to resist such challenges by whatever means necessary.

President Washington did not act alone in laying to final rest the principles of the Revolution. Certainly his strong action, gathering 15,000 troops from four states and sending them to march across Pennsylvania, was the crucial step. But the national legislature moved quickly to support the executive's decision. The upper chamber did so without reservation. In reply to the president's address, the Senate condemned self-created societies that misled the masses and added that,

> Our warm and cordial acknowledgments are due to you, sir, for the wisdom and decision with which you arrayed the militia to execute the public will, and to them for the disinterestedness and alacrity with which they obeyed your summons.
>
> The example is precious to the theory of our Government, and confers the brightest honor upon the patriots who have given it. We shall readily concur in such further provisions for the security of internal peace and due obedience to the laws as the occasion manifestly requires.[39]

The Senate, then, adhered to a theory that allowed the government unlimited authority to preserve its existence. It is axiomatic that any established government will take all possible measures to preserve itself, that its practices will refuse to accept external restraints unsupported by power. The point here is not that the president and the Senate were unusually willing to cast aside individual rights; rather, it is significant that the time had arrived when such an action was widely accepted. In the preceding twenty years, Americans had overthrown governments or established them quite regularly—British rule by force, colonial governments by de facto action, a confederation by a delegate assembly, a Constitution by means that some have likened to a coup d'etat. The "rights" extolled in the Declaration of Independence were freely exercised. But by 1794 unanimity existed for the principles espoused by Washington. Defenses against usurpation of rights had become "licentious invasions."

The House did not acquiesce as quickly or as fully to the new principles. Supporters of law and order were barely a majority, and on one roll call found themselves in a minority. Controversy centered on the role that the "self-created societies" mentioned in Washington's address had played in the uprising. Robert Rutherford of Virginia thought that the whole affair had been exaggerated. "This alarm is owing to an overgrown moneyed system, with which the people are not entirely satisfied," he declared, "but the moneyholders need not be afraid. The people will pay the public debt." Another Virginian, Josiah Parker, argued that since the disturbances had begun long before the Democratic Societies came into existence, it was absurd to relate them to the western insurrection. In his opinion the uprising originated as a reaction to an unfair excise tax to finance unjust funding. On the other side, Theodore Sedgwick, a hard line Federalist, bitterly attacked "illicit combinations" and expressed the hope that House action would "plunge these societies into contempt, and sink them still farther into abhorrence and detestation."[40]

It was a Pennsylvanian, Thomas Fitzsimons, who moved that a resolution expressing alarm at the Whiskey Rebellion be amended to note that self-created societies had been involved in fomenting strife. His amendment, a severe condemnation of Democratic Societies throughout the nation, was narrowly approved, by a vote of 47 to 45.[41] The vote foreshadowed future party strength with remarkable accuracy. Only four New Englanders opposed the added words. The four included Nathaniel Niles and Israel Smith of Vermont, both of whom voted against administration proposals more often than not. The other two came from Massachusetts: Henry Dearborn from Kennebeck, Maine, and William Lyman from Northampton, Worcester County. Lyman had consistently voted against all of Hamilton's tax proposals and Dearborn, while taking an equivocal position on that issue, had supported other anti-administration causes such as reduction of the military.[42] At this time, Massachusetts was divided for House election purposes into only four districts, each of which elected several representatives, so that it is impossible to associate a delegate with a precise area of the state. However, there was sufficient proto-Republican sentiment in the western counties and in Maine to elect one man in each district who represented that interest. All of Connecticut, Rhode Island, New Hampshire, and the other twelve members from Massachusetts voted for the amendment.

The South was as cohesive as New England. Twenty-nine of thirty-three voting members from Georgia, Kentucky, North Carolina, South Carolina, and Virginia opposed the condemnation of self-created societies. The four who voted for condemnation were William Dawson and William Barry Grove of North Carolina and Richard Lee and Samuel Griffin of Virginia. Dawson and Grove, representing northeastern and southcentral North Carolina respectively, had voted for the tax increases suggested by the secretary of the treasury and, except on issues involving the frontier, both supported the cause of law and order in all domestic matters. Griffin, representing Culpepper and Stafford counties in northern Virginia and Lee, representing the three counties adjacent to the District of Columbia, had long records of voting for selected administration proposals that extended back to the earliest roll calls of the First Congress. All the areas spoken for by these four men were heavily Federalist later in the decade.

In the Middle Atlantic region the situation was more complex. New Jersey cast all its votes in favor of the amendment but other states were split. Maryland divided evenly at three to three as no votes were cast by the two districts from Montgomery County westward. Samuel Smith, a nominally Republican merchant from Baltimore, joined Federalists William Vans Murray and William Hindman in voting for the amendment. Maryland's representatives had charted an uneven course from the very first recorded roll calls and, although this division is a fair indication of basic patterns in the state, the delegation never voted consistently. Perhaps this was due to the unique position of the state, with its old agricultural ties to the South and, at the same time, its rapidly increasing commercial interest in the North.

Three of nine New Yorkers, representing Long Island and the lower Hudson Valley, voted against censure of Democratic Societies. Two of the three had opposed tax increases and all of them had voted against a standing army and in favor of giving frontiersmen a free hand in dealing with Indians. The six to three margin by which New York proponents of censure outnumbered their opponents on this issue accurately reflected the division within the state's delegation as it had existed throughout the Second and Third Congresses.

Pennsylvania, scene of the Whiskey Rebellion, was sharply divided. The state had elected its representatives on a general ticket, but reference to place of residence and districts formerly or subsequently represented is revealing. Five of six delegates from the interior regions to the north and west opposed condemnation. Of these William Findley, John Smilie, and Daniel Hiester were strong adherents of the Republican cause. William

Montgomery was not counted on by any side, while Andrew Gregg, whom John Beckley referred to as a "trimmer," although sometimes going astray, became at least a lukewarm Republican. The other delegate from the interior, Thomas Scott, was a notable exception. Considered an opponent of the administration, during debate on the western insurrection he clearly joined its warmest supporters. He declared that "he knew that there were self-created societies in that part of the country, and he likewise knew that they had inflamed the insurrection. . . The speech of the President and the letter from the Secretary of the Treasury were, in every particular, strictly true." He added that "these deluded people were objects of real pity."[43] The "deluded" people of Scott's district defeated his bid for re-election; it is reasonable to assume that Scott's position on the Rebellion was a personal one not widely held by his constituents. James Armstrong, Thomas Hartley, and John Kittera, all from the York-Lancaster area, and Thomas Fitzsimons from Philadelphia agreed with Scott.

In terms of region, then, this vote foreshadowed future party strength. Administration opponents controlled Georgia, Kentucky, the upcountry of South Carolina, most of North Carolina, all of Virginia except the northern counties, half of Maryland, interior Pennsylvania, lower New York except New York City, Vermont, and small pockets in Massachusetts. Administration supporters were in command in New Hampshire, Rhode Island, Connecticut, most of Massachusetts, New York City, upper and western New York, New Jersey, Delaware, the older parts of Pennsylvania, half of Maryland, northern Virginia, a few counties in North Carolina, and the lowlands of South Carolina, especially around Charleston.

A subsequent amendment specifying that the condemnation of self-created societies applied only to the four western counties of Pennsylvania passed by the closest of margins, 47 to 46. To ardent Federalists such as Theodore Sedgwick, this represented a stunning defeat. The geographic pattern on this vote was essentially the same as on the original motion condemning all self-created societies.[44] Another clause, proposed by William L. Smith of Charleston, specifying that the insurrection was countenanced by self-created societies elsewhere was similarly defeated.[45]

The blocs that formed during House debate on the Whiskey Rebellion voted cohesively on other issues as well. Table 15 shows the voting behavior of proponents and opponents of condemnation of self-created societies on all roll calls in the two sessions of the Third Congress. Several conclusions may be drawn from this table, the most important of which is the extremely high level of polarity for the entire Congress. Significant cohesion differences occurred on 83 percent of all roll calls, with even greater polarity on

Table 15. Cohesion Differences: Proponents Against Opponents of Condemnation of Self-created Societies, Third Congress

	Range of Cohesion Difference			
Issue	*0–34%*	*35–64%*	*65–100%*	*Mean*
	Percent of Roll Calls in Each Range			
Government power	33	17	50	57
Frontier	25	31	44	54
Economic	9	59	32	54
Foreign policy	12	22	66	64
Miscellaneous and personal	28	43	29	50
ALL ROLL CALLS	17	38	45	57

foreign policy votes and on roll calls involving economic issues. Earlier accounts of legislative behavior before the Jay Treaty significantly underestimate the degree of consistency with which delegates coalesced.[46] As Joseph Charles noted, it is useless to argue about the precise moment when parties came to the foreground in the House. However, facile acceptance of the Jay Treaty as the crucial point has led to an emphasis on party machinery, correctly associated with Republican efforts to bring the treaty fight to the public—an emphasis that obscures the relationship between parties and policy outputs. The present study asserts that the first party system developed, at least in part, because factional groupings had formulated widely accepted solutions to the major problems that confronted the nation in 1789. Foreign affairs, economic policy, and western issues will be considered in detail later, but for the present it should be noted that the same delegates voted together on all roll call categories as early as 1794. The date is significant only because it marks the point at which the House offered major new policy outputs with sharply decreasing frequency. Let us return to the issue currently being analyzed, that is, to the effort to establish the limits of government power.

Ultimately, the House's reply to the president completely avoided the divisive phrase "self-created societies." However, its choice of language showed an essential willingness to support Washington's reduction of individual rights to a sacred limbo of rhetoric that could not restrain efficient government. "And we learn with greatest concern," said the House, "that any misrepresentations whatever of the Government and its proceedings, either by individuals or combinations of men, should have been made and so far credited as to foment the flagrant outrage which has been committed on the laws."[47] That concern with "any misrepresentations whatever" appeared again in 1798 and produced an act against sedition.

The nature of the debate over limits of government authority had changed. Between 1776 and 1794 men divided repeatedly on the matter of external restraints. Individuals and "combinations of men" believed not only that a community might form a civil government to meet common needs but also that the community retained the right to alter, in fundamental ways if necessary, the government it had established. Belief resulted in action. Anti-statism and suspicion of delegated power were widespread in the 1780s, but the balance shifted sharply after the Whiskey Rebellion. Men abandoned the question of restraints on federal power (except through states rights) in order to concentrate fully on attaining power, that is, on gaining control of a regime unfettered by external limits.

The shift from conflict over proper limits on federal authority to quest for control of a government exercising power restrained only by its own will was instrumental in causing the shift from faction to party that occurred during the 1790s. America's two-party system thrives on the contest for power; its mechanisms, from its earliest beginnings, emphasized acquiring office. Indeed, the essence of the failure of the Federalist party, as historian David Fischer demonstrates in *The Revolution of American Conservatism*, was its inability to match its Republican opponents in the business of winning elections. Party and quest for power are so closely associated in American politics that the statement "the party failed because it did not win elections" is periphrastic. However, if emphasis is placed on policy outputs, a severe decline in Federalist strength after 1800 is difficult to discern. And the fact that at a given point the two major parties seeking office do not offer policy alternatives seems to strengthen rather than weaken the political system. In many instances, there exists an inverse relationship between the vitality of the two-party system and conflict over policy outputs. The solution, by Washington and by factional groupings in the national legislature, of the deeply divisive issue of external restraints on government power contributed to the rise of America's first-two-party system. A similar resolution of other issues occurred at about the same time. The result was an ideological vacuum highly conducive to party contests for power. Therefore, to argue that the Federalist and Republican parties of the late 1790s arose out of congressional divisions earlier in the decade is misleading.[48] Unquestionably there is a relationship between the two phenomena, but the relationship is not one of similarity. Rather, presidential action and legislative blocs combined to resolve the major issues facing the new nation and then, with fundamental alterations in policy outputs rejected by all sides, parties arose to vie for control of the regime. This generalization is clearly applicable to the divisions of the late 1790s on the broad issue of restraints upon government authority.

From the Fourth Congress on, debate over the breadth and depth of federal authority rested upon tacit acceptance of government power limited only by its own volition. Party politicking and maneuvering for personal influence dominated legislative behavior that became increasingly predictable, interrelated, and impotent in terms of policy outputs. The Livingston Resolution, the Sedition Act, the "Logan Act" against usurpation of executive authority by private citizens, and the Judiciary Act all produced debates, but little modification of policies adopted earlier in the decade with regard to government authority.

The Livingston Resolution and the closely related Jay Treaty controversy mark the beginning of the primacy of party considerations in roll call voting. Edward Livingston, an eager first-term Republican from New York City, moved a resolution asking the president to "lay before this House a copy of the instructions to the Minister of the United States, who negotiated the Treaty with the King of Great Britain. . .together with the correspondence and the documents relative to the said Treaty."[49] With this action began a debate notable more for length and flourish of rhetoric than for productivity. The resolution itself passed rather easily by a vote of 62 to 37. The area south of the Potomac cast all but two of its votes in favor of calling for the treaty papers. The exceptions, Robert Goodloe Harper and William L. Smith, were both ardent Federalists from South Carolina. Maryland, Pennsylvania, and Delaware supported the Republican position by a two to one ratio as anti-administration votes came from western and northern Pennsylvania, Philadelphia, Delaware, and all of Maryland except the Eastern Shore. New York split evenly at five to five, but New Jersey opposed the resolution. Although New England formed the nucleus of the pro-treaty block, five of its delegates supported the Republican side.[50] Israel Smith of Vermont and Representatives Henry Dearborn, William Lyman, and Joseph Varnum of Massachusetts were to vote consistently against the treaty, but John Sherburne of New Hampshire did not. Israel Smith's tendency to oppose the administration had been exhibited on a variety of roll calls extending back to the Second Congress.

In Massachusetts, the redistricting of 1794 makes it possible to determine precisely the areas of Republican strength in the state. (The election of 1792 had been on the basis of four large districts, each of which elected several delegates.) Lyman represented the second western district, which included most of Hampshire County; Varnum spoke for the second middle district, which consisted of central Middlesex County plus nine towns in

Worcester County; and Dearborn represented the second eastern district in Maine. These areas were the least commercially oriented in the state and the most isolated in terms of lack of river transportation and good road connections with trading centers. The towns generally had been founded later than those in other districts, and Lyman's constituency included the centers of the Shayesite troubles of the previous decade.

The sizable anti-administration majority on the Livingston Resolution disappeared within the six weeks that elapsed before the treaty itself was voted upon. During the interval, Alexander Hamilton, who was without portfolio but by no means without influence, advised the president to refuse to furnish the requested documents to the House. Washington followed this advice, whereupon the treaty's opponents met in caucus to determine an appropriate course of action. Apparently at the lead of James Madison, this caucus decided to take a firm stand against the treaty but to "avoid as much as possible an overt recontre with the Executive."[51] To this end, a resolution was passed by a vote of 57 to 36, stating that the House had the right to deliberate on the expediency of any treaty that included regulations on subjects within the power of the House. The vote indicated no increase in Federalist strength, as demonstrated by opposition to the Livingston Resolution, and the small drop in Republican numbers was more the result of irregular attendance than lack of party zeal.[52] The same pattern held on passage of a resolve, in reply to Washington's refusal to furnish papers, that "it is not necessary to the propriety of any application from the House to the Executive for information desired by them, and which may relate to any Constitutional functions of the House that the purpose for which such information may be wanted or to which the same may be applied, should be stated in the application."[53]

In fact, on seven different roll calls from the Livingston Resolution until the actual Jay Treaty vote, Republicans outnumbered Federalists by nearly five to three. In order to achieve a majority, the administration had to hold all its own support and gain that of one in every five of its opponents. But victory, as events showed, was easily achieved. There was no gradual melting away of Republican votes; 20 percent disappeared almost overnight when the treaty itself was voted upon.[54]

The role of James Madison, who complained to Jefferson of a "melting away" of treaty opponents, was critical; it went beyond the mere casting of votes. The standard treatment of the entire debate, which portrays Madison as an astute party manager anxious to offer policy alternatives but sabotaged by several of his loyal followers, leaves several questions unanswered.[55] One issue that must be raised is just how far Madison was willing to go in blocking the treaty. Was he merely trying to make political mileage, or did he favor outright rejection and possible war with England? Was he willing to force an open confrontation and possibly a total break with the administration? The record of debate shows a clear answer to these questions. Madison moderated the Livingston Resolution by exempting certain delicate papers from the request. Subsequently, he advocated a firm stand but undercut that very possibility by urging the avoidance of a direct confrontation with the president. The same technique of avoiding a showdown, yet using an issue for propaganda purposes is evident in Madison's sponsorship of a motion to implement the treaty and at the same time declare it highly objectionable.[56] The attempt lost by one vote, and afterward Madison bemoaned his defeat on this motion more than on the treaty roll call itself. The motion was intended to express opposition to the administration, but in such a way as to guarantee that the treaty would be implemented. This political gesture implied Madison's acceptance of the treaty and made subsequent votes on Jay's work meaningless. Indeed, approval seemed certain at the time Madison introduced this motion, and a later vote against the treaty, by Madison and others, became a safe protest that could not involve any consequences at home or abroad. Whether Madison's role in approving the treaty by only half-hearted opposition indicates his placing the good of the country above party concerns is beside the point. The crux of the matter is that, once again, while appearing to lead Madison actually exerted a constraining influence upon the spearheads of the Republican interest.

Another possible explanation of Madison's role in the treaty question is that he was quite inept at managing a party. At several points he misjudged the situation rather badly. Madison himself wrote that Livingston's Resolution was ill-timed and that the House might only barely approve it. Yet it received the greatest support of any significant anti-administration measure in the entire decade. After Washington's refusal to furnish the requested papers, Madison gave a lengthy speech because he expected a "long and obstinate discussion" on a resolution asserting the rights of the House. The resolution immediately passed by a wide margin and with no oratorical displays from the Federalists. One may wonder why Madison did nothing to bring the question of implementation to a vote earlier in the session, before Hamilton's pressure and spreading war scares eroded Republican strength. Seven roll calls related to the treaty had all received comfortable anti-administration majorities, but a month elapsed before the crucial test. Inept management, however, can only partially account for the sudden defection of one in five treaty opponents. More significant is the characteristic which Madison apparently shared with a good many other Republicans: an unwillingness to pursue opposition to the point of a total break with the administration on a question of national consequence. The Livingston Resolution and the protestations that followed Washington's curt refusal to comply with the House's request were useful in party contests, but their strong rhetoric had no impact on policy outputs. Federal authority remained unfettered by external restraints and executive power within the government continued to expand at the expense of the legislature.

Table 16 portrays cohesion differences between proponents and opponents of the Livingston Resolution. Significant polarity occurred on three of every four roll calls for the two sessions of the Fourth Congress. Questions involving restraints on government power (mostly the Livingston Resolution roll calls), frontier, and foreign policy resulted in similar divisions. A significant exception exists in figures for roll calls involving economic issues. Levels of polarization dropped sharply relative both to other categories of questions in the Fourth Congress and to votes on economic issues in earlier Congresses. The reason for this exception is the House's consideration of a federal land tax for the first time. Here was a major policy alternative altering the structure of federal revenue in fundamental ways and changing the relationship between the people and their government. (The land tax proposal will be discussed in a subsequent chapter.) When initially debated, the proposal produced a factional voting pattern that contrasted markedly with legislative behavior on other issues.

Table 16. Cohesion Differences: Proponents Against Opponents of the Livingston Resolution, Fourth Congress

| | Range of Cohesion Difference | | | |
Issue	*0–34%*	*35–64%*	*65–100%*	*Mean*
	Percent of Roll Calls in Each Range			
Government power	0	0	100	92
Frontier	11	27	62	66
Economic	61	8	31	41
Foreign policy	12	41	47	60
Partisan politics	20	60	20	58
Miscellaneous and personal	46	33	21	43
ALL ROLL CALLS	24	29	47	59

The voting blocs that formed during the Livingston Resolution debate, which were similar to the grouping that existed on most other roll calls of the Fourth Congress, did not produce significant policy outputs. Washington's prestige was so great that his office suffered no restriction because the House had called for papers related to a treaty. Even the heated debate over the merits of Jay's treaty had little potential for altering the course of foreign policy already established by the Senate and the president. As delegates increasingly turned their attention to party considerations, to the matter of gaining office, they tacitly accepted the policies formulated by their predecessors earlier in the decade. Indeed, the quest for control of the regime became so overwhelming a consideration that it generated policy directions of its own. The behavior of delegates in the Fifth and Sixth Congresses, especially their votes on the Sedition Act, illustrates the triumph of party over policy.

The Sedition Act was no more than the logical extension of the principles espoused by the executive and endorsed by the legislature in response to the Whiskey Rebellion. In 1794 the House expressed its "greatest concern that any misrepresentations whatever of the Government and its proceedings, either by individuals or combinations of men, should have been made. . ." Washington's unilateral action, of course, precluded the need for positive legislation, but the Senate had clearly indicated its willingness to take any further steps the president might deem necessary. In 1798, Congress enacted an addition to the act for punishment of certain crimes against the United States that provided fines and imprisonment for the following:

> any persons [who] shall unlawfully combine or conspire to-
> gether, with intent to oppose any measure or measures of the
> government . . . any person or persons, with intent as aforesaid,
> [who] shall advise or attempt to procure any insurrection, riot,
> unlawful assembly, or combination, whether such conspiracy,
> threatening, counsel, advice, or attempt shall have the pro-
> posed effect or not . . . [anyone who shall write or print or
> utter] any false, scandalous and malicious writing or writings
> against the government of the United States or either house of
> the Congress of the United States, or the President of the
> United States, with intent to defame the said government, or
> either house of the said Congress, or the said President, or to
> bring them, or either or any of them, into contempt or dis-
> repute; or to excite against them, or either or any of them,
> the hatred of the good people of the United States or to stir
> up sedition within the United States, or to excite any unlawful

combinations therein, for opposing or resisting any law of the United States, or any act of the President of the United States done in pursuance of any such law, or of the powers vested in him by the constitution of the United States, or to resist, oppose, or defeat any such law or act, or to aid, encourage, or abet any hostile designs of any foreign nation against the United States, their people or government . . .[57]

The existence of a government limited in the exercise of power only by its own volition could hardly be stated with greater clarity. Yet historians who view the alien and sedition laws of 1798 as a temporary aberration, as a dangerous but limited flaw in the fabric of America's commitment to civil liberties, miss the underlying ideological continuity between Washington's response to the crisis of the Whiskey Rebellion and Adams' reaction to attacks on the government only four years later.[58] The Federalist party in 1798 openly attacked the exercise of individual rights that threatened, they believed, the government's security and stability. Republicans, however, offered no meaningful policy alternative. As historian Leonard Levy aptly phrased the situation, "Jeffersonian principles respecting freedom of political expression depended upon whose ox was being gored by the common law of seditious libel."[59] When Republicans controlled state governments, they argued that prosecution of sedition was the right of the state; when they controlled the federal government but were not in power at the state level, they argued for the concurrent right of the federal government to suppress seditious libel under the common law. Division over the Sedition Act did not reflect polarization along ideological lines. It did not array proponents of individual rights against advocates of suppression; rather, it pitted those in power against those who wished to gain power. Each side saw in its respective position a means of improving its chances for acquiring and holding office. Federalists hoped to brand their opponents as dangerous traitors. Republicans, appealing both to states rights and to libertarian arguments, saw potential political reward in the entire episode. But both sides miscalculated. The Virginia and Kentucky Resolutions alarmed southwesterners, who turned to the Federalist party in large numbers. On the other hand, especially in the pivotal Middle Atlantic states, Federalists failed in their efforts to characterize the contest for office as a fight between loyal Americans and traitorous French agents.

A brief analysis of voting behavior supports the conclusion that the Sedition Act was the outcome of the ascendancy of party goals over policy considerations. James Morton Smith's full account of the alien and sedition laws convincingly demonstrates that party needs dictated this legislation, and there is little need to retrace his thorough analysis.[60] However, it is useful to add depth to Smith's portrayal by considering the positions of these delegates on other issues.

Table 17 summarizes the votes of proponents and opponents of passage of the sedition law for all roll calls in the three sessions of the Fifth Congress. The two voting blocs being analyzed, in essence the Federalist and Republican parties, polarized against each other to a degree not even approached in previous years. The frequency of significant polarity (cohesion

Table 17. Cohesion Differences: Proponents Against Opponents of the Sedition Law, Fifth Congress

Issue	Range of Cohesion Difference			Mean
	0–34%	35–64%	65–100%	
	Percent of Roll Calls in Each Range			
Government power	3	18	79	78
Frontier	0	0	100	80
Economic	12	21	67	68
Foreign policy	10	17	73	73
Partisan politics	17	0	83	75
Miscellaneous and personal	18	36	46	58
ALL ROLL CALLS	9	18	73	73

difference above 34 percent) increased to 91 percent of all roll calls from 37 percent, 67 percent, 83 percent, and 76 percent for government power blocs in the four preceding Congresses. A more striking increase occurred in the frequency of extremely high polarity (cohesion difference above 74 percent and included in the 65 to 100 percent range in Table 17): from 6 percent in the First Congress, 12 percent in the Second Congress, 23 percent in the Third Congress, and 34 percent in the Fourth Congress, to 61 percent in the Fifth Congress, or nearly double the previous high figure. Because no new and innovative policies were introduced, delegates had little cause to engage in factious dispute, and cohesion differences were uniformly great on all categories of roll calls. The consistent alignment of delegates on all issues was not the product of elaborate party control in the legislature. Indeed, the caucus remained an infrequently used device of dubious value, and informal gatherings, especially among Federalists, were directed more often at internal maneuvering for power than at the opposition party. The absence of formal party discipline, however, did not diminish the strength of party as a motivating force in voting. The exigencies of acquiring and holding office were paramount not only in the contest over the sedition law, but also in debates on the Quasi-War against France and the tax program to pay for war.[61] With the search for new directions in policy outputs abandoned both by Federalists and by Republicans, party replaced faction in the House.

The inverse relationship between the desire to offer policy alternatives and the quest for office is amply demonstrated by voting patterns in the Sixth Congress. Except for the contest over the presidential election of 1800, its activities were rather inconclusive and inconsequential. By the winter of 1799, the imminent threat of war had passed and the House was left with little to do. It was too soon to dismantle the war effort in any major way and it was inexpedient, certainly, to increase it. Biding its time waiting for the outcome of renewed negotiations, Congress grappled with a variety of unimportant matters, which gave little for factions to feed upon. Without strong pressure from outside events, the House drifted aimlessly, talking much but accomplishing little.

Roll calls on the sedition law clearly fell within this pattern. A majority of the House opposed continuing the law and a different majority opposed repealing it. By default, the majority let it expire naturally on March 3, 1801. When the issue was raised, fifty delegates voted for Nathaniel Macon's motion of January 23, 1800, asking that the Sedition Act be repealed.[62] Only one of these fifty, Josiah Parker of Virginia, was to vote for Aaron Burr when the House decided the deadlocked presidential contest. None of the forty-eight opponents of Macon's motion subsequently voted for Jefferson. But James Bayard snatched victory from the hands of defeat for the Federalists when he moved that Macon's motion be amended to state that the repeal of the Sedition Act meant that the crimes it covered once again became punishable under the common law. Four delegates who had voted for Macon's motion—Edwin Gray and Josiah Parker of Virginia and Benjamin Huger and Abraham Nott of South Carolina—switched sides and voted for Bayard's amendment. Archibald Henderson, of western North Carolina, had voted against Macon's motion and he now voted against Bayard's amendment. As a result, the amendment was added by a vote of 51 to 47.[63] All efforts came to naught, however, when the House rejected by 87 to 11 the motion as amended.[64] Such action was typical: a lot of talk, some voting, and an overwhelming decision to do nothing.

A year later, when it was known that Adams would not be the next president of the United States, a desperate effort was made to extend the Sedition Act. A move to reject continuance failed on a tie vote, but engrossing of the subsequent bill for continuance also failed.[65] Thus Republicans were denied the delight of repealing the law, and Federalists suffered the pain of watching it expire.[66]

These two groups voted cohesively against each other throughout the two sessions of the Sixth Congress. Table 18 summarizes the voting of proponents and opponents of repeal of the sedition law. As was the case in the Fifth Congress, significant levels of polarity occurred on more than nine of every ten roll calls. Either delegates united consistently on a variety

Table 18. Cohesion Differences: Proponents Against Opponents of Repeal of the Sedition Law, Sixth Congress

	Range of Cohesion Difference			
Issue	*0–34%*	*35–64%*	*65–100%*	*Mean*
	Percent of Roll Calls in Each Range			
Government power	9	0	91	83
Frontier	12	25	63	72
Economic	0	16	84	77
Foreign policy	10	25	65	69
Partisan politics	6	18	76	75
Miscellaneous and personal	33	0	67	54
ALL ROLL CALLS	8	15	77	75

of issues, a phenomenon that Madison characterized as the rule of passion not reason, or issues that appeared different on the surface were in fact closely related. The possibility that men suddenly had become the victims of their passions, that parties are irrational, may be dismissed as an expression of the widespread bias against party among eighteenth-century political theorists, including Madison. There remains, then, the conclusion that categories of issues which were fundamentally different and productive of innovative policy outputs in the early 1790s had become meaningless by the latter part of the decade. The sedition law was simply an extension of the philosophy behind Washington's response to the Whiskey Rebellion, turned to the desire of a party to acquire office. A similar transformation took place on other issues and, as a result, the same delegates consistently coalesced against each other. The extent to which politicking superseded policy may be seen more fully by examining the other major activities of the Fifth and Sixth Congresses in the area of limiting federal power. Three efforts are particularly noteworthy: legislation regarding aliens, measures to prevent usurpation of executive authority, and a bill to expand the judicial branch of the central government.

The first law concerning aliens passed by Congress in 1798 expanded federal power, particularly that of the chief executive. Limited to two years' duration and operative in war and in peace, the law allowed President Adams to deport "dangerous" aliens. The cumbersome hearing procedure established in the bill did little to mitigate the thrust of the law, which was to imperil the philosophical foundation of individual rights by placing their continued existence at the pleasure of the president. That Adams did not choose to declare any aliens dangerous under this act is to his credit, but it hardly assuaged the coercive nature of the law. A second bill increased the residency requirement for naturalization from five to fourteen years and erected an elaborate registration system for ascertaining the whereabouts of all aliens. Registration of aliens has become an accepted and routine fact, but its initial passage in 1798, at a time when fear of government oppression ran high, increased apprehension among aliens about the safety of their lives and their property.

The third and final piece of legislation concerning aliens dealt specifically with alien enemies. The most important of the three acts, the Alien Enemies Law, "was a permanent wartime statute passed with *bipartisan* support."[67] Although Republicans opposed the extension of executive authority contemplated in the bill, many agreed with the measure's underlying assumptions. Thomas T. Davis, a Republican from Kentucky, supported the bill, and raised the spectre of French agents instigating expeditions against the United States.[68] Believing that the previously adopted law directed at all aliens represented a greater threat than the bill currently under consideration, Albert Gallatin, at this time the acknowledged leader of Republican forces in the House, surprised the Federalist leadership by adding his support to the effort to fashion a law to protect the nation from alien enemies in its midst.[69] As historian James Morton Smith concluded in *Freedom's Fetters*, the Alien Enemies Law "appears to have been virtually a Republican measure."[70] The failure of the Republican opposition to offer a meaningful alternative to the widely accepted policy of establishing a government unhampered by external restraints, with an executive whose power matched that of his European counterparts, is amply demonstrated in the words of the Alien Enemies Law:

> Whenever there shall be a declared war . . . *or any invasion or predatory incursion* shall be perpetrated, attempted, or *threatened* . . . and the President of the United States shall make public proclamation of the event, all natives, citizens, denizens, or subjects of the hostile nation or government,

> being males of the age of fourteen years and upwards, who shall
> be within the United States, and not actually naturalized, shall
> be liable to be *apprehended, restrained, secured, and removed*,
> as alien enemies.

The law went on to give the president wide latitude in establishing the
mechanism for restraining and removing such aliens. And in a rare attack
on the concept of private property, aliens *charged* with some crime or
"actual hostility" were afforded no protection for their "goods and effects."[71]

It took less than a fanciful imagination for French aliens to foresee
the imminent danger ahead. Without benefit of the constitutional guarantees afforded to citizens and with only a vague assurance that the president would provide for a "full examination and hearing," wary aliens em-
barked on the first available ship sailing for Europe. Precise figures are not
available, but fifteen ships loaded with Frenchmen sailed within a two-
month period, many passengers doing so out of fear of the various laws
passed against aliens.[72] Although President Adams employed neither the
Alien Act (applicable in war or in peace) nor the Alien Enemies Act, these
two measures, combined with the Sedition Act, made government power
formidable indeed.

The absence of ideological dispute and factiousness that characterized
the House's consideration of laws extending the authority of the state
over aliens also marked congressional action on the Logan Act, a measure
designed to prevent usurpation of executive authority. Republicans initially
opposed the bill and engaged in protracted debate, largely to further partisan aims. The act, which remains in force to this day, owes its name to
Dr. George Logan, a Quaker from Philadelphia who took it upon himself
to sail for France to reopen negotiations that had ended with the XYZ
affair. He carried with him a letter of introduction from Thomas Jefferson.
Just what Logan hoped to accomplish is a matter of conjecture; Federalists
were convinced that at the very least he intended to arouse undue interest
on the part of France in a change in administrations in the United States.
Legislative action consisted of maneuvers for political advantage curbed
less by philosophical considerations than by fears that the act might in-
advertently infringe on the flexibility of men of commerce. After overwhelmingly approving a resolution to frame a bill to prevent usurpation
of executive authority, the House moved to clarify its action. Amendments
were introduced to exclude from the bill persons seeking release of captured
American seamen or the restoration of property or debts as well as indiv-

iduals seeking redress for personal injury or loss. Other clauses were introduced to limit the bill to persons who "intended" to usurp authority or to "defeat" or "counteract" the government, whether such persons were government officials or not. After several weeks, the bill reached the House in its final form; it was little more than a partisan attack on Logan, an urban, eastern Republican whom several members of the party willingly abandoned for political reasons. The House had successfully avoided the underlying fundamental question, raised in debate by Albert Gallatin, of the relationship between America's desire to expand its commerce and the nation's near involvement in Europe's war. If the greed of merchants could bring the United States to the brink of war, asked Gallatin, then why could not an individual be equally bold in the quest for peace? The Logan Act failed to answer his question.[73]

The extent to which successful resolution of the limits of power issue in the early 1790s paved the way for partisan politicking later in the decade is also demonstrated in congressional action on restructure of the federal judiciary. The weakness of this branch of government reflected the intentions of delegates to the First Congress. They had rejected Hamilton's suggestions for the creation of a uniform body of laws throughout the states to be administered by a complex system of lower courts that would undermine state court authority by carving out districts of common law authority within each state. Instead, the Judiciary Act of 1789 established only a Supreme Court (as required by the Constitution), two circuit courts, and thirteen district courts. More importantly, original jurisdiction was sharply restricted; even the adjudication of cases under the Constitution, federal laws, and treaties were to be initiated in the state courts.[74] The balance of power shifted even further towards the states when the Eleventh Amendment became law in 1798. Adopted in direct response to the Supreme Court's contention in *Chisholm v. Georgia*, the amendment denied federal jurisdiction in cases involving one of the states and a citizen of another state or foreign power. Thus the situation was ripe for meaningful legislative action in the area of extending the authority of federal government through a restructure of its judiciary. Hamilton, among others, had been ready for years with detailed plans for such an endeavor.[75] President Adams, in his third annual address, noting the rebelliousness of "seduced" Pennsylvanians who were resisting the new federal land tax, but lacking his predecessor's flair for the bold and dramatic response, used their actions to argue that "a revision and amendment of the judiciary system is indispensably necessary." "On the one hand," said Adams, "the laws should be executed; on the other, individuals should be guarded from oppression. Neither of these objects is sufficiently assured under the present organization of the judicial department."[76]

But any serious plans for altering policy outputs came to naught as party patronage needs loomed ever larger. During its entire first session, the Sixth Congress did little more than agree to postpone consideration of revisions of the judiciary.[77] After the election of 1800, when it became apparent that Adams would shortly be vacating the executive branch, Federalists in the House rallied around a Judiciary Act that avoided basic issues to concentrate on creating seemingly safe jobs. Understandably perhaps, the next president placed a high priority on adopting an appropriately political response to such a partisan maneuver. At Jefferson's request, the Seventh Congress abolished the new positions. Neither passage of the "reform" nor its repeal involved the issue of the limits of federal power in any serious way.

*   *   *   *   *

This chapter has examined a variety of roll calls recorded in the House of Representatives during its first twelve years. Although these measures touched upon many subjects, a central theme united them: the search for the limits of federal power. During the 1790s the legislature, in conjunction with the executive, steadily challenged and overrode external restraints on government authority. Surfacing in the controversy over amendments to the Constitution, reapportionment, and the response to the Whiskey Rebellion, factious groupings waged the same debate that, in its essence, had actively engaged political theorists in the United States since the 1760s. The Revolution, the state constitutions, even the adoption of the Federal Constitution of 1787, all demonstrated that sovereignty resided in the people, that government's power was limited by individual rights, by legitimate sub-states, by the will of its creators. But after 1794, after Washington placed the Revolution on an unreachable and unique pedestal, after Congress agreed that "any misrepresentations whatever of the Government" were dangerous and licentious, the balance shifted. Parties concerned primarily with acquiring control of a regime unlimited in the exercise of power replaced factions that had fought over the policy outputs that produced such a regime. As long as a factious spirit dominated the legislature, men fell into different opinions on different issues. But once factions reached accepted policy outputs on a variety of issues, the same names began to appear consistently on the same side, no matter what the apparent content of the roll call. This occurred neither because delegates were the slaves of party discipline nor because the people elected irrational representatives after 1794; rather, the success with which factions had formulated policy created an ideological vacuum in which the quest for office overrode the desire to implement alternative policies. Ultimately, the needs of party became so important that policy itself was turned to partisan ends. The recently acquired unlimited power of government to protect its continued existence became a tool to be used to preserve the position of individuals within the government. Thus, the controversy over the Sedition Act can be understood most correctly as a contest over the application of policy to a particular group rather than as a debate over the policy of unrestrained government power. The issue of limiting federal authority arose again after 1800 and, on each occasion, the strength of the two-party system declined as factional blocs struggled to reach acceptable policy outputs. But the basic outline of the solution of 1794—government power limited only by its own volition—remained.

4

POLITICS AND ABUNDANT LAND

In the course of calling the attention of his colleagues to "The Significance of the Frontier in American History," Frederick Jackson Turner concluded that, "The legislation which most developed the powers of the national government, and played the largest part in its activity, was conditioned on the frontier."[1] Made in the context of a sweeping, intentionally provocative essay, the statement would not pass a coldly scientific and quantitative test. Nevertheless, congressional policy outputs dealing with western issues are well worth analyzing. The issues themselves are widely known. "The first frontier," wrote Turner, "had to meet its Indian question, its question of the disposition of the public domain, of the means of intercourse with older settlements, of the extension of political organization, of religious and educational activity." Each successive frontier raised similar issues.[2] Varying only in the precise choice of words, most students of the West have framed their work in terms of Turner's set of questions and, not surprisingly, they have come to similar conclusions concerning the perpetuity of western problems and of national reaction to those problems. Most conclude that the federal legislature, in the 1790s and later as well, failed to formulate permanently acceptable policies to deal with frontier issues. Most portray each generation as beginning totally anew the process of producing legislation to meet the needs of an advancing frontier.

Analysis of the specific western problems noted by Turner—Indians, land distribution, relationship of new settlements to old—has reached a state of diminishing return that can be reversed only by modifying the framework within which such specific questions are studied. Indian policy has been considered in the context of land security, but, to borrow a perceptive phrase employed in an essentially related problem, one must ask: "security for what?"[3] Land distribution has most often been analyzed as a contest between speculators and settlers, but such an approach finds crass, personal economic motives at the cost of failing to focus upon national goals and policies. The relationship of new settlements to old has been viewed primarily as a political problem, especially with regard to sectional balance, but the most important insights here may well be in the understanding of a society, insights that can be gained by studying that society's attempt to reproduce the best in itself.

David Potter's brilliant analysis of the factor of abundance in forming the American character confronted Turner's frontier hypothesis directly and produced the key for breaking through the circles of rhetoric that had encased the old master's idea. Casting aside Turner's agrarian dogma as a confusing and unnecessary piece of intellectual baggage, Potter preserved the vital concept of free land and viewed it as abundance in its most tangible, visible, alluring form. Deeply influenced by Western Europe's critical shortage of acreage, Americans believed that land, no matter how uncleared, inaccessible, or infertile, was the key to wealth, to a form of abundance peculiarly under God's beneficent watch. Ultimately, Americans demonstrated remarkable flexibility and ingenuity in turning from the abundance of land to the exploiting of industrialization, but in both instances the ultimate goal was the same: to convert potential abundance to actual wealth. The conversion process, of course, converted the people as well and, Potter concluded, produced an "American" character.[4]

In analyzing legislative behavior on western issues, then, the focus is on a basic, necessarily abstract, concept: the relationship between the political process and formation of national character through interaction with abundance. Specific roll calls recorded in the House of Representatives during the 1790s involved much more mundane and practical issues, but the end product of a series of such votes was a broad policy reflecting the nation's attitude towards abundance, towards the acquisition of wealth. In their dealings with Indians, Americans looked upon themselves as a community, united in carrying out the will of God and the laws of nature, that must eliminate the misuse by outsiders of potential abundance. The security that frontier settlers sought to achieve by removing the Indian involved freedom from physical danger but, more importantly, security meant full exploitation of the wealth of the land. In its policies concerning land distribution, the legislature gave less attention to mediating the speculator versus settler conflict than it did to finding the most rapid means for realizing the full economic potential of the West. In attempting to recreate itself on the frontier, American society, through its legislature, reflected the impact of abundance—emphasis upon education as the prerequisite for equality of opportunity, faith in a democratic system meaningful only in an abundant society, protection of inequality in levels of acquisition of wealth, the ultimate subservience of individual desire to the needs of the community.

Although creation of a national domain is correctly noted as an accomplishment of the Confederation period, the best means of converting potential abundance to actual wealth eluded Congress before 1789. Some beginnings had been made in the ordinances adopted in 1784 and revised three years later, but the rapid settlement of trans-Appalachian territory, crystallized for House delegates in the admission of Kentucky and Tennessee to the Union, brought other problems to the foreground, problems that raised fundamental questions about the American character. The answers provided by the policy outputs of Congress in the 1790s established the outlines of the nation's symbiotic association with abundance. Protection of the association from outsiders, division of the association's fruits among members of the national community, and perpetual reproduction of the association formed the triad goal of frontier policy in the early national period. In examining the pursuit of this goal, the relationship between faction and party in legislative behavior once again will receive attention.

Security on the frontier meant acquisition of the potential abundance of virgin land. But the goal was more easily stated than implemented. Tension, mistrust, and misunderstanding marked the relationship between western delegates in the House and their eastern counterparts on the issue of security. Westerners viewed the Indian menace in highly personal terms, arguing passionately for a free hand in dealing with savage incursions that threatened their very families. They resented the law and order admonitions of easterners who had not known the terror of an Indian raid for over one hundred years. Eastern delegates, on the other hand, believed that the provocative actions of frontier settlers were largely responsible for the constant hostilities that plagued the West and retarded the conversion of potential abundance to actual wealth. This is not to say that easterners were particularly concerned with the rights of Indians. Indeed, even the nobility of the savage, a concept that found expression in American literature, never swayed debate in Congress. But the majority in the House was moved less by arguments of personal danger than by its conviction that Indian use of land was inevitably misuse, that only the white American, deeply imbued with a belief in the sanctity of hard work, could produce abundance from God's gift of land. Thus, the ultimate thrust of a series of roll calls dealing with Indian treaties, frontier defense, military expeditions in the West, and restrictions on whites traveling in Indian territory was to forge a policy of national control over security that placed primary emphasis on full utilization of land. A detailed examination of particular roll calls demonstrates the dimensions of this policy.

The first occasion on which the House divided over the issue of security occurred on August 12, 1789, when twenty-three delegates voted against an appropriation of $40,000 to be used in the negotiation of Indian treaties.[5] Nearly a year later, a bloc of twenty-six representatives moved to do away completely with "bribe" money in conducting Indian relations. The effort was turned back by a single vote.[6] The switching of individuals and of entire states on these two roll calls indicated complex voting patterns at this early point. Nevertheless, cohesive groups emerged in these two votes.

One consisted of fourteen delegates who opposed authorizing money for treaty negotiations in the first place and who, after being defeated, voted for the amendment a year later that would have done away with bribe money.[7] Fully half of this group strongly supported amendments to the Constitution proposed for the purpose of sharply limiting federal power; none came from frontier areas. The group did not have any other common characteristics, and it may tentatively be concluded that lack of interest in Indian affairs, combined with a desire to limit the scope of the central government whenever possible, governed its votes. Previously, the state legislatures directly involved had granted money for treaties with hostile savages.

Opposing this bloc were nineteen representatives who initially voted for the $40,000 appropriation and subsequently voted not to eliminate the money.[8] All six delegates to the First Congress who spoke for the West were part of the group. It is not at all surprising that these men—Abraham Baldwin, John Brown, George Matthews, John Page, Thomas Scott, and John Steele (not present on the earlier roll call)—voted together, since they had a common interest in establishing peace with the Indians as long as it did not interfere with the freedom of white settlers. Two significant pressures account for the votes of the remaining proponents of treaty money. Pennsylvania and Virginia had been struggling against hostile Indians for years and their representatives were generally only too glad to receive some assistance from the federal government. A second influence, one that is more difficult to isolate, was the desire of nationalists, some of whom had investment ties to frontier lands, to impose law and order in the West. Ten of the thirteen non-westerners voting for "bribe" money were classified earlier as nationalists on the basis of their opposition to all amendments that might restrict federal power.[9] This nationalist position in favor of establishing a strong government presence on the frontier eventually clashed with the aims of westerners who desired a free hand in running their affairs. However, the strings attached to federal aid did not yet constrict the actions of remote settlers, who actively supported early efforts at nationalizing Indian policy.

Table 19, which summarizes the voting behavior of delegates who adhered to a consistent position on the issue of money for Indian treaties, supports the conclusion that westerners and proponents of strong federal government combined to forge a policy that enlarged national control over Indian affairs. Roll calls concerning foreign policy, location of the capital, and economic issues clearly did not involve the motivating forces that caused delegates to polarize on western issues. However, the voting blocs that formed on treaty money were not accidental, random, or temporary. Table 19 reveals a positive correlation between votes on frontier issues and roll calls involving the extent of government power. It foreshadowed policy outputs produced later in the decade, in particular the desire of a majority in the legislature to play an active role in assuring the rapid acquisition of the West's abundance.

Table 19. Cohesion Differences: Proponents Against Opponents of Indian Treaty Money, First Congress

Issue	*Range of Cohesion Difference*			*Mean*
	0–34%	*35–64%*	*65–100%*	
	Percent of Roll Calls in Each Range			
Government power	25	65	10	43
Frontier	33	0	67	68
Location of the capital	44	56	0	36
Economic	82	15	3	20
Foreign policy	50	50	0	26
Miscellaneous and personal	55	36	9	33
ALL ROLL CALLS	54	40	6	33

That this majority ultimately would antagonize and exclude western settlers became apparent when the House debated a Senate amendment to the military appropriations bill for 1790. The measure initially adopted by the House had specified the number of men from the militia of Pennsylvania, Virginia, and Georgia that the president might assign to defense operations against Indians. The Senate eliminated the upper limit on executive troop calls, thereby arousing western fears that the militia companies formed by remote settlers for their own defense might be off on a useless foray directed by incompetent easterners at a time when the troops were sorely needed for local protection. Representatives from frontier areas also expressed concern over the possibility that a federalized militia would direct its efforts less at Indians than at the imposition of law and order among white settlers. For these reasons, none of the six western delegates who had voted for Indian treaty negotiation money supported this Senate amendment. In so doing, the six voted against the overwhelming majority of their former nationalist allies on treaty money and brought about the defeat of the Senate's proposition by a substantial margin.[10]

The efforts of the First Congress to solve the problem of securing western land from the menace and misuse of the Indian proved to be ineffective. Legislators blamed insufficient appropriations and use of undisciplined, unwilling state troops for the government's failure. Years of blundering, of which Brigadier General Harmar's 1790 fiasco was only one example, culminated in a major crisis when forces under Major General Arthur St. Clair, governor of the Northwest Territory, met defeat in 1791. Unlike previous expeditions, in which few knowledgeable leaders had placed much faith, the support, prestige, and wisdom of President Washington himself guided St. Clair's mission. After offering assurances to Great Britain that the move did not threaten its interests, a combined force of regular army and militia moved north from Fort Washington (near the present site of Cincinnati). But hopes were soon dashed as a band of Indians overwhelmed St. Clair's bewildered troops less than one hundred miles north of the fort; "the catastrophe paralyzed American military operations for nearly a year."[11]

Congressional disbelief and anger turned quickly to recrimination and the establishment of a House committee to inquire into the circumstances surrounding the defeat.[12] From the outset, a substantial number of delegates, led by William Giles of Virginia, hoped to uncover evidence against Alexander Hamilton, whose position as secretary of the treasury made him responsible for army supply contracts. The investigation dragged on for nearly a year and culminated in a report that indicted William Duer, Hamilton's disgraced and jailed agent, but exonerated Hamilton himself. Memory of the defeat faded quickly and a year later the House approved by a two to one margin a bill to compensate St. Clair for earlier efforts at negotiating treaties with Indian tribes in the Northwest.[13]

The Second Congress did not confine its response to St. Clair's failure to investigations aimed at discovering individual incompetence. Far more important in the establishment of long-range policy was the defeat's impetus to efforts to develop a strong federal presence on the frontier. Early in its first session, on February 1, 1792, the House approved a measure, by a vote of 29 to 19, for making more effectual defense of the frontier. In the First Congress, before the St. Clair disaster, westerners opposed to national control of military operations against Indians joined with easterners opposed to any expansion of federal power to limit President Washington's requests for a large, permanent military establishment. By 1792, however, a majority in the House favored some action along the lines proposed by the executive branch. Indeed, several members from districts bordering the southwestern frontier opposed the pending bill because it did not do enough for them.[14] With the exceptions of Israel Jacobs of Pennsylvania and James Gordon of New York, all other votes against the measure came from New England; this voting pattern was nearly opposite that recorded on earlier roll calls.[15]

However, the bill to defend frontiers underwent such drastic revision that, when appropriations for it came up for final action on April 21, 1792, John Page of Virginia, in urging rejection, declared:

> If the bill were what its title says it is, I should be the last man in the House to vote against it . . . Sir, it is not a bill for the protection of frontiers, but for the encouragement of fisheries, and for the increase of the Sinking Fund. It is about to pass . . . as a compromise for the assumption of State debts, and an encouragement to the manufacturers and fisheries.[16]

As the breakdown of the vote clearly shows, Page's analysis was essentially correct.[17] Southerners who had opposed the bill earlier as not being strong enough continued to do so but, except for them, the original supporters and opponents changed sides. Abraham Baldwin of Georgia, Thomas Tucker of South Carolina, and Joshua Seney of Maryland had originally voted for passage but now opposed the bill, as did a majority of the Virginia delegation. New Englanders, who had previously opposed defense of frontiers by a three to one ratio, now strongly supported the "defense of frontiers" bill that aided Cape Cod fisheries. The sole opposition in that area now came from the Smiths of New Hampshire and Vermont. The Middle Atlantic states supplied the margin by which the bill passed, as only Cornelius Schoonmaker and Thomas Tredwell of New York opposed it. The two roll calls serve to delineate eastern attitudes toward western defense needs: inconsistent, ambivalent, self-serving. The votes, however, do not clarify the position of frontier representatives, several of whom clouded the picture by voting for the final bill. These included John Steele of North Carolina, who often supported measures strongly favored by the executive, but the votes of William Findley of Pennsylvania and of John Brown and Andrew Moore of Virginia represent a definite break in their normal pattern. Either they did not agree with Page's contention that the frontier defense bill was in reality a bill to aid fisheries or else they felt that a bad bill was better than none at all. Other delegates from outlying areas opposed the measure and one can only surmise that some westerners were not so strongly against eastern fisheries and manufacturers as to prevent them from voting for a bill that was also in their interest.

Frontier solidarity was more in evidence on a motion introduced on December 18, 1792, authorizing offensive operations against the Cherokee Indians. On this measure western delegates outside New England, forgetting their earlier warnings against nationalization of local militia, united to support unlimited presidential use of state troops in carrying out "offensive" raids in the southwest.[18] To the dismay of frontier representatives, a majority in the House opposed authorizing the raids, which aroused eastern fears of a long, costly war against Indians that would do nothing to promote effective land use. Several delegates pointed out that the territories involved, in western Georgia and Tennessee, were as yet beyond the edge of productive settlement. Because such offensive operations would promote neither productivity nor law and order on the frontier, most nationalists voted against the proposition, which lost by a tally of 27 to 21. The roll call is significant, not because it indicated a commitment to peace or justice in dealing with Indians, but because it demonstrated that a majority in the House, particularly eastern delegates, supported military operations against Indians only when the potential result appeared to be immediate improvement of land productivity. Westerners, on the other hand, were willing to engage in warfare that promised no tangible economic gain and that even threatened the orderly conversion of potential abundance to actual wealth. However, these divisions did not extend uniformly to other issues that came before the legislature.

Table 20 summarizes the voting behavior of the two groups that opposed each other on the question of offensive Indian operations. As was the case with Indian treaty blocs two years earlier (see Table 19), extent of government power remained the overwhelming consideration in voting on western issues. Indeed, the low levels of cohesion difference that existed on the category "frontier" prove that the word "offensive" preceding Indian operations is the key to explaining the break that occurred on this roll call between westerners and their nationalist allies, a split that deepened in the next Congress.

Early in 1794 a determined bloc of representatives, believing that local militia would never succeed in bringing stability to the frontier, urged the legislature to establish a permanent, national military force. A fierce debate ensued, during which proponents of a standing army quickly abandoned the pretense that the troops were needed for defense against Great Britain and admitted that a national army might be used on the frontier. The question of executive tyranny was once again a source of opposition to strengthening the army. Fisher Ames, more willing than most administration supporters to confront the issue directly, asked, "Why were we afraid to entrust

Table 20. Cohesion Differences: Proponents Against Opponents of Offensive
Operations Against Indians, Second Congress

	Range of Cohesion Difference			
Issue	*0–34%*	*35–64%*	*65–100%*	*Mean*
	Percent of Roll Calls in Each Range			
Government power	30	67	3	42
Frontier	76	16	8	24
Economic	63	37	0	32
Foreign policy	50	50	0	32
Miscellaneous and personal	65	35	0	27
ALL ROLL CALLS	55	43	2	33

the President with the power of raising ten thousand men? Can any body of
men to be raised in this country tread down the substantial yeomanry?"[19]
The answer was that many delegates thought so. The entire question of the
military establishment involved a number of motivations for voting—distrust of standing armies, dislike of any federal force, fear of an executive
with too much power, desire to avoid serving in the army, and unwillingness to pay the cost of maintaining a military establishment. The extent to
which each of these factors operated is difficult to determine; debate did
not always reveal inner convictions and roll calls involved overlapping considerations. Nevertheless, the central thrust of the argument of proponents
of expanding the military was that the need to turn the frontier from a
lawless, wasteful, unproductive wilderness into an integrated part of an
abundant nation justified the costs and risks involved. Their opponents,
some committed to finding abundance in eastern plantations, others more
concerned with the myth of frontier individualism than with national
wealth, preferred to rely on local militia, a system that was disorderly but
exciting.

Despite the scare of war with England, a majority in the House rejected,
on two occasions, efforts to increase the national military establishment—
on May 19, 1794, by a vote of 50 to 30 and eleven days later by a margin
of 50 to 32.[20] Proponents of "assisting" the frontier by providing for defense against Indians came almost entirely from northern coastal districts:
six from Connecticut, three from Maryland, nine from Massachusetts, one
from New Hampshire, two from New Jersey, six from New York, one
from Pennsylvania, and two from Rhode Island.

The Senate, however, did not give up easily. A House bill authorizing
the president to call out local militia, if the need arose, was amended by
the Senate with a provision to establish a standing army of 1,140 men to

defend the southwestern frontier. In the House, William Giles, ever alert to schemes for undermining individual liberties, protested that, "Proteus never assumed a greater number of shapes than this attempt has done. The people of the United States did not wish to be trodden down by a Continental army." John Nicholas, a fellow Virginian, added that "a bill had been wanted to protect the frontiers, but, by this amendment, the bill would scourge them." Two western representatives reminded the House of their own frontier experiences and pointed out that a standing army was useless; only the local militia could handle Indian defense. Thomas Carnes of Georgia asserted that a federal force would do more mischief than service and that they "always lose to the Indians who slip between their forts."[21] After a bit more torrid rhetoric, the House defeated the Senate's proposal by a vote of 42 to 26 as, once again, coastal delegates stood alone in favor of increased aid to the frontier.[22]

The two groups that polarized during the Third Congress on the question of establishing a permanent federal military presence on the frontier differed substantially from the blocs that coalesced in earlier Congresses on western issues. The figures in Table 21 reveal the dramatic shift that had occurred: before 1794 (see Tables 19 and 20) voting patterns on measures to increase national control on the frontier did not correlate closely with other categories of roll calls, except moderately with "government power" issues; beginning in 1794, the two groups that polarized on frontier issues also voted cohesively against each other, not only on government power issues, but also on economic questions and even on roll calls involving personal or inconsequential matters. The single exception, and it is significant, is in the category "foreign policy"; low levels of polarization occurred on these roll calls. As will be shown later, the legislature did not divide deeply over outputs in the foreign policy area before 1794. On the other

Table 21. Cohesion Differences: Proponents Against Opponents of Establishing a Standing Army on the Frontier, Third Congress

Issue	*Range of Cohesion Difference*			*Mean*
	0–34%	*35–64%*	*65–100%*	
	Percent of Roll Calls in Each Range			
Government power	33	17	50	46
Frontier	20	36	44	58
Economic	19	58	23	49
Foreign policy	61	10	29	32
Miscellaneous and personal	14	72	14	52
ALL ROLL CALLS	30	39	31	47

hand, the question of the proper limits of government power had been a source of divisiveness for years. Its solution, through Washington's response to the Whiskey Rebellion, was close at hand. Similarly, disagreement over domestic economic policy immediately produced polarization in the legislature, and by 1794 the lines of factional formation on the issue had hardened. Thus, voting behavior on frontier policies correlated closely with voting behavior on two categories of issues in which widely accepted policy outputs were rapidly being reached, but did not correlate with voting patterns in the area of foreign policy, an issue that the legislature had only begun to consider. To recall once again Madison's definition of party as the rule of passion producing legislative discipline, the situation was one of transition from policy-oriented factions to office-seeking parties.

After several years in which rapidly shifting blocs of delegates produced the broad outlines of a frontier policy by forming temporary alliances and then quickly disbanding, it had become clear that the national government would take whatever steps it deemed necessary to assure the orderly conversion of the West from potential abundance to actual wealth. These steps included full control over Indian affairs, the right to restrict the self-defense measures of white settlers, and the supervision of local government arrangements. By 1794 this policy was widely accepted, at least by those with the power to make their opinions significant. Subsequent disagreements were over details of implementation rather than over meaningful alternatives. This circumstance, combined with the resolution of other basic issues, formed the milieu in which a two-party system developed and flourished. Westerners, so deeply concerned about the national government's ability to protect them that they had heartily joined efforts to adopt a new Constitution, now broke their policy alliance with proto-Federalists and turned to partisan politicking. Easterners, both northern and southern, certain that federal authority had been established on the frontier, courted western votes for reasons of office rather than policy.

The implementation of this policy of federal control, however, did not always take place with the unanimous consent of the House. Several sharp divisions occurred, in most cases as a result of the continued desire of western settlers to handle their own Indian affairs. Although these divisions did not alter the basic agreements on frontier policy that had been reached by 1794, they did severely test the accords reached in the House.

On February 27, 1795, westerners, freshly alerted by Washington's response to the Whiskey Rebellion to the darker side of federal assistance on the frontier, united with southern anti-administration forces to defeat

Senate-initiated legislation to "prevent depredations on the Indians south of the Ohio River." Forty-three members favored rejection while thirty-seven voted for the bill. The states most directly affected by the proposed legislation—Georgia, Kentucky, North Carolina, and Virginia—were unanimous in their opposition, casting a total of twenty-five ballots. Twenty of twenty-three New Englanders voted for the protection of Indians, but a split among delegates from the Middle Atlantic states tipped the balance in favor of the frontier position against federal interference.[23]

The victory proved ephemeral, the result of parliamentary maneuver, misunderstanding, and absence. On the very next day, as the House considered a similar bill, westerners suffered a decisive setback. A portion of the proposed legislation to protect Indians made it a crime for unauthorized persons (anyone but federal troops) to bear arms while on Indian lands. This was a forceful, unequivocal provision intended to make certain that high-spirited, violence-prone frontiersmen would no longer provoke skirmishes with Indians. The resultant peace in the West, it was hoped, would promote prosperity. Western delegates, more interested in vengeance than abundance, united behind a proposed amendment to exempt from criminal prosecution persons "immediately in pursuit of Indians who shall recently have committed hostilities." Supporters of the amendment appealed to the sacred right to defend home and family. Opponents pointed out that the aggressive self-defense tactics of westerners had resulted in costly wars that brought no gain to the nation as a whole. By a vote of 46 to 40, the House defeated this attempt to effectively circumvent the purpose of the bill. In so doing the majority reaffirmed the determination of the federal government to oversee the orderly development of western wealth.[24]

In the aftermath of Pinckney's Treaty with Spain, frontier delegates launched yet another effort, also unsuccessful, to undermine federal control in the West. It was generally assumed that the treaty would help reduce the level of hostilities with the Creek Indians on the southwestern frontier. Once again, opponents of a federal army argued that a strong military force was expensive, unnecessary, and dangerous, and that reliance should be placed on the local militia. Those delegates who favored reduction of the army were in the majority in the House on all eight recorded roll calls dealing with the question, but they lacked sufficient strength to override the executive veto that ultimately put an end to their efforts.[25] The reductions voted upon were as follows: to reduce the light cavalry by 80 percent; to reduce the standing army by 25 percent; and to eliminate completely the post of major general, held at the time by Anthony Wayne.[26] But Washington vetoed the bill incorporating all three proposals, and on March 1, 1797, the House failed to override, as 36 of 91 members voted to support the president. The core voting blocs consisted of twenty-three delegates who opposed any reduction of the military establishment and twenty-six who favored all three proposed reductions and who also voted to override Washington's veto. The remaining half of the House took a mixed position, favoring some reduction but not the full amount advocated by extreme opponents of the military establishment. An analysis of the two groups that took consistent positions for or against all reductions reveals that the underlying issue in these roll calls was not defense of the West but, rather, federal control over the frontier in order to assure the orderly development of its potential abundance.

The twenty-three opponents of reduction came from districts that had not been troubled by Indians for several generations, areas where very few federal troops had ever been stationed. Six of these delegates were from Massachusetts, five from Connecticut, two from Rhode Island, three from New York, three from Pennsylvania, two from Maryland, one from New Jersey, and one from South Carolina.[27] The single exception was William Cooper, representing western New York, whose support of the Jay Treaty, financing of frigates to protect commerce, large standing armies, great tracts of western lands, and new furnishings for John Adams can only be ascribed to a personal inclination that did not necessarily reflect the wishes of all his constituents. Through a complex and occasionally questionable series of deals, Cooper had acquired huge holdings in western New York. All other strong supporters of the army represented districts that had seldom seen a federal soldier on duty but were certain that law and order must be imposed on the West. All twenty-three voted against the Livingston Resolution and for the Jay Treaty. Only one member of the bloc opposed appropriations to outfit frigates for defense and expansion of commercial operations. Pro-army, pro-commerce, and pro-administration, this bloc was instrumental in upholding and extending the policy forged two years before by factional groups in the Second and Third Congresses: national control over western affairs to promote the orderly acquisition of the wealth of the land.

There was, however, an even larger group of representatives dedicated to reducing the federal military establishment whenever possible.[28] This group of twenty-six, more than half of whom came from Virginia or North Carolina, included delegates from every frontier area except western New York and Georgia. Factors other than geographical location influenced the delegates from these two areas. William Cooper has been mentioned previously; Georgia's representatives opposed the elimination of the post of major general out of loyalty to Anthony Wayne, but otherwise they favored army reductions. Sixteen of the twenty-six consistent opponents of a standing army represented frontier areas. These delegates, and their predecessors, had opposed federal troops for years, especially after it had become clear that the national government was more concerned with curtailing lawlessness among whites than with protecting settlers against Indians. The remaining ten delegates in the group hoped to curb centralized power that they believed already threatened the liberty of the states and of the people.[29]

But neither of the two blocs offered any new policy alternatives, nor did their efforts against each other result in any change in previously formulated policy outputs. Table 22 shows the now familiar voting pattern of opposing groups concerned more with partisan politicking (in this case the reputation of the outgoing administration) than with forging new responses

Table 22. Cohesion Differences: Proponents Against Opponents of Reducing the Military Establishment, Fourth Congress

	Range of Cohesion Difference			
Issue	*0–34%*	*35–64%*	*65–100%*	*Mean*
	Percent of Roll Calls in Each Range			
Government power	0	25	75	81
Frontier	11	5	84	80
Economic	54	8	38	43
Foreign policy	12	28	60	68
Partisan politics	0	80	20	62
Miscellaneous and personal	21	44	35	50
ALL ROLL CALLS	18	25	57	65

to important issues. On more than four of every five roll calls proponents and opponents of reducing the military establishment polarized against each other to a significant degree. They did so whether the issue was foreign policy, restraint on government power, sale of western lands, or outright politicking. The significant exception that exists on economic issues, when levels of polarization dropped sharply, occurred because the House began consideration of a federal land tax, an innovative policy proposal that generated factional voting behavior. (See Chapter 3, especially p. 57, Table 16, for parallel data supporting the conclusion that the land tax question was a new policy alternative, standing in sharp contrast to the lack of innovation in other legislative matters.)

The willingness of westerners and easterners to accept the broad outlines of the frontier policy formulated by 1794, that is, to allow the federal government to oversee and promote the rapid and peaceful conversion of potential wealth to actual abundance, ran deep. Even discussion of the policy, admittedly directed more at party needs than at offering viable alternatives, ceased after 1796. The pressures of threatened war with France, of course, turned the legislature's attention to the Atlantic rather than the Appalachians. Nevertheless, Congress found time to consider excluding Mississippi River transportation from an embargo on trade with France and its allies, to conduct a lengthy investigation of Winthrop Sargent's activities as governor of the Territory of Mississippi, and to authorize President Adams to accept the Western Reserve cession. But none of the 249 roll calls recorded in the Fifth and Sixth Congresses challenged federal control over western policy, or questioned the assumed relationship between establishing order on the frontier and realizing the full potential of landed abundance. Thus, the most important segment of the government's triad frontier policy was firmly established and implemented by the mid-1790s. The land was secured for effective development, against the misuse of Indians as well as the wasteful human frailties of white settlers.

This much accomplished, the legislature turned to the question of dividing the fruits of abundance among members of the national community. As William Appleman Williams perceptively concluded, "the idea that expansion was the key to prosperity and republicanism soon matured and came to govern American politics for at least a century."[30] In analyzing the years immediately following the writing of the Constitution, Williams succeeded in avoiding the alluring pitfall of dwelling too long on the greed of individual speculators and, instead, formulated a cogent summary of a critical national goal: to replace "quasi-colonial" dependence on England with an independent economy fueled by expanding wealth in an expanding West.

The goal was not achieved without many a false start, diversionary action, and blind fumbling. The most widely discussed of these was the activity of speculators, the grand and the not so grand. Faced with the harsh reality of needing immediate revenue, state and national governments easily lost sight of long-range plans and scrambled for the tantalizing panacea offered by a Robert Morris, a Manasseh Cutler, or a Yazoo Land Company. But the story of such schemes ought not to be confused with divisions over fundamental policy. Obviously, legislators heavily involved in the buying and selling of land voted with one eye on their personal accounts, but the sheer enormity of frontier abundance effectively neutralized such considerations. The trough overflowed, and even after feasts that landed more than a few in debtors prison, enough remained to provide the basis for a national policy. Though self-righteous men of lesser business acumen fulminated against speculative schemes, no policy alternative could eliminate such activity. The greedy always remained a step ahead—by selling national debt certificates short to buy land long, by hedging national debt holdings through purchase of state debt notes, by investing in banks so as to share in the profits that flowed from their own borrowing operations—unless, of course, they fell victim to the greater sharpness of a fellow gentleman of wealth. Short of returning to a primitive barter economy (which delegates alluded to only when they were especially angry or wearied by long debate), efforts to forge a national land policy could change the mode but not the extent of speculative activity.

Inability to define the national community among whom wealth would be divided proved to be a more significant obstacle in the drive to promote American prosperity through western expansion. In essence, the problem was that the leaders most committed to development of the frontier were often least able to accept a view of the nation based on a harmonious, or at least mutually dependent, relationship among the various segments of the society. As a result, men such as Madison, Jefferson, and Gallatin were troubled by their expansionist policies, even as they pursued them ever more successfully. The trouble was that expansion produced wealth for a nation which, these men believed, had not yet developed a sense of community, and which was still divided into the hostile factions that Madison had hoped the Constitution would render impotent. Jefferson's view of commerce as the "handmaiden" of agriculture was typical of his contentment with a vacuous but catchy phrase on a point that begged for rigorous analysis. It offered no solution to the dilemma of how to divide the fruits of landed abundance. Ultimately, Jefferson chose the path of least resistance and acquired future land while doing little to develop existing holdings. Gallatin, as secretary of the treasury, and Madison, in the last year of his presidency, faced the question of internal improvements squarely, thereby confronting the issue of distribution of western wealth to the national community, but both retreated to the safety of ambiguous, unworkable solutions.

The makers of policy in the 1790s—Washington, Adams, and Hamilton—stood at a very different point on the ideological spectrum of western positions. They had no philosophical difficulties, at least in their own minds, in defining a national community. Yet they too proved unable to develop and distribute landed abundance throughout the nation. President Washington, casually assuming that the nation was but a grand reflection of his own plantations, failed to see that the primary step in producing abundance was to fill the land with settlers, with men who freely chose this way of life, with men who were long on hope but short on cash. No one held a firmer conception of community than did John Adams, but for him the essence of community was the need to overcome sin and innate depravity. Understandably, Adams did not favor giving away God's land to let men run amuck; consequently, he emphasized control of the passions rather than acquisition of wealth. Alexander Hamilton, despite the narrow range of his personal experience, or perhaps because of it, predicated his copious suggestions for improving the economy on the premise that agriculture, commerce, and manufacturing were symbiotically associated, that a policy that benefitted one group might aid the others as well. But the secretary of the treasury, obligated by his office to emphasize short-term needs and circumscribed by Anglophilia, was not very interested in the frontier.

The inability of prominent leaders to offer ways to make effective use of western wealth paralleled the failures of lesser men. Between 1789 and 1801 the national legislature reached accord on a new land sale policy only once, and even then the result did not facilitate frontier settlement. Delegates recognized that the highest priority had to be given to encouraging actual settlers, but they disagreed sharply over the means of achieving this goal. Several forces combined to stalemate all legislative efforts before 1796. The response of the First Congress to Hamilton's *Report on a Uniform System for the Disposition of the Lands, the Property of the United States* was typical. The secretary outlined plans to sell to "moneyed individuals and companies who will buy to sell again," to associations of individuals who might pursue a new communal life, and to single families who wished a fresh start. Not surprisingly, detailed proposals on price, credit terms, surveying arrangements, and land office locations reflected Hamilton's willingness "to meet the financial demands of the hour without a proper consideration of the future." Briefly in its second session and at length in its third, the First Congress debated the secretary's proposals. Many amendments were offered, a few of which the House adopted, but its efforts came to naught when the Senate failed to act at all. Indifference about the West and deep division over the role of speculators in frontier development combined to block any legislation, and therefore any land sales, until the middle of the decade.[31]

Prospects for some sort of legislation improved sharply, however, following Major General Anthony Wayne's highly publicized victory at Fallen Timbers on August 20, 1794. Further impetus came in the following year, when the House suffered the indignity of having several of its members approached concerning their receptivity to a bribe for favors in connection with a grant of twenty million acres in Michigan. William L. Smith of South Carolina, chairman of the Land Office Committee, revealed that he had been approached, whereupon a host of prominent representatives, among them James Madison, William Giles, William Vans Murray, and Daniel Buck, announced that they too had been sounded out. At least one delegate's delay in reporting the bribe attempt was mildly embarrassing. An aroused House did little more than slap the wrists of the bribers, but it did resolve firmly to pass land sale legislation.

The resulting Land Act of 1796 failed to promote settlement on federal lands, the necessary prerequisite to converting potential abundance to actual wealth. The act specified sale at two dollars per acre, a price out of the reach and interest of most settlers when states were selling equally good land at fifty cents per acre. Provision under the act for minimum tracts of 640 acres and inflexible credit terms reduced buyers to a trickle. Indeed, the legislation did little more than harass squatters and delay expansion into the Ohio Territory until after 1800. Although Congress failed to solve the problem of encouraging orderly and productive expansion of land use, a heated debate and a little known pair of roll calls do offer some insight on policy positions at mid-decade.

Minimum tract provisions occasioned the House's most searching analysis of western land policy. James Holland, a delegate from interior North Carolina, offered an exhaustive treatment of the case for dividing federal lands into 160-acre tracts as opposed to lots of at least double that size. He wished to see the land sold to genuine settlers who did not intend to hold only for resale. In an attempt to lure the support of congressmen more concerned with immediate revenue than with frontier needs, he reasoned that the increased number of potential buyers of smaller lots would drive up land prices and provide a windfall for the government. Large tracts, he maintained in appealing to a different group of delegates, gave rise to monopoly and increased the danger to free government. He concluded his remarks with a plea that included an astute comment on the foundations of the young republic: small tracts, he said, "would accommodate the poorer class of citizens. To live as tenants of others had a tendency to vitiate and debase their minds, instead of making them free, enlightened, and independent. By this amendment [160-acre tracts], this class of citizens would be enabled to become possessed of real property—a situation incident to freedom, and desired by all."[32]

In some of its facets, the issue appeared to be more complicated than rich versus poor, speculator versus settler. Proponents of large tracts argued that they might be surveyed rapidly and, the sooner the land was sold, the sooner the national debt might be discharged. But discharge of the debt was hardly of concern to potential buyers of small tracts, and even creditors were divided on the matter by Hamilton's argument for the utility of a continuing debt. Some delegates claimed that large tracts would ultimately assist the poorer classes by encouraging first purchase by speculators who might provide the credit assistance that the government would not offer to buyers of small tracts. Opponents countered with the observation that the inevitable result of passing land through the hands of speculators was to raise its price. The debate droned on, but no one chose to seriously dispute Holland's argument, and the issue voted upon was quite clear: should lots be 160 acres, thereby allowing the poorer classes a better chance to acquire them?

Two roll calls were recorded. A motion to survey 320-acre tracts lost by a vote of 45 to 40 and immediately thereafter the House approved 160-acre lots by a 45 to 42 margin.[33] Forty delegates opposed 320 acres and voted for 160-acre lots; thirty-six representatives favored 320 acres and voted against 160-acre lots. The remainder abstained, voted for both proposals, or voted against both measures. In any event, their positions cannot be determined with certainty. Table 23 displays the voting pattern of the seventy-six delegates who voted consistently for or against reducing minimum lot size. Significant polarization occurred on two of every three roll calls, a ratio substantially lower than existed for blocs voting against each other on reduction of the military establishment (see Table 22). The figures for extreme polarity reveal more fully the policy commitment involved in the tract size vote: Table 23 shows that only 3 percent of all roll calls resulted in cohesion differences above 64 percent; Table 22 shows that, for military establishment blocs, 57 percent of the same roll calls occasioned cohesion differences above 64 percent. By 1796 the issue of reduction of the army in the West had become a political football devoid of policy considerations; consequently, delegates voting against each other on this issue consistently opposed each other on most other roll calls. But on the question of land sales, the House still groped toward acceptable policy outputs and delegates sometimes ignored partisan allegiances in their quest for ways to realize the potential wealth of the frontier.

The forty representatives who voted for the smaller tracts opposed administration-supported measures more often than not, but they did not do so as a highly disciplined party.[34] Thirty-five of them voted for the

Table 23. Cohesion Differences: Proponents Against Opponents of Reducing
Minimum Tract Size to 160 Acres, Fourth Congress

Issue	*Range of Cohesion Difference*			*Mean*
	0–34%	*35–64%*	*65–100%*	
	Percent of Roll Calls in Each Range			
Government power	0	100	0	56
Frontier	11	72	17	53
Economic	54	46	0	36
Foreign policy	32	68	0	40
Partisan politics	60	40	0	31
Miscellaneous and personal	58	42	0	28
ALL ROLL CALLS	34	63	3	41

Livingston Resolution and only three opposed it, but ten favored implementation of the Jay Treaty. On the question of building frigates to protect commerce, ten would prove to be hard core opponents while four would vote in favor of building the ships. None of the forty consistently opposed reduction of the military establishment, but only sixteen delegates in the group always voted for reduction. Most of the group ran for Congress as Republicans, but several were prominent Federalists, notably William Barry Grove of North Carolina, Richard Thomas of Pennsylvania, and John Van Alen of New York. The geographic distribution of the group was significant; none came from New England, New Jersey, or Georgia, and only one was from Maryland. New England and the land-poor coastal states were not interested in promoting frontier settlement that threatened to drain them of their work force. Georgia's delegates were more concerned with the state's own western lands. Support for 160-acre tracts was substantial in the other states: thirteen in Virginia, seven in North Carolina, six in New York, six in Pennsylvania, four in South Carolina, two in Kentucky, and one in Delaware. Frontier delegates from New York to North Carolina were only one short of unanimous in their support of the small lots. They achieved victory, albeit only temporarily, because they received the votes of easterners who were willing to pay the added cost of surveying 160-acre tracts in order to make western lands more easily available to the poorer classes.

Analysis of the thirty-six opponents of small tracts, sarcastically referred to as "garden plots" by New York's William Cooper, sheds further light on the interests that formed on this issue.[35] Most were counted as administration supporters; twenty-two opposed the Livingston Resolution; twenty-five ultimately voted to implement the Jay Treaty; eleven would fully support appropriations for frigates to protect commerce; and sixteen opposed any reduction in the size of the military establishment. On the other hand, a sizable minority of the bloc voting against garden plots were prominent opponents of the administration. Thirteen delegates in the group voted for the Livingston Resolution and ten voted against the Jay Treaty to the bitter end. Two would oppose frigates consistently, and three favored every proposed army reduction. The geographic distribution of the thirty-six opponents of 160-acre tracts showed a large proportion in New England, New Jersey, and Maryland, with scattered support from coastal areas in other states. The group divided among the states as follows: one in Vermont, three in New Hampshire, nine in Massachusetts, two in Rhode Island, five in Connecticut, two in New York, two in New Jersey, one in Pennsylvania, four in Maryland, one in Virginia, three in North Carolina, one in South Carolina, and two in Georgia. Outside New England, where every delegate who took a consistent position opposed 160-acre tracts, votes against the small lots came from coastal areas and from delegates who feared that the increased desirability of western federal lands would reduce values in their own areas. Members falling into this last category included some Republicans of considerable note—Edward Livingston, Gabriel Christie, Aaron Kitchell, Nathaniel Macon, and John Nicholas.

Roll calls on size of western lots demonstrate, once again, the relationship between interest group and party. Most supporters of the small tracts accepted the label Republican and most opponents considered themselves Federalists, but party connection did not motivate voting on this issue. When men as important as those Republicans noted above were on the "wrong" side and when other stalwarts such as Albert Gallatin and James Madison took equivocal positions in favor of both 320- and 160-acre tracts, party discipline can be dismissed as an explanation for policy positions. Two groups existed, motivated by the extent and mode in which they desired to see the frontier opened to settlement. Large tracts meant continued holding by speculators or no sales at all; smaller lots encouraged the possibility of settlement by a wider range of citizens. The West was nearly unanimous in its support of 160-acre tracts. Other delegates divided, not according to party, but on the basis of their attitude toward encouraging western migration. This attitude may have been based on economic interest—protecting eastern land values or large western holdings—or it may have been based on the principle of assisting the poor. The relationship of party affiliation to this attitude or interest was more than incidental, but it was not causal.

Congress was not satisfied with its efforts to forge a means for realizing the potential wealth of the national domain but, even in failure, legislative patterns established in the 1790s molded the dimensions of future policy. Utopian visions of a tax free society constantly enriched by sale of its greatest natural resource did not materialize, nor was the land used to provide unlimited opportunity for the poorer classes. The balance struck between these extremes tilted moderately from time to time, but never deviated far from its fulcrum. The barriers of high price, inflexible credit, and inadequate transportation prevented the lure of landed abundance from capturing the labor of the poor and undermining eastern economic development. On the other hand, the national domain did not become the exclusive preserve of the wealthy; men of means realized that capital investment in eastern industry provided rewards at least equal to the profits of speculation in western lands. Thus the legislature, in a fumbling and occasionally unthinking way, successfully guided the national economy beyond the outdated and ultimately self-defeating mercantilist policy of "colonizing" new territory, away from the irrational myth of an agrarian utopia, and toward integration of the two factors uniquely present in the United States: natural resources and technology. By avoiding a total commitment to either land or industry, Congress made the most of the reality that both existed in bountiful supply.

Having secured the national domain from the misuse of Indians and while avoiding the lure of exploiting the land to the detriment of eastern industrial needs, the nation turned to the last aspect of its triad goal for the West: to reproduce on the frontier the best in itself. Seldom did Americans, and their delegates in Congress, analyze their own society more carefully than at those times when the opening of new land offered the prospect of a societal rebirth. Nowhere are such beliefs as the wisdom of representative republican government, the value of education, and the immorality of slavery more cogently expressed than in writings on society and the new frontier—in Jefferson's plan of 1784 for the old northwest, in John Quincy Adams' joyful diary entries after concluding a transcontinental treaty with Spain, in the bitter, often penetrating debate over the admission of Missouri. The problem of societal rebirth is an ongoing one that must be examined over several generations. The present study of legislative behavior in the 1790s can offer only a brief and partial glimpse of this process of procreation.

By the end of the decade Congress formulated a policy that may be summarized as follows: frontier settlers were free to determine specific forms for governing themselves, but the parent national legislature retained the right to judge the handiwork of its citizens in order to assure

the perpetuity of republican government. In most instances direct intervention proved unnecessary. The exceptions, brought to light during debate
over the admission of Tennessee in 1796 and the organization of the Territory of Mississippi in 1800, offer tangible evidence of congressional insistence on its obligation to nurture a healthy commitment to parental
values in its frontier offspring. Speaking in favor of the admission of Tennessee, Robert Rutherford of Virginia, a man with a remarkable gift for
reducing complex problems to domestic metaphors, concluded with a direct allusion to the rebirth theme:

> He would have them taken out of leading-strings, as they were
> now able to stand alone; it was time to take them by the hand,
> and to say, we are glad to see you, stand on your own feet.
> We should not . . . be too nice about their turning out their
> toes, or other trifles; they will soon march lustily along.[36]

For some delegates the question of admitting Tennessee was not quite
that simple. William L. Smith of Charleston, among others, was alarmed by
the sheer upishness of these crude westerners. They had not consulted with
Congress or even informed it of their intention to become a state. They
had conducted a population count in a fashion contrary to that used for
the federal census and peculiarly calculated to assure a full count. Instead
of enumerating everyone in the territory as of a given time, Tennessee
spread its census over several months, enumerating one county at a time
and insisting that anyone present in a county be included regardless of
permanent residence. The practice was defended on the basis that people
who intended to settle might not yet have built a residence, but the possibility of counting the same person twice was obvious. When the census
revealed a total population of 67,000, only 7,000 more than the minimum required for statehood, some delegates raised questions. The questions turned to fury when a handful of Tennessee's warmest supporters
in the House audaciously proposed that the state be assigned two representatives, as its population justified, rather than the single representative
normally allotted pending federal enumeration.[37]

A major issue lurked behind the census squabble. It soon became apparent that Tennessee had first established itself as a state, elected a governor, a legislature, two senators, and a representative and only then applied for admission to the Union. Delegates sensed that they were at the
precipice of a constitutional crisis, for to deny admission to the state was
to continue its de facto existence as an independent entity of some sort,
though representatives disagreed over the exact status of Tennessee at the

moment. Clearly, the territory had exhibited too much independence and resourcefulness to suit some members of the House, but the majority agreed with Nathaniel Macon that the best course of action was to hope that dangerous precedents or constitutional challenges did not exist and to move immediately to the North Carolinian's easier test for admission: "Was the new Government Republican?" and "Were there 60,000 inhabitants in the Territory?" Forty-three delegates answered yes to both questions and voted to admit the state.[38] The partisan intensity of the recently concluded Jay Treaty debate caused representatives to be less concerned with the policy issues raised by Tennessee's admission than with the anticipated votes of its representative and two senators. Table 24 summarizes a pattern of extreme polarization between proponents and opponents of Tennessee's admission for all Fourth Congress roll calls except those dealing with the land tax. The array of delegates against each other, and the motivation for their votes, are similar to the voting behavior that occurred on the reduction of the military issue (see Table 22). In this instance, then, the legislature forgave the wayward actions of territorial settlers, but in future it intended to exercise firmer control.

Table 24. Cohesion Differences: Proponents Against Opponents of Admitting Tennessee, Fourth Congress

	Range of Cohesion Difference			
Issue	*0–34%*	*35–64%*	*65–100%*	*Mean*
	Percent of Roll Calls in Each Range			
Government power	0	0	100	91
Frontier	18	17	65	64
Economic	53	16	31	39
Foreign policy	20	36	44	59
Partisan politics	20	60	20	50
Miscellaneous and personal	57	29	14	37
ALL ROLL CALLS	29	25	46	55

A partial opportunity to do so arose in 1800, when the House moved to establish a government for the Territory of Mississippi. However, attempts to deal with the substantial issues were undermined by the presence of Winthrop Sargent as governor of the territory. Though his revolutionary ardor had cooled considerably over the years, Sargent still spoke proudly and often of his fine war record. His subsequent service as governor of the Northwest Territory had been marred by an unpleasant incident or two, but Sargent remained a model frontier leader, at least in the eyes of his Federalist supporters back East. Westerners viewed the man in a different light. Thomas T. Davis, one of Kentucky's spokesmen in the House, charged that Sargent "pursued the principles of despotism," that he "practiced avarice, extortion," and that his appointees were "obnoxious for their intrigues and foreign influence." William Claiborne, another Kentuckian, urged the House to investigate Sargent's "want of disposition to have the General Assembly organized."[39] Speaker Theodore Sedgwick appointed a committee of reliable Federalists to investigate the charges. On the last day of the session the committee presented its report, which reduced the attack on Sargent to two specific charges. On the first, interference with a local election, the committee concluded that Sargent had interfered "accidentally," and ordered a new election. On the second, failure to convene the legislature, the committee uncovered extenuating circumstances for the governor's delay and declined to intervene "on the grounds suggested, of a presumption that those powers will not be fairly and discreetly exercised in this instance." The report concluded that no further action should be taken against Sargent, a conclusion that was more a statement of fact than a recommendation since the House was within hours of final adjournment. Nevertheless, an obstinate majority refused to accept the report and, with a new administration coming to power, Sargent vacated the governorship without the benefit of congressional exoneration.[40]

The entire episode typified the tendency of the Sixth Congress to lose itself in a quagmire of investigating charges and countercharges, eventually to emerge with a meaningless, highly partisan vote to do nothing. But in this case, at least one important policy decision emerged. The House approved and then insisted upon, despite Senate objections, an amendment to the bill on the Mississippi Territory that denied the governor (Sargent or anyone else) the right to prorogue the legislature at his pleasure. In the spring of 1800 many Federalists, still victimized by their own rhetoric, believed that a conspiracy existed against order and liberty. The same mentality that produced an act against sedition two years earlier now led some delegates to defend the monarchical principles that their opponents had once falsely accused them of harboring. By any reasonable standard of judgment, so drastic an undermining of legislative power was a step backward, a measure at total variance with the carefully thought out provisions in the Constitution for preserving a balanced, stable, republican government. To set up potential gubernatorial monarchs in frontier territories threatened fundamentally the process of societal procreation that Congress was attempting to preserve. A majority in the House recognized the threat and, in some instances laying aside partisan attachments, voted to maintain a balance between executive and legislative functions in the territory. But,

Table 25. Cohesion Differences: Proponents Against Opponents of Allowing a Territorial Governor to Prorogue the Legislature, Sixth Congress

Issue	Range of Cohesion Difference			Mean
	0–34%	35–64%	65–100%	
	Percent of Roll Calls in Each Range			
Government power	9	0	91	81
Frontier	12	25	63	74
Economic	0	16	84	75
Foreign policy	10	20	70	68
Partisan politics	6	18	76	72
Miscellaneous and personal	33	0	67	55
ALL ROLL CALLS	9	15	76	71

as Table 25 indicates, the forty-six delegates willing to allow proroguing of a territorial legislature by its governor polarized consistently against their fifty-five opponents on most other issues as well.[41]   Party solidarity was great throughout the Sixth Congress, even in the consideration of ideological issues that earlier in the decade had generated what Madison called the rule of reason not passion. Intense partisanship made it difficult for the House to examine in detail the nature of American society and to forge policies to assure successful procreation on the frontier. Only the most blatant violations of widely accepted norms for republican government aroused the House from its pursuit of apparent party needs.

*   *   *   *   *

At the outset of this chapter, the frontier was described as an especially attractive form of abundance, to which the national legislature directed its attention in order to achieve three related goals: (1) to secure potential abundance from the misuse of those outside the national community, (2) to apportion landed abundance among members of the community in a just and widely beneficial way, and (3) to use the frontier to perpetually recreate the best in the community. Analysis of specific legislative outputs in the first twelve years under the Constitution reveals numerous false starts, diversions, complicating factors, and misunderstandings. Yet the general trend of policy outputs is clear. Congress pursued security on the frontier, not in the safety envisioned by western settlers who emphasized violent defense, but rather in the permanent acquisition of land for use by law-abiding white farmers protected by a federal army from themselves as well as from Indians. The House coped less successfully with the problem of distributing the fruits of abundance, but even in failure it established a policy that allowed exploitation of the frontier without disruption of eastern economic development. It provided an opportunity for the speculator who did not dream on too grand a scale, and a potential start for the settler of proven industriousness. The legislature seldom faced concrete problems in guiding societal rebirth on the frontier but, acting as the proud parent of a promising offspring, the House gave firm guidance when necessary. In forging these policy outputs, delegates divided primarily on the merits of the particular question at hand. Especially before 1795, blocs that coalesced on frontier issues did not polarize consistently against each other on other categories of roll calls. In the latter half of the decade, after the pressing western need for security had been fulfilled, representatives turned away from substantive issues in order to pursue the acquisition of office, most often through rapidly growing party machinery.

5

MONEY, PARTY, AND FACTION

> But the most common and durable source of factions has been
> the various and unequal distribution of property. Those who
> hold and those who are without property have ever formed
> distinct interests in society. Those who are creditors, and those
> who are debtors, fall under a like discrimination. A landed in-
> terest, a manufacturing interest, a mercantile interest, a mon-
> eyed interest, with many lesser interests, grow up of necessity
> in civilized nations, and divide them into different classes, actu-
> ated by different sentiments and views. The regulation of these
> various and interfering interests forms the principal task of
> modern legislation, and involves the spirit of party and fac-
> tion in the necessary and ordinary operations of the govern-
> ment.[1]

No more incisive statement on American politics exists than these words
of James Madison. The subject of intensive inquiry from Charles Beard to
Douglas Adair, they remain a simple, necessary basis for understanding the
nation's development.[2] Unfortunately, several generations of historians
too often reduced a powerful analysis to a useless slogan by too heavily
emphasizing the polarization between "those who hold and those who are
without property." Formulators of such neat boxes as "Beardians," "neo-
Beardians," and "anti-Beardians" serve no function except to create confusion and, in the process of reducing an argument to absurdity, they cast
aside Madison's fundamental point. The brilliant insight in Number 10 of
The Federalist is not the statement, true though it is, that the "most common and durable source of factions" is "unequal distribution of property";
rather, it is the inclusion in that sentence of the word "various" and the
immediate emphasis on a wide range of propertied interests. In a society
of abundance, in which "haves" outnumbered "have-nots" (especially
since slaves were property, not people) and even the "have-nots" generally
acted on the belief that they would soon join the ranks of the "haves,"

95

the destitute did not constitute a politically meaningful interest. But the balancing and control of "various and interfering" propertied groups did form the "principal task" of government. Again, Madison showed remarkable foresight in specifying four major economic interests: agriculture, manufacturing, commerce, and banking. Representatives of these four groups coalesced into rapidly shifting factions in the early 1790s and produced policies so successful in promoting and balancing the economy that issue-oriented factionalism gave way to Federalist and Republican parties that offered few meaningful policy alternatives, thereby making it possible for politics to cut across lines of economic interest. By overcoming attachment to narrow economic interests, the legislature forged policies for establishing an expansive, independent economy in which the shares of various groups might be unequal, but at least they promised to be large. The relative prosperity of the early 1790s, combined with nearly universally optimistic forecasts, encouraged delegates to compromise on short-range interests and solve problems that had perplexed the nation for a decade. The Constitution provided the potential for strong national legislation and Congress produced the reality.

The ultimate goal of the legislature was to promote economic growth while maintaining a just balance among conflicting interests. There were, of course, no roll calls on the merit of this goal, and if any existed no doubt they would have been unanimous. What does exist is a maze of proposals and counterproposals reflecting disagreement over the best means of achieving the common goal. Any sorting out and categorization of the numerous roll calls recorded during the decade is subject to qualifications, but within the area of domestic economic legislation several types of issues gave rise to distinct factional formations, and in this instance analysis of component parts is necessary before reaching conclusions about the ultimate goal.

Representatives understood that the acquisition of a secure revenue base was prerequisite to government action in promoting the economy, and in any other area as well. In Number 35 of *The Federalist* Hamilton had expressed, more clearly than most delegates could, the advantages of employing a variety of taxes falling by design on different economic interests. In theory no one disagreed, but in practice representatives were loath to support levies that burdened important interests in their particular constituencies. Consequently, fundamental factional voting patterns are difficult to discern and trace over time. Further complications arise because some delegates voted against revenue measures to protest the use of tax dollars rather than the means of acquiring them. Nonetheless, distinct divisions occurred on four types of revenue sources: tariff and tonnage duties, consumption taxes, domestic production taxes, and land taxes. Tariff and tonnage duties were used to produce revenue and to aid domestic shipping interests, but not to protect local manufacturers. Consumption taxes were used to produce revenue and, on a few occasions, to promote moral positions such as opposition to smoking and drinking. Domestic production taxes were not widely employed, but the single exception of the levy on spirits makes the type important. Land taxes, initially supported by Hamilton's opponents, were imposed only when the need for revenue became desperate. Each of these sources of division in Congress will be treated subsequently in some detail.

The establishment of government credit followed immediately upon acquisition of revenue as a major goal of domestic economic policy outputs. Hamilton's desire to ally moneyed interests with those of the new government was obvious to all, but the more significant advantage of establishing credit was the great flexibility that accrued to the nation. When opportunity or need might arise—to purchase, to build, or to fight—good credit would mean the ability to exceed the narrow limits of current revenues and to fully exploit fleeting chance. Funding of national debts and assumption of state debts incurred during the Revolution allied creditors to the new government, expanded federal power and flexibility, and, at the very least, denied state governments an opportunity to do the same.

Regulation of economic expansion in order to create a national market was another closely related goal of national legislation.[3] To foster a stable currency and controlled credit expansion, Congress established a bank and a mint. It adopted a uniform bankruptcy law, intervened to aid fisheries and cloth manufacturers, and provided business for shipbuilders. Intervention in the economy remained somewhat haphazard, predicated more on the wishes of individual legislators than on overall plans for growth, but Congress did firmly establish its right to regulate for a national market. Lack of positive action reflected the belief that all was going well rather than a commitment to laissez-faire.

Each of these three broad subdivisions of domestic economic policy—acquiring revenue, establishing credit, and regulating growth—produced distinct legislative behavior. In all three areas the first secretary of the treasury provided forceful leadership; he molded policy by offering cogent analyses of current problems and concrete proposals for improving the economy. The legislature, however, did not simply acquiesce in rubberstamping Hamilton's program. Delegates in the House acted on their own initiative in several critical areas and, even when approving major portions of the secretary's reports, Congress deliberated fully upon the merits of what it was accepting and the strengths of alternative proposals. In the process legislators divided and re-divided into factional blocs that forged meaningful, innovative policy outputs. By the middle of the decade all politically powerful economic interest groups accepted the broad outlines of Hamiltonian policy. Continued fulminations against the moneyed classes served to further partisan desire for office but were no longer aimed to upset established policies.

The roll call analysis that follows demonstrates several propositions concerning economic policy and legislative behavior: (1) issue-oriented factions dominated Congress until the mid-1790s; (2) these factions produced widely accepted policies in the areas of revenue, credit, and regulation for growth; (3) in the late 1790s delegates felt no pressing need to produce new policy outputs; (4) as a result, partisan considerations centering upon acquisition of office produced a legislative stalemate characterized simultaneously by avoidance of divisive issues and by highly polarized voting patterns. The actual record, of course, is not as tidy as the bare statement of four propositions might imply, but in the maze of votes and the flourishes of rhetoric there was a discernible shift from faction to party, from the exercise of power for policy goals to the quest of power for the rewards of its exercise.

The *sine qua non* of successful government in 1789 was revenue; delegates in the House made its acquisition their first order of business. On April 8 of that year, the earliest day on which matters of substance could come before the House, James Madison initiated debate on a bill to impose import duties. He began not with economic arguments but with an appeal to overcome the "state of imbecility" that had beset government under the Articles. All delegates agreed on the "impotency" of the past, and only this overwhelming agreement on the necessity of doing something prevented the lengthy debate that followed from degenerating into a morass of personal interest claims. Congress spent days on such matters as a penny more on rum, twenty-five cents less per fisherman, and the date to commence collection of duties on hemp. In nearly every case the arguments ranged widely, from the morality of using the product to be taxed to the need to protect domestic manufacturing and on to the role of God in affairs of the pocketbook. But to detail these debates would be misleading, for the crucial point is their outcome.

After six weeks of deliberations, interrupted only for the presidential inauguration, the House passed a bill imposing duties of sufficient magnitude to assure adequate revenue for the new nation.[4] Thus, at a time when other branches of government had not yet formed and the Senate dallied over the matter of titles, the House atoned for a decade of "impotency" and subservience to local interest. Successful passage of a far-reaching tariff schedule is a legislative accomplishment of considerable magnitude at any point in American history. Coming at the very outset of government under the Constitution, passage of a tariff bill in 1789 set the tone of legislative action for the next few years. Delegates, at least some of them some of the time, compromised narrow economic interests and formulated policies they believed were in the national interest. Understandably, representatives from Massachusetts continued to argue that promotion of fisheries was in the national interest and Virginians felt the same way about tobacco production. But both accepted a share of the burden necessary to finance "energetic" government.

Sixteen additional pieces of tariff legislation passed both houses of Congress during the next eleven years, but none substantially modified the policy agreed upon in 1789: import duties would provide the mainstay of national revenue but were not to be employed primarily to benefit particular sectors of the domestic economy.[5] The relationship of import duties to foreign policy questions, of course, was not as harmonious an issue, nor did debate over the proper uses of revenue produce universal agreement. Nevertheless, at least until the Embargo of 1807 the tariff policy formulated in 1789 remained intact, and it was not effectively replaced until the Tariff Act of 1816.

Import duties provided a major portion of the new government's revenue and occasioned the least divisive policy debates of the decade on economic matters. Other forms of taxation, though less important in terms of absolute percentage of total revenue, brought factional groupings more fully to the foreground. Domestic excise taxes, occasionally laid for convenience on the producer but inevitably paid by the consumer, provoked bitter debate and raised fundamental questions about the role of government. The analysis that follows necessarily deals with a maze of seemingly different issues—taxes on whiskey, salt, sugar, carriages, and so forth—but certain consistent voting patterns will be demonstrated. Opponents of domestic excise taxation desired limitation of the government's "energy," opposed full payment of creditors, and tried to establish the regressive nature of such levies. Proponents sought a wide revenue base for expansion of governmental power, favored taxing those who spent their money "unwisely" anyway, and placed obligations to creditors on a sacred plateau. Some delegates shifted from group to group according to the particular tax under consideration, but a majority in the House voted consistently with one bloc or the other. This pattern continued until nearly the middle of the decade, when domestic excise taxation became an accepted policy and legislators turned their efforts more fully to the quest for office.

Two roll calls serve to illuminate factional patterns in the First Congress: an excise on distilled spirits approved on March 3, 1791, and an import duty on salt in the tariff revision passed on August 10, 1790. Both measures became necessary following the decision to fund the national debt and and to assume state obligations as well. Hamilton's decision to press for an excise tax, particularly the levy on domestically distilled spirits, outraged the same segment of the population and section of the country that made no gain from assumption.[6] Of all the roll calls recorded on the issue of obtaining revenue, none is more indicative of early opposition to domestic taxation than the vote on an amendment to levy duties only on imported spirits. The delegations of Georgia and North Carolina unanimously supported the amendment, but all the representatives of New England, New York, and New Jersey were as strongly for adding the domestic tax.[7] Pennsylvania split along intrastate regional lines. George Clymer, Thomas Fitzsimons, and Henry Wynkoop, all from the Philadelphia area, wanted to retain the domestic tax on whiskey, but three representatives from the interior opposed it. Virginians voted for the domestic tax by five to three, the minority consisting of two western delegates and one from the poorer southeastern section of the state. Thomas Sumter of upcountry South Carolina formed his usual minority of one in that state and voted to eliminate the tax on domestic spirits, while Michael Stone was the only one of three Maryland representatives voting who favored retaining the levy. Fighting a hopeless cause with great determination, opponents of domestic excise taxation delayed the bill for a time, but they suffered a final setback on January 27, 1791, by a margin of 35 to 21.[8]

Table 26 portrays the voting behavior of proponents and opponents of domestic excise taxation for all roll calls recorded in the First Congress. Several conclusions may be drawn from the data. Lack of consistent polarization on the issue of location of the capital indicates that the excise tax blocs were not primarily sectional in character. In other words, North and South did not vote against each other on taxation, even after passage of funding and assumption. A somewhat higher correlation exists between voting blocs on domestic excise levies and voting patterns on the issue of limiting the power of government. This finding is consistent with the statements of a number of opponents of further taxation, who expressed a desire to curtail the rapidly growing energy of the new government by nar-

Table 26. Cohesion Differences: Proponents Against Opponents of an Excise Tax on
Domestically Distilled Spirits, First Congress

Issue	Range of Cohesion Difference			*Mean*
	0–34%	*35–64%*	*65–100%*	
	Percent of Roll Calls in Each Range			
Government power	55	40	5	34
Frontier	100	0	0	7
Location of the capital	58	42	0	30
Economic	40	37	23	42
Foreign policy	75	25	0	24
Miscellaneous and personal	73	27	0	28
ALL ROLL CALLS	54	37	9	34

rowing its revenue base. The high level of polarity on economic issues is
very significant. In marked contrast to the compromising spirit of the 1789
tariff debate, the House polarized sharply and repeatedly on a variety of
economic issues, ranging from assumption to banking and to revenue acquisition. The category "Economic" in Table 26 includes thirty-five roll calls,
recorded over a period of nearly three years. Clearly, there existed two
blocs of delegates, together comprising over 90 percent of the voting members of the House, who consistently opposed each other on economic policies but who did not do so on other types of issues. Chapters 2, 3, and 4
of this study demonstrate the existence in the First Congress of distinct,
issue-oriented factions polarizing on three questions—location of the capital,
limits of government power, and the frontier. To these may properly be
added factions uniting primarily on economic issues.

Further evidence concerning the nature of voting behavior on economic
policy may be gained from a brief examination of the unsuccessful effort
of a number of House delegates to lower the duty on imported salt from
twelve to nine cents. Any import duty on this vital household product offered the prospect that domestic producers would raise their prices as well.
The small amount of revenue to be gained appeared inconsequential to delegates whose primary concern was with the sharply regressive nature of the
tax. Never before, others claimed, had a government taxed a more essential
item, one for which there was no substitute. The self-sufficient yeoman
who might avoid most of the federal tax burden had to purchase salt. But
the same arguments that convinced some delegates to favor lowering the
duty on salt led a majority to reach the opposite conclusion. Apparently
acting on the belief that even the most isolated and poorest citizen should
relate to his government by sharing some of its tax burden, thirty delegates voted to retain the twelve cent duty.[9]

Table 27 shows the voting behavior of these thirty, and of the twenty-eight representatives who favored lowering the duty to nine cents, by contrasting the votes of these two blocs with the votes of the two groups that emerged during the domestic excise tax debate. The salt tax blocs did not polarize as consistently and deeply as did the domestic excise factions.

Table 27. Cohesion Differences (CD%): Taxation Policy Blocs, First Congress

Blocs	*Percent of Roll Calls on Which CD% Exceeded 34%*		
	All Roll Calls	*Economic*	*Non-Economic*
(1) Salt tax opponents vs. whiskey tax opponents	2	6	0
(2) Salt tax opponents vs. whiskey tax proponents	28	49	15
(3) Salt tax proponents vs. whiskey tax opponents	33	54	21
(4) Salt tax proponents vs. whiskey tax proponents	0	0	0
(5) Salt tax opponents vs. salt tax proponents	19	34	11
(6) Proponents vs. opponents of whiskey tax	46	60	38

Nevertheless, certain patterns are evident. Rows 1 and 4 of Table 27 show that delegates who favored a higher salt duty also supported an excise tax on whiskey. Those who desired a lower salt duty opposed the whiskey tax. A comparison of rows 2 and 3 with rows 5 and 6 extends the conclusion: cohesive, issue-oriented factions emerged during the First Congress to contest economic policy outputs.

The new Congress that convened in the fall of 1791 was not as innovative and productive as its predecessor. The furious pace of legislative output that began with Madison's tariff proposals and increased when Hamilton revealed his bold plans did not quite grind to a halt, but the Second Congress did drift into a consolidation and adjustment phase. Even the presentation of Hamilton's *Report on the Subject of Manufacturers*, justly hailed by historian Richard B. Morris as the secretary's "most constructive and far-sighted" economic paper, failed to stir legislative action.[10] In its consideration of revenue acquisition, the House recorded votes on only two matters: a new whiskey tax rate and a duty on imported cotton. Although neither item involved a fundamental change in previously agreed-upon policy, both produced heated debate and sharply divided voting patterns. An examination of these two roll calls reveals that the factional behavior of the First Congress continued into the Second, though with less substantial matters to feed upon.

The proposed duty on raw cotton brought sectional allegiances to the surface and nearly reversed previous voting patterns on revenue matters. The proposal lost by a vote of 32 to 32, with only ten of the affirmative votes cast by delegates from the North and only five of the negative votes cast by southerners.[11] Unlike other revenue roll calls, a majority of southerners voted for the proposal and a majority of northerners were against it. Even at this early stage of cotton production in the South and of manufacturing in the North, both sections defended their economic interests. The compromising of local interest that had characterized legislative behavior early in the First Congress already was giving way to sectional attachment. But the extent of position reversal that occurred is significant. The ten northerners who voted for this duty generally opposed Hamiltonian policy and the five southerners who opposed the tariff revision consistently supported the administration.[12] This indicates a cohesive and total reversal of an earlier factional grouping rather than a shift to a different and unrelated pattern. That is, the pressure of sectional interest caused issue-oriented blocs to take uncharacteristic positions, but it did not cause the factions to disintegrate.

Delegates returned to more familiar positions on a roll call establishing the rate at which to continue the excise on domestically distilled spirits. Proponents of a levy of eight cents per gallon suffered a setback, by the narrowest of margins, to advocates of a lower rate. Although the defeat proved to be temporary, the roll call illuminates issue-oriented voting behavior in the Second Congress. After a lengthy debate that revealed the inability of Hamilton's opponents to offer constructive alternatives and provided a few good laughs about the evils of excessive drinking, the House rejected an eight cent rate by a vote of 26 to 27.[13]

Table 28 portrays the voting behavior of proponents and opponents of a lower tax on distilled spirits for all roll calls recorded in the Second Congress. The data demonstrate a continuation and extension of patterns that emerged during First Congress voting on revenue questions: lack of deep and consistent polarization by economic factions on frontier and foreign policy issues, a moderate correlation between behavior on economic policy and on government power issues, and highly cohesive voting on most economic questions. Similarity in voting patterns is one indication of continuity; another is the presence of the same delegates on one side or the other in both Congresses. Twenty-eight representatives voted on the domestic spirits excise in 1791 and on the eight cent rate proposal in

Table 28. Cohesion Differences: Proponents Against Opponents of a Lower Rate of
Excise on Distilled Spirits, Second Congress

Issue	0–34%	35–64%	65–100%	Mean
	Range of Cohesion Difference			
	Percent of Roll Calls in Each Range			
Government power	30	64	6	42
Frontier	85	15	0	23
Economic	17	74	9	49
Foreign policy	50	50	0	27
Miscellaneous and personal	65	25	10	29
ALL ROLL CALLS	40	53	7	39

1792. Of these, all but three took a consistent position. The exceptions, Samuel Livermore of New Hampshire and James Madison and Alexander White of Virginia, all voted for the excise in 1791 but favored a lower rate in 1792.[14] Throughout the First Congress the three supported the acquisition of sufficient revenue to finance energetic government, even after passage of assumption, but they returned to the Second Congress ready to oppose the administration, especially if an opportunity arose to attack a policy closely associated with the secretary of the treasury. But there was no massive movement of delegates from one faction to the other; most maintained a consistent position on economic policy throughout the first four years under the new government.

Reliance upon domestic taxation increased sharply in 1794. Rising debt service costs and the desire to mount an effective campaign against Indians on the western frontiers made the need for more revenue apparent to all. Hamilton's hesitancy to suggest changes in tariff schedules at a time when Jefferson's long-awaited report on the treatment of America's commerce was before the House, combined with the general uncertainty about the war in Europe, caused the House to consider a series of domestic levies. In such circumstances the effect of any proposed tax on a particular district weighed heavily in the casting of votes and, to an extent, ameliorated the pressures of factional alliances. Nevertheless, the influences of regional and personal interest did not entirely eliminate broader economic considerations. The Third Congress considered at length a multitude of sources of revenue and recorded votes upon a carriage tax, a stamp tax, a tobacco tax, increased tonnage duties, a retail liquor license tax, and an auction tax.

Since each of these taxes threatened to burden particular elements of the general population and certain areas of the country it is impossible to

generalize about positions on increasing taxes from the roll call on any particular proposal. In every instance certain representatives aligned themselves
on the basis of how hard the tax would hit their constituencies. A proposal
that never came to a vote—to tax stock transfers at five cents per hundred
dollars—gave rise to debate that exemplified the degree to which personal
interest might be involved in voting. Fisher Ames, who favored taxing
almost everything, argued that the purpose of taxes was to support public
credit but that,

> This tax on the transference of the Public Funds tended to in-
> jure it, by sinking their value . . . taxation of the Public Funds
> is nothing more or less than the debtor taxing the creditor . . .
> the progress of this measure would degrade the Public Debt
> into a paper rag.[15]

Richard Winn of North Carolina, who opposed most taxes, responded by
asking who the holders of public funds were and how they had acquired
such wealth. He concluded that they deserved to be heavily taxed.[16] Such
logic characterized debate on other proposals as well.

The tax on carriages that the House debated in May of 1794 was to be
an annual levy ranging from $10 for a coach to $2 for a two-wheeled vehicle. If one could judge by the arguments, a sectional issue was involved:
the more substantial citizenry in the older areas with good roads, it was
said, would pay the tax while large portions of the frontier would escape
entirely. Another argument against the tax, which probably did not sway
too many votes, came from Samuel Smith of Maryland, a state with many
carriages. He reasoned that,

> This was a tax on population. A young man gets a wife and a
> carriage to drive her to church in. You tax him. In due time he
> has a number of children, and must have a second carriage for
> giving them an airing. You tax him. Thus, sir, you tax a person
> for doing you the greatest service that can be done you—
> peopling your country.[17]

New Englanders favored the tax by 23 to 2 and Virginians, perhaps not for
the reasons given by Smith, opposed it in about the same ratio. Other states
were less cohesive.[18] Areas that probably had a small number of carriages
were not strong proponents of the tax, and the breakdown on this vote
closely reflected divisions that occurred on domestic excise questions in
previous Congresses.

Voting on two other taxes, on retail liquor licenses and on property sold at auction, did not occasion any significant change from the pattern that developed on the carriage tax vote.[19] New England's delegates voted for both taxes and Virginians opposed them while other states were divided. There was no significant debate on these two levies.

In contrast, the tobacco and snuff tax was the subject of extensive argument. Madison and Giles spoke at length of the unfair burden that would fall on Virginia. Nathaniel Macon of North Carolina, in opposing the $4 per hundred weight tax on snuff, pointed out that "this was the first instance in history where a raw material was taxed more than its value." Proponents of the levy, such as Samuel Dexter of Massachusetts, argued that the use of tobacco "is certainly a mere luxury, or, rather folly; and all who use, and of course, pay the duty, are volunteers."[20] A motion to eliminate the tax was strongly supported by delegates from Virginia and Maryland, but other states did not shift significantly from the positions they had taken on levies on carriages, liquor licenses, and goods sold at auction.[21]

The proposed stamp tax would have affected almost all legal actions, including mortgage deeds, at both the national and state level. On May 8, 1794, the House approved the measure in a preliminary vote of 58 to 35 as the pattern established on other tax proposals held firm. New Englanders favored the levy by 24 to 3, and were joined by the delegations of Maryland, New Jersey, New York, and South Carolina. Virginia and North Carolina opposed the tax by a three to one ratio and Pennsylvania repeated the five to five split that was characteristic of the state on the entire question of raising revenue.[22] When the bill came up for final approval on May 27, however, a vote of 50 to 32 eliminated the stamp tax. As sufficient income could be derived from other proposed levies, a large number of New Englanders switched sides and voted against the tax. Connecticut and Massachusetts, which had favored the stamp duties by 19 to 1 earlier, now opposed them by 11 to 7. Similar shifts occurred in Maryland, New Jersey, and South Carolina. Pennsylvania remained at five to five, but states that had originally opposed the tax did so even more forcefully on this occasion.[23]

Opposition to the stamp tax by delegates generally in favor of increased taxation appeared belatedly and was not unanimous. The question of raising tonnage duties resulted in a clearer division. Members who had favored all other proposed taxes were violently against this proposition, and representatives who had spoken at length on the evils of taxation were quick to exempt this one from their arguments. New England, excluding Vermont, voted to eliminate a duty of six cents per ton on

United States ships employed in foreign trade by 22 to 1. Other states seemed torn between their opposition to any taxes and the chance to vote for a levy that would hit hard at commercial interests. North Carolina, Pennsylvania, and Virginia favored the increased duty while Maryland, New Jersey, and New York opposed it. In all these states, however, the votes were divided.[24] A move to tax American tonnage also failed, with state alignments similar to those that existed on the defeat of the foreign tonnage duty.[25]

The patterns that existed on revenue acquisition votes and the trend of most of the House debate over the issue reflected local interests and, at first glance, the absence of broader ideological considerations. A closer examination of the actual votes, however, reveals two major blocs opposed to each other. A large group of delegates strongly favored increasing taxes, even when it affected their constituencies adversely. These men stood for expansion of federal power, payment of government creditors, promotion of commerce, and wide distribution of the tax burden. Most of them, and their predecessors, had done so consistently for five years. Although the term Federalist party is inappropriate for a group that was so disdainful of electoral machinery, these men may properly be considered an issue-oriented faction. Their opponents called them the representatives of the "moneyed classes."

At the other end of the ideological spectrum there evolved a cohesive, interstate faction that had initially emerged during the first domestic excise debates in late 1790. The group consisted partly of representatives of agriculture (whose long-standing aversion to big government turned to outright hostility when national power appeared to rest with eastern speculators, friends of England, and men of commerce who made money without really earning it). Increasingly, the bloc included frontiersmen who sought protection and received restrictions on their way of life. Added strength came from New Yorkers and Pennsylvanians who failed to share in the wealth they believed was flowing into New York City and Philadelphia. As an issue-oriented faction, the group was hopelessly outnumbered. Later in the decade it achieved overwhelming majorities, largely by abandoning policy positions to concentrate on electoral success.

But let us return to patterns in 1794. There were forty-five consistent proponents of increased taxation. At the extreme, five delegates—John Beatty of New Jersey, Thomas Fitzsimons of Philadelphia, James Gillespie of North Carolina, James Gordon of New York, and John Hunter of South Carolina—voted in favor of all six proposed taxes. Eighteen delegates strongly supported this nucleus by voting for all but one of the levies, the exception being the duty on tonnage which, because it adversely affected commercial interests, was scarcely an exception.[26] To these twenty-three may properly be added twenty-two delegates who favored all levies but voted against the stamp tax only after it became clear that the revenue would not be needed.[27] Altogether, then, a bloc of forty-five delegates, including representatives from every state except Vermont and Kentucky, joined together to produce a federal tax policy that greatly increased dependence on domestic levies.

Opposition to this policy shift came largely from a bloc of twenty-four delegates who consistently voted against new taxes. Four members—Isaaç Coles and Abraham Venable of Virginia, John Smilie of Pennsylvania, and Thomas Tredwell of New York—voted against every proposed tax. Coles and Venable had opposed Hamiltonian policy for years, but Smilie and Tredwell were equally firm in their adherence to that interest. Supporting these four, by opposing five of the six proposed taxes, was a group of eleven delegates, most of whom could not resist voting for increased tonnage duties but who were, nevertheless, solid opponents of expanding the national government further.[28] A less consistent bloc of nine representatives, favoring not only tonnage duties but one of the other taxes as well, tended to vote against the administration-sponsored domestic proposals that came before the House.[29]

There existed in the Third Congress, then, two cohesive blocs: one supported increased reliance on domestic levies, the other opposed the shift. The average total by which the House approved particular taxes ranged from 53 to 58 affirmative against 32 to 36 negative. Factional voting by these blocs therefore accounted for 67 to 80 percent of all votes cast and represented the most important single factor in determining action taken on revenue measures. Despite all the speeches and complaints about local hardships, the deciding influence was an ideological one: the proper extent of government power and the most appropriate way to finance energetic national authority. The significance of interest groups is even more evident when viewed on a state by state basis. Table 29 summarizes the categories discussed above.

The large number of pro-tax delegates shown for New York and North Carolina illustrates a basic characteristic of factional development and its relationship to party. Hard core factions could only achieve majorities in the House by forming alliances with blocs that did not always share similar views. The hard cores and the allies they recruited on the question of taxation were not exactly the same as those that formed when foreign policy was debated or when efforts to limit the executive were underway. To an

Table 29. State Distribution of Tax Factions, Third Congress

State	Pro-Tax	Anti-Tax	Inconsistent	Absent
Connecticut	7	–	–	–
Delaware	1	–	–	1
Georgia	1	–	1	–
Kentucky	–	–	1	1
Maryland	1	2	2	5
Massachusetts	9	1	1	3
New Hampshire	2	–	–	2
New Jersey	3	–	2	1
New York	7	2	1	–
North Carolina	6	3	1	–
Pennsylvania	3	3	3	3
Rhode Island	1	–	1	1
South Carolina	3	1	1	2
Vermont	–	2	–	–
Virginia	1	10	4	4
TOTAL[a]	45	24	18	23

[a]Exceeds 105 because five delegates were replaced during the session.

extent, then, one can properly speak of certain delegates as being, at the same time, economic Federalists, foreign policy Jeffersonians, and independent westerners. Such representatives cannot be classified as non-party or inconsistent; rather, they were members of three different factions, which in action on the House floor resulted in constantly shifting majorities.

In the Third Congress, however, as demonstrated in Table 30, distinctive factions that voted cohesively only on one type of issue rapidly gave way to blocs that polarized against each other on all categories of roll calls. Cohesion differences between pro-tax and anti-tax blocs were greatest on economic issues, an indication that broad ideological considerations outweighed the influence of local pressures in voting on such matters. But polarization was consistent and deep on other issues as well—on foreign policy questions, especially efforts to implement Jefferson's report on commerce; on limiting government power, particularly the appropriate response to the Whiskey Rebellion; on frontier issues, primarily the establishment of a standing army. In virtually every matter of concern to the legislature, delegates found themselves appearing on the same side at the calling of the roll. Greatly outnumbered in their efforts to offer viable alternatives to administration policy, opponents opted for a more successful approach to politics. They turned to newspaper propaganda, to development of effective electoral machinery, and to vacuous slogans. The result—unparalleled

Table 30. Cohesion Differences: Proponents Against Opponents of Increased
Taxation, Third Congress

Issue	*Range of Cohesion Difference*			*Mean*
	0–34%	*35–64%*	*65–100%*	
	Percent of Roll Calls in Each Range			
Government power	33	17	50	53
Frontier	19	32	49	58
Economic	10	44	46	62
Foreign policy	15	40	45	59
Miscellaneous and personal	14	57	29	47
ALL ROLL CALLS	16	40	44	57

success for the Republican party—rested upon general acceptance of policies
produced by the mid-1790s. Opponents of the administration continued to
criticize its revenue policies, but they no longer offered innovative counterproposals. The Fourth Congress approved no new excise or tonnage taxes;
the Fifth approved modest increases but ultimately moved to a different
form of taxation; the Sixth routinely continued levies initiated in 1794
that otherwise would have expired. A brief survey will reveal the absence
of important policy changes on this issue during the late 1790s.

After the flurry of tax legislation produced by the Third Congress, three
years elapsed before the House approved additional revenue measures.
Soon after his inauguration, John Adams decided to call a special session
of Congress to confirm his intention to try to negotiate with France again
while, at the same time, showing the potential enemy that the United
States was prepared for all contingencies including, if necessary, war itself.
In contrast to his specific calls for coastal defensive operations and reorganization of the militia, President Adams stated only that his program
would necessitate raising additional revenue. In response, the House adhered closely to established policies and ultimately decided upon a retail
liquor license tax, a stamp tax, and an increase in the salt duty. All these
levies previously had received detailed examination and Congress moved
quickly to approve them, recognizing, however, that they would not produce revenue adequate to finance a war.[30] The only innovative proposal
was Robert Goodloe Harper's insistent request for a tax on certificates of
naturalization, a provision more important as a forerunner of several acts
concerning aliens than as a revenue measure.[31]

Using votes for and against these four taxes, delegates may be assigned
to one of several groups: (1) the forty-seven who supported all new taxes,
(2) the nine who supported all but one new tax, (3) the four who opposed
two new taxes and supported two other new taxes, (4) the eighteen who

opposed all but one new tax, and (5) the twenty-three who opposed all new taxes. Table 31 summarizes the voting behavior of these five groups for all roll calls recorded in the Fifth Congress.[32] The data support the contention that blocs voting against each other on tax legislation also polarized on other types of issues. Significant levels of polarization occurred on at least 90 percent of all recorded roll calls (note figures for 1 vs. 5, 1 vs. 7, 5 vs. 6, and 6 vs. 7). Moderates moved rapidly to more extreme positions (note figures for 1 vs. 2 and 4 vs. 5) and those genuinely in the middle on the four tax roll calls later joined administration opponents (note figures for 3 vs. 6 and 3 vs. 7).

Table 31. Cohesion Differences: Tax Groups, Fifth Congress

	Range of Cohesion Difference			
Groups[a]	*0–34%*	*35–64%*	*65–100%*	*Mean*
	Percent of Roll Calls in Each Range			
1 vs. 2	85	15	0	24
1 vs. 5	9	15	76	71
1 vs. 7	8	17	75	70
3 vs. 6	43	27	30	46
3 vs. 7	85	11	4	25
4 vs. 5	97	2	1	20
5 vs. 6	10	18	72	59
6 vs. 7	9	23	68	68

[a] 1 = for all taxes   2 = for most taxes
3 = evenly divided   4 = against most taxes
5 = against all taxes   6 = groups 1 and 2 combined
7 = groups 4 and 5 combined

Voting behavior in the Sixth Congress fell into a similar pattern: consistent polarization on all categories of issues. The House agreed to continue the "emergency" salt tax passed in 1797 and the carriage, retail liquor license, and auction taxes first authorized in 1794. In addition to continuations, the legislature imposed a new levy on sugar. The votes were 54 to 38 for the salt tax, 54 to 28 for the sugar tax, and 46 to 31 on carriage, liquor license, and auction taxes.[33] Table 32 portrays the voting behavior of delegates for and against these taxes on all roll calls recorded in the Sixth Congress. Polarization was deeper and more consistent than in any preceding Congress. Indeed, on more than half the roll calls cohesion differences exceeded 84 percent, an indication of near unanimity within each of the two blocs.

The contrast between these figures and those for tax groups in the early 1790s strongly supports the conclusion that issue-oriented factions

Table 32. Cohesion Differences: Proponents Against Opponents of Continued and New Taxes, Sixth Congress

	Range of Cohesion Difference			
Issue	*0–34%*	*35–64%*	*65–100%*	*Mean*
	Percent of Roll Calls in Each Range			
Government power	9	0	91	84
Frontier	12	12	76	75
Economic	0	16	84	82
Foreign policy	10	15	75	71
Partisan politics	9	15	76	78
Miscellaneous and personal	33	0	67	59
ALL ROLL CALLS	10	11	79	74

gave way to highly predictable voting blocs motivated by something other than the issue at hand. Even in the absence of hard mechanisms to impose party discipline, the rule of passion that Madison had sought to counteract in 1787 reappeared a decade later. Wide acceptance of the innovative policy outputs of the early 1790s—the removal of external restraints on government power, the orderly conversion of the frontier to actual abundance, and the secure acquisition of revenue—provided the milieu in which divisive policy positions could be avoided so that men might devote their full energies to the quest for office.

But the shift from faction to party was not total. Occasionally, matters did arise that forced delegates to examine the issues carefully and to take a stand. On such roll calls "normal" voting patterns gave way to temporary alliances that cannot be termed factions only because they lacked longevity. Nevertheless, these votes support the hypothesis that a strong inverse relationship existed between consistent polarization on a variety of issues and the forging of innovative policies. The effort to add to national revenues by imposition of a land tax was such a policy, and the course of its adoption illuminates the limits of party solidarity in the late 1790s.

The idea of a federal tax based on land values (and on buildings and slaves as well), of course, was not new. But when the House considered the proposal in 1797 it found itself faced with a fundamental alternative to Hamiltonian economic policy. The plan's leading proponent, Albert Gallatin, pointed out for the benefit of less perceptive representatives from agricultural districts that such a tax would bring the people closer to their government and would promote a zealous concern with federal expenditures. In addition to supplying this external restraint on national power, the tax would sweep away the administration's most persuasive argument for a foreign policy that, under the cloak of neutrality, favored

England. Shifting its revenue base from import duties to a domestic land tax would break the government's dependence upon the commercial interests and would allow a foreign policy devoted to national needs rather than to the payment of creditors. Jefferson's report on commerce, finally presented to Congress in December 1793, had been too idealistic and impractical and Madison's fight against the Jay Treaty had focused on politicking, but Gallatin's proposed land tax attacked established policies in a meaningful, fundamental way.[34] Although the proposal ultimately lost because of hostility among members of the Committee on Ways and Means and a series of stopgap indirect taxes, a roll call favorably reporting a land tax from the Committee of the Whole merits examination.

The vote followed two others on similar matters, and the final tally— 49 for a land tax, 39 against—accurately reflected positions taken on this critical issue.[35] Some strange alliances emerged. Fisher Ames, bulwark of the moneyed interests, joined young Andrew Jackson in opposition; Albert Gallatin and Chauncey Goodrich voted in the same way on only one significant issue during their six years together in the House, and this was the occasion; Nathaniel Macon opposed James Madison. The Virginian ultimately voted for the land tax, but earlier he had supported an amendment, to equalize rates by state, that Gallatin was convinced would cripple the bill. Gallatin's comment was, "the amendment proposed [and seconded by Madison] would be a total defeat of the resolution for laying a direct tax."[36] These examples are not atypical. The temporary groups that formed on the land tax roll call took a position on a fundamental issue, one of the few raised in the Fourth Congress. The two groups did not polarize on other roll calls, an indication that the same issue did not appear under a different guise and, when viewed in conjunction with evidence previously offered on Fourth Congress voting, a further confirmation that other roll calls generally did not come to grips with major policy questions.

Table 33 summarizes the voting behavior of delegates for and against the land tax on all roll calls recorded in the Fourth Congress. It is apparent that representatives willing to consider a fundamental alteration of Hamiltonian economic policy did not vote as a group on any of the measures usually treated as major issues of the period. Cohesion differences between the two groups were only 16 percent on the Livingston Resolution, 11 percent on the Jay Treaty, 10 percent on the admission of Tennessee, 9 percent on an adulatory response to President Washington's last annual message, 7 percent on army reduction, and 9 percent on the building of frigates. These votes, correctly used by historians to demonstrate the in-

Table 33. Cohesion Differences: Proponents Against Opponents of a Land Tax, Fourth Congress

	Range of Cohesion Difference			
Issue	*0–34%*	*35–64%*	*65–100%*	*Mean*
	Percent of Roll Calls in Each Range			
Government power	100	0	0	20
Frontier	100	0	0	13
Economic	77	8	15	24
Foreign policy	100	0	0	11
Partisan politics	100	0	0	14
Miscellaneous and personal	93	7	0	16
ALL ROLL CALLS	95	2	3	16

creasing role of party attachment in the legislature, then, are clearly at variance with votes on the significant, innovative policy matter of a land tax.

The complexity of motivations involved in voting for a land tax increased when the matter again came before the House during the Fifth Congress. On this occasion the basic issue of reliance on commerce for revenue was overshadowed by the pressing need for new money sources created by preparations for war against France. The direct tax imposed in 1798—on land, improvements, buildings, and slaves—was temporary in nature and for many it indicated no desire to permanently alter the government's tax base. The major shift in sentiment, which resulted in passage of a proposal that had been defeated a year earlier, occurred among strong backers of the administration. They swallowed hard and, bowing to necessity, joined with former proponents of a land tax to produce acceptance of the measure by a wide margin. Token opposition came from delegates less concerned with basic questions of revenue acquisition than with the opportunity to say no to President Adams.

Although a single policy question was involved less clearly on the land tax in 1798 than in 1797, the issue nevertheless produced a significant shift from voting patterns that held on most other roll calls in the Fifth Congress. The magnitude of the shift is evident from the summary of voting patterns in Table 34. Polarization occurred most frequently and most sharply in two pairings: (1) opponents of the land tax vs. opponents of lowering the tax rate on land relative to the rate on buildings and improvements (2 vs. 4) and (2) opponents of the land tax vs. proponents of other forms of taxation (2 vs. 5). On these pairings, levels of polarization matched the figures already established for "normal" groupings in the Fifth Congress (see figures for 5 vs. 6 in Table 34, which is taken from Table 31). The explanation for this is simple: opponents of the land tax also opposed the

Table 34. Cohesion Differences: Land Tax Groups, Fifth Congress

| Groups[a] | Range of Cohesion Difference | | | Mean |
	0–34%	35–64%	65–100%	
	Percent of Roll Calls in Each Range			
1 vs. 2	14	69	17	50
1 vs. 3	24	76	0	42
1 vs. 4	99	1	0	16
1 vs. 5	100	0	0	19
1 vs. 6	14	58	28	54
2 vs. 3	98	2	0	17
2 vs. 4	10	22	68	69
2 vs. 5	10	19	71	62
2 vs. 6	98	2	0	13
3 vs. 4	16	73	11	47
5 vs. 6	9	23	68	68

[a]1 = for land tax

2 = against land tax

3 = for lower rate on land relative to buildings

4 = against lower rate on land relative to buildings

5 = for other taxes (group 6 of Table 31)

6 = against other taxes (group 7 of Table 31)

administration on other levies; the delegates included in the group coalesced consistently, but their allies were more numerous on roll calls other than the land tax. Proponents of a land tax constituted an unusual group—delegates ready to approve the tax because it would facilitate war preparations combined with delegates opposed to war preparations, who agreed with Gallatin's earlier argument and hoped for a permanent shift of the government's revenue base away from commercial activity. As might be expected, polarization between these delegates as a group and other "normal" blocs occurred less frequently and less deeply, due to the lack of unity among land tax proponents on other issues. Even in the late 1790s, then, the forging of an innovative policy broke voting patterns that reflected an increasing commitment to party needs.[37]

At the end of this survey of voting behavior on revenue acquisition in the period 1789–1801, several conclusions are in order. Under the leadership of James Madison, Congress set a high priority on adopting a tariff schedule based on revenue needs rather than intervention on behalf of particular sectors of the domestic economy. Driven in part by a desire to atone for the national government's impotence in this area in the 1780s, delegates overwhelmingly approved reliance on import duties. Minor adjustments in particular rates followed, but a fundamental alteration of policy did not occur until 1816. Gallatin's espousal of a land tax was a bold alternative but, although it temporarily shattered the acquiescent party divisions of the late 1790s, too many delegates failed to grasp the relationship between revenue acquisition and foreign policy. An emergency land tax finally passed, but its adverse effect on the political fortunes of the incumbent administration caused both parties to abandon the quest for such radical alternatives to established policy. Following the dictates of practical necessity as well as ideological inclination, Secretary of the Treasury Alexander Hamilton urged Congress to supplement import duties with a series of domestic levies. His plans aroused fierce opposition of a factional, issue-oriented nature. Delegates who moved in a variety of ways on other matters, united consistently on domestic tax issues until 1794. But later in the decade the pressures of electoral politics loomed larger and the House did not consider viable alternatives to previously accepted policies. The balance between import duties and domestic levies shifted in harmony with external developments, particularly the level of fighting in Europe, rather than at the will of the legislature. Avoidance of divisive policy issues and concern with acquisition of office reinforced each other, so that the factional voting patterns of the early years disappeared almost entirely after 1795.

Acquisition of a secure revenue base was a major concern, but an efficient, energetic new government also required the establishment of public credit. There is no need to denigrate the successes of the Confederation and of the individual states in establishing credit in the 1780s. Indeed, recent scholarship demonstrating the economic strength of the states supports the conclusion that federal efforts to establish good credit were also aimed at undermining the power of potentially competitive state governments.[38] Hamilton's plan for assumption was not an attack on states about to wither and die of poverty anyway; rather, it was a bold effort to take something of value (creditors) from the states and attach it to the national government. "If all the public creditors receive their dues from one source, distributed with an equal hand," wrote Hamilton in his report on public credit, "their interest will be the same. And, having the same interests, they will unite in the support of fiscal arrangements of the Government." The "plain and undeniable truths," he noted, are "That exigencies are to be expected to occur, in the affairs of nations, in which there will be a necessity for borrowing. That loans in time of public danger, especially from a foreign war, are found an indispensable resource, even to the wealthiest of them."[39]

The salient features of Hamilton's compromise proposal for funding of the national debt and assumption of debts incurred by the states during the Revolution have been considered in depth by E. James Ferguson.[40] The present study deals with the issue from a somewhat different vantage point: the voting patterns generated in the House by the secretary's proposals and the relationship of these patterns to national politics in the 1790s.

Despite the absence of a recorded roll call vote on the question of funding the national debt, men at the time and historians since have agreed that the general idea received nearly unanimous approval. Sharp differences of opinion occurred only on specific aspects of the plan that were of relatively less consequence. Nevertheless, these minor divisions provide useful information on the voting behavior of delegates in the First Congress. One such division involved consideration of old Continental money, most of which had long been in the hands of speculators. Hamilton had advised its redemption at forty to one, which gave a high rate of return to its holders. By a vote of 31 to 25, the House finally adopted the Senate's proposed ratio of one hundred to one. The issue was whether even this gave too much to the speculators, and so a negative vote on the roll call generally indicated a desire for an even higher ratio or else the position that Continental money should not be redeemed at all.[41]

A subsequent roll call on whether to pay back interest on Continental money now funded at one hundred to one revealed the limits of House concern for speculators. The date from which interest would be calculated was not specified, but debate implied a commencement date as far back as 1781. Such a plan would have resulted in an added windfall for the speculators holding these "worthless" scraps of paper. But delegates from the Middle Atlantic region, who had overwhelmingly supported the one hundred to one ratio, voted convincingly against this radical amendment, thereby assuring its defeat.[42]

Table 35 summarizes the voting behavior of the "losers"—those who opposed the one hundred to one ratio and those who favored paying back interest on funded Continentals—for all roll calls recorded in the First Congress. These two blocs may be termed, respectively, the "enemies" and the "friends" of the speculator. In general such stark labels, even though they were used at the time, should be avoided, for a maze of conflicting pressures usually affected voting behavior. But in this instance it was widely known that old Continentals were almost solely in the hands of speculators and that, while individual holders stood to gain a tidy profit, the total sum involved was not so great that it might imperil overall fiscal policy. Attitude toward speculators motivated both opponents of funding Continentals and proponents of paying back interest, though in opposite directions of course. With this conclusion in mind, the data in Table 35

Table 35. Cohesion Differences: Enemies and Friends of the Creditor Interest,
         First Congress

	Range of Cohesion Difference			
Issue	*0–34%*	*35–64%*	*65–100%*	*Mean*
	Percent of Roll Calls in Each Range			
Government power	75	15	10	31
Frontier	33	67	0	47
Location of the capital	16	59	25	52
Economic	43	45	12	38
Foreign policy	100	0	0	19
Miscellaneous and personal	91	0	9	22
ALL ROLL CALLS	47	37	16	39

are highly revealing. Unlike other First Congress factions, these two blocs
polarized consistently and deeply on the sectional issue of locating the capital. This is hardly surprising since eighteen of twenty-five "enemies" of
the speculator came from the South and fourteen of fifteen "friends" came
from Massachusetts, New Hampshire, or South Carolina.[43] However, on all
other issues, including even roll calls involving economic policy, the two
blocs did not consistently and sharply polarize against each other. The
reasonable conclusion to be drawn from this phenomenon is that the speculator interest, in both its positive and negative aspects, did not decisively
influence voting. This is not to say that strong concern over speculators did
not exist; indeed, two-thirds of the delegates in the House are included in
Table 35 as enemies or friends. But it is clear that more complex motivations must be ascribed to voting on issues, even directly economic questions, in the First Congress.

Two other roll calls related to funding gave rise to patterns more indicative of legislative response to Hamilton's proposals. These votes were occasioned by differences between the House and Senate over the rate of
interest on indents and the time when interest should commence on those
securities to be issued under the funding program upon which payment of
interest was to be deferred to a later period. The Senate proposed an interest rate of 3 percent on indents, whereas the House had agreed to 4 percent.[44] Voting positions of every delegate were identical with those on
the question of paying interest on the new deferred stock after seven
years, as the House proposed, or after ten years, as the Senate had agreed
upon. Eventually the House gave way because (according to Theodore
Sedgwick) it would have been unwise to commit the new government to
more than it could possibly pay. The members who opposed the lower

rate of indents and the longer deferral on payment of interest included ardent Hamilton supporters such as Fisher Ames, Egbert Benson, and Jonathan Trumbull, as well as several of the secretary's notable opponents, Isaac Coles, James Jackson, James Madison, John Page, and Thomas Sumter. The votes of these opponents against the Senate proposals are not explained in the debate. It is hardly possible that these delegates agreed with Fisher Ames' contention that the 3 percent figure was a "manifest and glaring violation of the contract between the Government and its creditors."[45] Possibly Madison hoped to make the cost of funding national obligations so high that it would become impossible to assume state debts.[46]

Support for the higher interest rate on indents and the shorter deferral of interest on new stock apparently came from two distinct groups, which opposed each other on other economic questions. Table 36 shows the two separate groups, as identified by a subsequent vote on assumption of state debts. Seventeen delegates, who voted against assumption, favored the higher interest rate on indents and the shorter deferral of interest on new stock.[47] This group, predominantly from the South (14 of 17), which had

Table 36. Characteristics of Delegates Who Favored a Higher Interest Rate on
Indents and a Shorter Deferral of Interest on New Stock, First Congress

Characteristic	Anti-Assumption	Pro-Assumption
Classified as nationalists		
(see Chapter 3)	2	10
Classified as anti-nationalists	7	0
Favored 100 to 1 ratio on Continentals	5	7
Opposed 100 to 1 ratio on Continentals	10	3
Favored national bank	7	9
Opposed national bank	7	1
Favored domestic excise taxation		
(see Table 26)	2	10
Opposed domestic excise taxation	10	0
Represented New England	1	5
Represented Middle Atlantic	2	4
Represented the South	14	1
TOTAL NUMBER	17	10

few indents, generally opposed strong central government. They opposed funding of Continental money at one hundred to one by a vote of ten to five. They divided evenly on the question of establishing a national bank, but solidly opposed the revenue bill imposing domestic excise taxes. This seemingly inconsistent position, in favor of increasing government expenses by voting for higher interest rates while opposing plans for obtaining revenue, can only be explained in terms of a desire to burden the national government to the extent that taking on further obligations would become impossible.

For entirely different reasons, a group of ten delegates also supported higher interest rates on indents and earlier payment of interest on new stock.[48] This bloc, all of whom had voted against restrictive constitutional amendments, represented the area from Philadelphia northward and unanimously favored assumption. They voted for funding of Continental money by a margin of seven to three. All but one advocated a national bank and all ten voted for the revenue bill.

Proponents of a lower interest rate and longer deferral of interest on new stock also came from two groups having different motives. Table 37 summarizes some key differences between the two blocs. Twenty-one delegates voted for assumption and for longer deferral of interest on new stock.[49] They opposed higher interest rates on indents only on the practical ground argued by Theodore Sedgwick—the government simply could not afford to pay any more without risking the defeat of assumption. The group overwhelmingly favored strong central authority (12 of 15). They backed the other important aspects of Hamilton's economic program: funding of Continentals by 15 to 4, establishment of a national bank by

Table 37. Characteristics of Delegates Who Favored a Lower Interest Rate on Indents and a Longer Deferral of Interest on New Stock, First Congress

Characteristic	Anti-Assumption	Pro-Assumption
Classified as nationalists (see Chapter 3)	4	12
Classified as anti-nationalists	4	3
Favored 100 to 1 ratio on Continentals	3	15
Opposed 100 to 1 ratio on Continentals	8	4
Favored national bank	6	14
Opposed national bank	5	6
Favored domestic excise taxation (see Table 26)	3	17
Opposed domestic excise taxation	8	2
Represented New England	1	8
Represented Middle Atlantic	5	6
Represented the South	6	7
TOTAL NUMBER	12	21[a]

[a]Includes Daniel Huger of South Carolina, who clearly favored assumption but who was absent on the day of the vote.

14 to 6, and domestic excise taxation by 17 to 2. The delegates in this bloc came from all areas of the country: eight from New England, six from the Middle Atlantic states, and seven from the South.

Twelve delegates who favored longer deferral of interest on new stock subsequently voted against assumption.[50] They were divided on the question of drastic constitutional amendments limiting the scope of the national government and on the establishment of a national bank, but they opposed most aspects of the Hamilton program by nearly a three to one ratio. Only one of the twelve came from New England.

The four-bloc pattern formed by combining the roll call on interest rates on indents with that on assumption occurred because of the distinctly different economic interests, public and private, involved. Assumption provided the greatest gain to Massachusetts, Connecticut, and South Carolina. Delegates from these states did not wish to risk the defeat of assumption by greedily adding 1 percent to the interest rate on indents. The funded federal debt involved in deferral of interest on new stock was distributed in the Middle Atlantic states and in New England. Pennsylvania, New York, and New Jersey gained more from funding than from assumption. They were more willing than New Englanders to risk the defeat of assumption by voting for a more expensive funding plan. Patterns were obscured still further by the votes of those delegates who opposed or favored fullest payment of all kinds of creditors, without consistent regard for the interests of their particular state. Fisher Ames of Massachusetts, for example, surely favored assumption; yet he risked its defeat by voting for the more expensive funding plan. Thomas Scott came from Pennsylvania, a state that gained from funding; yet he opposed both assumption and the more expensive funding plan.

Table 38 summarizes by state the four blocs formed by combining votes on assumption and funding (from Tables 36 and 37). It is of considerable note that every state delegation was internally divided.[51] The reasons for divisiveness varied from state to state, but certainly a simple conclusion of state interest is inadequate as an explanation of voting patterns on funding and assumption. Emerging political parties cannot account for the common votes of Theodore Sedgwick and Aedanus Burke, or Abraham Baldwin and Thomas Hartley, or Fisher Ames and Alexander White. One hesitates to conclude that the delegates did not know what they were doing or that they were trying to confuse future historians. What, then, accounts for this four-way pattern?

Several factors were involved. The ten delegates favoring assumption and the more expensive funding plan supported the principle that all debts

Table 38. Distribution by State of Combined Funding-Assumption Factions, First Congress

State	For More Expensive Funding		For Less Expensive Funding	
	Pro-Assumption	*Anti-Assumption*	*Pro-Assumption*	*Anti-Assumption*
Connecticut	2	–	2	–
Delaware	–	–	1	–
Georgia	–	2	–	1
Maryland	–	3	2	1
Massachusetts	2	–	6	–
New Hampshire	1	1	–	1
New Jersey	1	–	2	–
New York	3	2	–	1
North Carolina	–	.3	–	2
Pennsylvania	–	–	3	4
South Carolina	–	1	4	–
Virginia	1	5	1	2
TOTAL	10	17	21	12

should be paid fully and previous interest commitments honored. They did so even on a minor issue, 3 or 4 percent on indents, that endangered the major question, assumption. The twelve delegates opposing assumption and the more expensive funding plan supported the principle that old debts should not be paid in full, at least not by the federal government. They opposed all aspects of the Hamilton plan, including those that assisted their own states. Other delegates acted less from principle than from practical considerations. One percent more or less on indents and a three-year delay in interest payment on new stock were not as important as assumption. One bloc hoped to prevent assumption by raising the cost of funding, and the other hoped to smooth the way for assumption by reducing the cost of funding. Both groups took tactical positions on funding, which was sure to pass anyway, in preparation for the assumption fight yet to be resolved.

Table 39 shows the voting behavior of these four groups on all roll calls recorded in the First Congress. The figures confirm the conclusion that delegates jockeyed for position on cost of funding but did not align themselves in a pattern of long-range significance.

The situation differed on assumption, the most controversial aspect of Hamilton's policy and, for many members, the one that involved the hardest decisions. In addition to economic considerations and the implication of strong national government, there was the difficulty of weighing the plan in relation to prior state action on debts. Further, there was the vexing

Table 39. Cohesion Differences: Funding-Assumption Blocs, First Congress

Groups[a]	Issue	Range of Cohesion Difference			Mean
		0–34%	35–64%	65–100%	
		Percent of Roll Calls in Each Range			
1 vs. 2	Economic	31	43	26	48
	Government power	40	50	10	41
	Location of the capital	17	36	47	59
	All other roll calls	83	11	6	26
1 vs. 3	Economic	91	3	6	24
	Government power	95	5	0	21
	Location of the capital	40	60	0	38
	All other roll calls	100	0	0	19
1 vs. 4	Economic	29	34	37	53
	Government power	70	15	15	33
	Location of the capital	30	25	45	55
	All other roll calls	78	22	0	26
2 vs. 3	Economic	46	34	20	42
	Government power	65	35	0	30
	Location of the capital	89	11	0	22
	All other roll calls	67	27	6	31
2 vs. 4	Economic	77	17	6	28
	Government power	80	20	0	25
	Location of the capital	80	20	0	23
	All other roll calls	94	6	0	21
3 vs. 4	Economic	54	34	12	37
	Government power	75	25	0	27
	Location of the capital	80	20	0	27
	All other roll calls	78	22	0	25

[a]1 = for assumption and for expensive funding

2 = anti-assumption and for expensive funding

3 = for assumption and anti-expensive funding

4 = anti-assumption and anti-expensive funding

question of the general settlement of accounts that should have eliminated any possibility of inequities in assumption. However, it was widely feared (events proved justifiably) that this redistribution of debt incurred during the Revolution would never actually take place. The result was that more than half the states had a tangible economic interest in this feature of Hamilton's plans. South Carolina, Massachusetts, and Connecticut were strong backers of assumption, while Maryland, Virginia, North Carolina, and Georgia opposed it.[52] The remaining states, as their voting patterns revealed, were less deeply concerned.

Despite the great pressure of state interest, the final votes on assumption showed that in the South basic economic-issue patterns were not totally obscured. Thomas Sumter of South Carolina voted to reject assumption in the crucial 32 to 29 vote of July 24, 1790, thus once again breaking with the remainder of his delegation.[53] Apparently his proto-Republican principles overruled the interests of his state. Two Marylanders, Daniel Carroll and George Gale, opposed the majority in that state and voted with the Hamiltonians, as did Michael Stone of Maryland on the next occasion that assumption came to a vote.[54] In fact, the only southern state to vote unanimously on the issue was North Carolina. The famous bargain between Hamilton and Madison and Jefferson that traded Pennsylvania votes to locate the capital on the Potomac for the support of Virginia's Richard Lee and Alexander White on assumption complicated the situation in that state.[55] Even excluding the two traded Virginia votes, however, assumption found enough support in the South to assure its passage. Daniel Huger of South Carolina, who was absent, definitely favored the plan and Theodoric Bland of Virginia, who had died, had expressed support.[56]

State interest was stronger in New England than in the South or, at least, unanimous voting was more common. Only New Hampshire divided, as two of the state's three delegates voted against assumption. In doing so, Nicholas Gilman and Samuel Livermore thought they were expressing the best interests of their state, but such pressures did not sway Abiel Foster, who voted for the Hamilton plan. Foster consistently favored strong central authority, law and order in the West, a powerful chief executive, and full payment of all financial obligations.

The exceptions to state interest voting—Foster in New Hampshire, Sumter in South Carolina, and several delegates in Virginia and Maryland—although not dominant, were significant. In each case, these "exceptions" voted in accordance with principles and interests that reflected the factional nature of legislative voting behavior. The men involved consistently supported certain positions, even when they ran contrary to state interest.

The presence of broader considerations was more evident in New York and Pennsylvania, states that did not have nearly so direct a stake in the question of assumption. The three New Yorkers isolated as hard core opponents of expanding federal authority during voting on amendments all opposed assumption, and the remaining three delegates, who favored the plan, had voted with the nationalist bloc. The same three to three split occurred on the revenue bill and on roll calls related to the imposition of limitations on presidential authority.[57] The division in Pennsylvania paralleled earlier splits (such as that on discrimination against British trade) that had shown signs of consistent adherence to principle.[58] Thus, in the midst of the issue on which the highest degree of state cohesion might be expected, there were several signs of the influence of the other basic sources of divisiveness that characterized politics in the early 1790s.

Again, the figures in Table 39 reveal the strength of association between voting on assumption and positions taken on other issues. Groups 2 and 3, composed of delegates who voted "inconsistently" on funding and assumption, did not polarize against each other on other matters. Groups 1 and 4, composed of delegates at opposite ends of the spectrum of response to Hamilton's plans, were heavily sectional in character and opposed each other not only on location of the capital but also on many government power issues. The level of polarization exhibited by these groups, however, was substantially less than the levels that occurred later in the decade. Viewed in the larger context of the entire period 1789-1801, voting blocs on funding and assumption were heavily issue-oriented. They were factions, in the sense in which Madison used the term, dedicated to the forging of meaningful and innovative policy outputs. That these outputs served the interest of certain sectors of society much more fully than they did others is perfectly consistent with the Virginian's understanding of the motivation of factions.

Most accounts of assumption conclude with the passage of legislation in 1790. The issue of public credit, however, continued to generate sharp controversy and polarized voting for several years. On various occasions Congress considered such related matters as debts owed to the United States by private citizens, Hamilton's conduct of office, and the long delayed general settlement of accounts. Although action on these questions did not result in significant alteration of policies formulated in 1790, the initial decision to firmly establish public credit through funding and assumption came under severe attack. Issue-oriented factions dominated the course of this ongoing controversy.

The general settlement of accounts promised to redress inequities that resulted from assumption of outstanding state debts incurred during the Revolution. The settlement concept was simply to calculate the cost of the Revolution, divide the cost among the states, and subtract for each state the amount it had already paid. Some plain arithmetic would make certain states creditors (those which had paid more than their share) and others debtors (those which had paid less than their share). The obvious problem was that no one could agree on the proper amounts to be filled in for each factor in the equation for settlement. The thankless task of doing the impossible was assigned to the Office of the Commissioners of

Accounts. While awaiting its verdict, some legislators sought ways to use the settlement to strengthen public credit still further.

Early in 1793 Hamilton's supporters in the House introduced a proposal to authorize a loan, to be paid by the national government, in the debt of states that would become creditors of the United States under the general settlement of accounts. The language of the bill was complex, but the purpose was clear: to induce creditors of those states that turned out to be creditors of the nation to turn directly to the nation for payment. Even John Page of Virginia, who was usually among the last in the House to understand such matters, awoke to the danger and urged his colleagues to defeat a measure that would "seduce" creditors "from their attachment to their State."[59]

The bill precipitated the same sort of speculative fever that had characterized consideration of assumption, though on a less grand scale, and this spurred opposition on slightly different grounds. The lure of windfall profits motivated speculators to purchase debt notes, which often reflected the impecuniousness of the states that issued the notes by circulating at substantially less than par (only 50 percent of par, charged John Mercer of Maryland), in the hope that the effective assumption of these notes under the general settlement would increase their value. Mercer, building on the lesson of the 1790 assumption battle, proposed an amendment aimed directly at the speculators: no payment on notes transferred after January 1, 1793. Reaction came swiftly, the arrogance of which is captured fully in Thomas Hartley's comment on the proceedings. "I regret exceedingly," he said, "the great inequality of fortune, which has arisen among citizens, by the speculators in our paper, but in a great and mighty revolution, some partial evils must be expected to obtain a general good. We are bound to pay our debts."[60] The House rejected Mercer's amendment. A more crippling proposal, to limit assumption to debt "for services rendered, or supplies furnished, during the late war" also met defeat. Proponents of turning the settlement of accounts into a vehicle for further speculation recognized that "We must act now upon principle, without knowing how the balances will operate. If the creditor and debtor States were known, it would be found exceedingly difficult to reconcile the several interests." On this note the House pushed rapidly for passage of the bill, doing so by the narrowest of margins, 33 to 32, on January 28, 1793. Senate opposition ultimately prevented the bill from becoming law. Nevertheless, votes in the House provide the basis for understanding the nature of legislative behavior on the issue of public credit.[61]

Table 40 depicts the voting records of proponents and opponents of enhancing national public credit through the general settlement. As in the preceding Congress on the question of assumption, issue-oriented factions led the way. These groups did not join forces on roll calls involving frontier policy or limitation of government power, but on 85 percent of all economic issues they polarized sharply. The divisiveness that had marked consideration of Hamilton's plans in 1790 remained three years later.

Table 40. Cohesion Differences: Proponents Against Opponents of Using the General Settlement of Accounts to Enhance Public Credit, Second Congress

	Range of Cohesion Difference			
Issue	*0–34%*	*35–64%*	*65–100%*	*Mean*
	Percent of Roll Calls in Each Range			
Government power	53	44	3	35
Frontier	69	31	0	27
Economic	15	43	42	60
Foreign policy	25	50	25	39
Miscellaneous and personal	50	40	10	38
ALL ROLL CALLS	40	41	19	44

Finally, on December 4, 1793, Congress received the official report on balances due in the general settlement of accounts. To the consternation of administration opponents, the long-sought document showed that the states that had gained most from assumption would profit again. Amounts due to the states were: Georgia, $19,988; New Jersey, $49,630; New Hampshire, $75,055; Rhode Island, $299,611; Connecticut, $619,121; South Carolina, $1,205,978; and Massachusetts, $1,248,801. The crushing blow came in the list of balances owed by the states: Pennsylvania, $76,009; Virginia, $100,879; Maryland, $151,640; North Carolina, $501,082; Delaware, $612,428; and New York, $2,074,846. Whatever the merits of the method of calculation (and some delegates pushed for an investigation of the accounting procedures used), the political arithmetic necessitated a compromise. Debtor states held 61 of 105 seats in the House.[62] After months of debate about what all knew would eventually be done, Congress agreed to drop serious efforts to force debtor states to pay amounts due and passed a bill that arranged for some winners but no losers. The polarized factional behavior that had previously characterized voting on the issue gave way to ephemeral state interest considerations.[63]

Public credit had been established, and continued fulminations against the "moneyed interest" and Hamilton's conduct of office revealed more about the shift to partisanship than the process of policy formulation. For, as Thomas Hartley had said, some would gain and some would lose, but the nation had to be preserved. Hamilton's plan worked and, although success did not vanquish the opposition, the advantages of sound public credit persuaded them to direct their attacks at secondary issues.

The final element in the triad goal of economic policy in the 1790s was the development of a national market. Voting patterns on this issue are less clear than those on revenue acquisition and establishment of credit. Sectional jealousies, confusion and uncertainty about the consequences of particular proposals, and the continuing presence of an agrarian myth led to inaction on many matters and no more than partial success on others. Uniform bankruptcy legislation, considered essential in 1787, did not pass for more than a decade and, even then, failed to facilitate creation of a national market. Bills to aid shipbuilders, fisheries, and cloth manufacturers set important precedents for government intervention in the economy, but national legislation did not greatly alter the position of these industries. Establishment of a national bank and a mint, correctly cited as major policy outputs of the decade, aroused deep sectional antagonism that overshadowed consideration of the purely economic issues involved. Finally, the absence of any meaningful response to Hamilton's report on the subject of manufacturers indicated an unwillingness to move far along the path of positive action to shape a national economy. On the closely related question of revenue and public credit, Congress vigorously carried out programs made possible by the Constitution. On development of a national market, however, the agreements of 1787 remained as the perimeter of government action until at least 1815.

Discussion of the constitutionality of establishing a national bank raised the issue to a level very different than that on which delegates actually voted. First proposed by Hamilton in December 1791, a heated but relatively rapid debate led to passage of the bank bill on February 8, 1792, by a ratio of nearly two to one. In view of the animosities left in the wake of the assumption fight, the depth of support for the bank requires some explanation. On four separate roll calls New Englanders voted overwhelmingly for the bill, a position that surprised no one. But the key to understanding the course of this legislation is the vote of delegates from the Middle Atlantic states. New Yorkers and Pennsylvanians, who had divided sharply on revenue and public credit measures, unanimously supported establishment of a national bank. They did so for a practical reason, the location of the bank in Philadelphia, and for an ideological consideration, the future development of manufacturing in the middle states. Delegates from this region knew from experience the benefits of strong banking operations and voted accordingly. Representatives from the South, now ready to oppose anything proposed by Hamilton and fearful that establishment of a national bank in Philadelphia would damage their sectional interests and threaten the agreement to locate the capital on the Potomac, cohesively opposed the bill.[64]

Table 41 shows the voting pattern of proponents and opponents of establishing a national bank for all roll calls in the First Congress. The sectional nature of these two groups emerges clearly; only on location of the capital did the two blocs polarize significantly. This is the single economic issue of the First Congress that gave rise to purely sectional groupings (see Tables 26, 35, and 39). It follows that considerations of constitutionality and of broad economic policy, to the extent that they existed at all, coincided with sectional attachments in a way that did not occur on other issues.

Table 41. Cohesion Differences: Proponents Against Opponents of a National Bank, First Congress

Issue	Range of Cohesion Difference			Mean
	0-34%	35-64%	65-100%	
	Percent of Roll Calls in Each Range			
Government power	70	30	0	23
Frontier	100	0	0	11
Location of the capital	28	49	23	47
Economic	51	37	12	39
Foreign policy	100	0	0	24
Miscellaneous and personal	55	45	0	24
ALL ROLL CALLS	51	37	12	36

The force of sectionalism abated quickly, however, and in the Second, Third, and Fourth Congresses legislation involving development of a national market gave rise to distinctive factional formations. A roll call recorded on March 26, 1792, to establish a national mint illustrates the alignments that characterized these years. Proponents and opponents of the bill polarized against each other on 63 percent of all roll calls involving economic issues but on less than one-third of all other roll calls. Supporters of the bill included twelve New Englanders, nine delegates from the Middle Atlantic states, and eleven from the South. The opposition consisted of four, seven, and eleven delegates from the three areas, respectively. A similar division occurred in the Second Congress on the question of raising the duty on raw cotton.[65] Within four years the blocs that emerged on roll calls involving regulation for a national market polarized on most other issues as well. On May 25, 1796, the House agreed to sell government-owned shares

in the Bank of the United States. Three days later many of the same delegates joined to remove the existing floor on the price of government debt
shares bearing 6 percent interest. These blocs voted cohesively against each
other on more than two of every three roll calls in the Fourth Congress.[66]
By the end of the decade, the partisan considerations that dominated the
issues analyzed in previous chapters also determined the shape of legislation aimed at development of a national market.

Table 42 portrays the voting behavior of proponents and opponents of
a uniform bankruptcy law. Levels of polarization were typical for blocs in
the Sixth Congress; the mean cohesion difference for all roll calls was 73
percent.[67] Within the limited range of legislative output on this issue, then,

**Table 42. Cohesion Differences: Proponents Against Opponents of a Uniform
Bankruptcy Law, Sixth Congress**

Issue	Range of Cohesion Difference			*Mean*
	0–34%	*35–64%*	*65–100%*	
	Percent of Roll Calls in Each Range			
Government power	9	0	91	90
Frontier	12	24	64	70
Economic	8	0	92	77
Foreign policy	10	20	70	72
Partisan politics	9	15	76	74
Miscellaneous and personal	33	11	56	55
ALL ROLL CALLS	11	12	77	73

voting behavior followed the now familiar pattern for the decade. Issue-
oriented factions formed in the early 1790s to create the broad outlines of
national policy. After 1795 delegates divided into two consistently hostile
camps, but both stayed within the boundaries of earlier policy decisions.

*   *   *   *   *

As James Madison had predicted, the regulation of "various and interfering [property] interests" did involve "the spirit of party and faction" in
the "operations of the government." But as with so many of the Virginian's
insights, reality turned the prediction on its head. For half a decade the
House acted as Madison knew it would: delegates fought bitterly for legislation that advanced the interests of particular property groups. Convinced
that the goals of their special groups also served the nation as a whole, issue-
oriented factions acted with speed and great energy to forge the outlines
of early national economic planning. They achieved agreement on creation
of a wide revenue base, establishment of public credit, and development of

a national market. The policy outputs of these years—import duties, domestic levies, funding, assumption, a national bank—shaped economic development for several decades and assured an energetic national government. Wide acceptance of these policies brought about a situation that Madison had not foreseen. Party activity and highly polarized, predictable voting dominated legislative behavior after 1795, but the goal shifted from policy formulation to quest for office. Even the pressure of war preparation failed to spur innovative action by the Federalist majority. And the long-awaited Republican victory in 1801 was no revolution at all.

6

THE SEARCH FOR SECURITY,
WEALTH, AND PEACE

Men who supported the Constitution because it offered a way to balance conflicting, self-interested factions were equally realistic in their approach to foreign policy. In Number 4 of *The Federalist* John Jay stated the problem most baldly: "nations in general will make war whenever they have a prospect of getting anything by it." Indeed, considerations of power pervaded the thinking of the founding fathers. Violent rhetoric and accusations against a French party and a British party served their purpose—to elicit support from the electorate in contests for office—but such propaganda did not determine the foreign policy outputs of the decade.

America sought two objectives in its relationships with other nations. One was the widest possible control over the course of events in the New World, and the other was to develop an extensive network of markets for American goods. The former involved the nation in wars against Indians, diplomatic pressure on Spain, alliance with a nation seeking to expand its influence in the New World, and ultimately a war against the remaining land power in North America. The search for markets brought the nation into the thick of Europe's war, shaped domestic politics, and dominated the business of government.

The search for these two goals, security and wealth, took place within a range of agreed-upon realities that narrowly circumscribed the young nation's ability to create a foreign policy. Since Great Britain and the United States were each other's best customers, it followed that alteration of trade patterns between the two would have significant and immediate impact. Great Britain was the European nation most able to threaten seriously American security in the New World. That nation's naval supremacy gave it effective veto power over America's commerce, a fact that loomed particularly large in time of war. By 1790 the alliance with France had become a debt to be paid, repudiated, or negotiated; it no longer offered meaningful protection to the United States, nor did it advance the search for markets. Throughout the decade relations with France played a secondary role in America's foreign affairs, as a weapon to be used in the

larger struggle against Great Britain. Spain's weakness in the New World offered the United States an opportunity to pursue a belligerent, aggressive
approach to the search for security on its southern and western borders.
Relations with other nations, especially Holland, the German states, and
Russia, involved little risk of open hostility but only modest market opportunities. These, then, were the major realities within which the nation
pursued security and wealth.

So much for areas of agreement, for the politics of foreign policy during
the decade was divisive in the extreme. Every point of agreement proved to
be a fulcrum for disagreement. Yes, Anglo-American trade patterns were significant for both nations, but what was the significance and which nation
could best withstand or gain most from a disruption of the relationship?
Yes, Great Britain was the major threat to America's security, but should
America ally itself with strength or against it? Yes, the British navy dominated the Atlantic, but should the United States build a counterforce? Yes,
the French alliance no longer benefitted America, but how should the debt
be paid? Yes, Franco-American relations were secondary, but how could
they be employed most effectively in the contest with Great Britain? Yes,
Spain was weak, but should America move aggressively into the southwest
and Florida? Yes, other nations were less important in the New World and
in trade, but should their favor be cultivated more actively? And most
divisive of all, what should be done when security seemed attainable only
by sacrificing the quest for markets or when development of new trade opportunities reduced security?

These questions rose repeatedly in the 1790s. Debate over discriminatory
duties, Jefferson's reports on commerce, the Jay Treaty, the Quasi-War,
the building of frigates, and the role of the army saw the emergence of
sharply polarized voting blocs that agreed on goals and the realities of the
situation but disagreed fundamentally on appropriate responses. Because
the focus of this study is on legislative behavior, it will not be possible to
explain fully why particular actions were taken or avoided. Such explana-
tions required detailed investigation of the decision-making process in the
executive branch and of the records of other nations.[1] Nevertheless, Congress played a significant role in the major foreign policy decisions of the
decade, a role that often has been misunderstood because of a failure to
consider foreign affairs within the broader context of legislative behavior
on domestic issues. The focus here, then, is on the effort of the House of
Representatives to further the nation's security and to develop markets for
America's produce. One of the consequences of pursuing these goals was
armed conflict, a fact that allows detailed analysis of legislative response to

war. Once again the emphasis will be on the interaction between faction and party, between consideration of policy and desire for office.

Continuities between foreign policy issues in the 1780s and those of the next decade provide little assistance in understanding developments during the Federalist era. The Constitution fundamentally altered the dimensions of the policy making apparatus. Where only empty fulminations and humble pleadings had existed, the Constitution provided the potential for strong, concerted action: treaties could be negotiated and enforced; trade regulations would be uniform; a powerful and united nation would confront its foreign neighbors. Power was the essence of policy, and the Constitution greatly expanded the limits of national power. Impotence had muffled disagreement (with the notable exception of the Jay-Gardoqui negotiations); conversely, strength provided something worth contesting.

James Madison, quick to recognize the new possibilities, presented the first of many proposals aimed at upsetting Anglo-American trade patterns. Great Britain stood as the most formidable obstacle to expansion of American markets and, simultaneously, as the greatest threat to the young nation's freedom of action in North America. Commercial retaliation against unfriendly nations had found favor throughout the 1780s among the supporters of strong government, but they had been powerless to act in the face of independent state action. As the Tariff Act of 1789 atoned for the impotence of the Confederation years, so discriminatory tonnage rates, the Virginian believed, would forcefully demonstrate the nation's power and determination. Tonnage discrimination was only a modest step, affecting shippers but not necessarily producers; it satiated patriotic pride without forcing great alteration of consumption patterns. Madison at first intended to go no further, but William Smith of Maryland then introduced discrimination on distilled spirits as well. Tariff levies, as indicated in the preceding chapter, provided revenue but not protection. Rates were sufficiently high, however, that additional discrimination against non-treaty nations, principally Great Britain, might force a change in trade patterns. Madison was unwilling to go that far and, noting the need to avoid loss of revenue, expressed preference for only token discrimination, enough to establish a principle. "I am certain," he said, "that there is a disposition to make a discrimination, to teach the nations that are not in alliance with us that there is an advantage to be gained by the connexion; to give some early symptom of the power and will of the new Government to redress our national wrongs, must be productive of benefit." The House agreed, and by a wide margin it passed a bill including both tonnage and tariff discrimination.[2]

The vote involved considerations other than trade with England, however, and it did not accurately foreshadow positions on discrimination. As anticipated, the Senate struck out all references in the bill to treaty and non-treaty nations and returned the measure to the House. Debate now revealed great concern over the prerogatives of the two legislative bodies, and perhaps the distaste felt by certain of the people's representatives for submitting to the pretensions of the upper chamber counted for more than the particular issue at hand.[3] Although the debate leads to such a conclusion, the vote that followed does not.

On the final calling of the roll, thirty-one of fifty delegates opposed tonnage and tariff discrimination. New England and New York gave the majority its greatest support as only Jonathan Grout of Massachusetts, John Hathorn of New York, and Jonathan Sturges of Connecticut voted to retain the House version of the bill. During more difficult economic times under the Articles of Confederation, many northern merchants, who stood to gain from discrimination while southern planters bore the brunt of higher tonnage duties, had advocated the plan Madison now supported. But as prosperity returned, commercial warfare against Great Britain became less attractive to men of trade. It was true that prosperity augured well for the potential success of discrimination, but the immediate consideration of protecting profits loomed large—in 1789 there was something to lose in altering Anglo-American trade patterns. Georgia and South Carolina, far removed from New England geographically and politically, contributed six of their seven votes to the majority, the lone exception being Thomas Sumter, an upcountry representative who often found himself opposed to the rest of South Carolina's delegation. The other six voted for the interest of their planter-dominated constituencies. Tonnage discrimination and the British retaliation that would surely follow meant higher transportation costs, and planters knew from bitter experience that a portion of the increase would come from their profits. For this reason Madison failed to control even his own state's delegation, one-third of which voted for the Senate bill. The northeast and the deep South, then, joined forces to defeat discrimination. Only in the Middle Atlantic and the upper South did Madison's proposals find favor. In this area, particularly in Philadelphia, Baltimore, Wilmington, and Norfolk, merchants were on the make, aggressively seeking new markets and suffering consequently from British restraints. Gouverneur Morris' reports of continued English intransigence convinced a willing majority of the delegates from this area to try discrimination.[4]

The two blocs that contested tonnage and tariff discrimination in 1789 did not polarize against each other on other issues. Table 43, which summarizes the voting behavior of proponents and opponents of discrimination for all roll calls recorded in the First Congress, reveals the uniqueness of the issue. Only on rare occasions—and these owing largely to quirks of attendance rather than principle—did cohesion differences exceed 34 percent. The absence of sharp polarization by these two blocs on other issues

Table 43. Cohesion Differences: Proponents Against Opponents of Trade Discrimination Against England, First Congress

Issue	Range of Cohesion Difference			Mean
	0–34%	*35–64%*	*65–100%*	
	Percent of Roll Calls in Each Range			
Government power	85	15	0	17
Frontier	100	0	0	7
Location of the capital	86	14	0	25
Economic	83	17	0	21
Foreign policy	75	0	25	28
Miscellaneous and personal	91	9	0	12
ALL ROLL CALLS	85	14	1	19

and the fluidity of positions on discrimination (which originally received the acquiescence of a majority in the House) leads to several questions about the standard historical interpretation of this critical issue. Alexander DeConde termed commercial discrimination a "political issue" that "loomed large in the Jefferson-Hamilton feud and in the formation of political parties."[5] But the division of delegates was unlike that on location of the capital, assumption, establishment of a national bank, and strengthening of national authority—all of them issues that fueled party development. Although less hostile to Hamilton than is DeConde, historian Jerald Combs also finds the young secretary's "hand in defeating" discrimination.[6] Clearly, Hamilton opposed retaliation against Great Britain even at this early date and he was not one to use his influence with restraint. However, it is equally certain that Hamilton did not sway the votes of the eleven southerners, a majority of those who voted, who opposed discrimination. The most significant conclusion to be drawn from the 1789 discrimination debate is that the pressure of geographically circumscribed economic interest in the North and South favored maintenance of existing Anglo-American trade patterns. Even the most modest proposal to exert newly available power in commercial matters failed to secure the support of a majority. Madison's efforts to establish American mercantilism, as William Appleman Williams in *The Contours of American History* perceptively titled the quest for security and wealth, faced obstacles that proved to be insurmountable in the 1790s. Of course Hamilton was one of them, but the attachment of political leaders, especially southerners, to local economic interests severely undermined Madison's cause and, as will be demonstrated, led the Virginian himself to advocate compromise and ultimately acquiescence.

In 1790, however, Madison remained an ardent spokesman for the use of discriminatory tariff and tonnage rates against Great Britain. In May of that year, in response to a petition from merchants in Portsmouth, New Hampshire, Congress again gave initial approval to higher tonnage duties for foreign-built ships belonging to non-treaty nations. Madison directed his arguments primarily at his fellow southerners, appealing variously to patriotism, thriftiness, the general welfare of the nation, and fear of war. "We can do better without Great Britain," he asserted, "than she can do without us; articles of luxury can be retrenched with advantage." The South was "deeply connected with the British," and he "lamented that measures calculated to promote the general good, should militate with any particular interest." But the connection was perilous, for "in case of war the Southern States would be the first objects of attack." Pushed perhaps by the apparent depth of support for retaliatory measures, Madison then proposed absolute prohibition of the carrying of non-manufactured items in ships of non-treaty nations. This was too much for many in the southern bloc and their chief spokesman, James Jackson of Georgia, opposed Madison's plan on the simple and incontrovertible ground that "our produce would be left on our hands." It took six weeks for the pro-discrimination majority to disappear, but by the end of June the House defeated the measure.[7]

Madison's majorities on discrimination disappeared with great frequency despite the enormous respect he received from fellow delegates who, in the Committee of the Whole, were loath to kill his plans without a hearing. But the statesmanlike deference accorded the Virginian did not extend to sacrifice of economic interest. Madison's inability to distinguish between respect and support was again shown when, after acknowledging the defeat of discrimination, he proposed the "principle of reciprocity." The idea was alarmingly simple: British restrictions on American trade would be countered with similar legislation against Great Britain. At this point Jackson abandoned legislative niceties. The proposals "will annihilate in a great measure the trade of Georgia to the West Indies, and he believed of North Carolina, too," and "he thought it extraordinary that the gentleman from Virginia should come forward with one exceptionable proposition after another." While praising Madison's brilliance, a majority in the House agreed to postpone consideration of the extraordinary plans until "to-morrow." But tomorrow never came, as Congress adjourned without further discussion of Anglo-American trade.[8]

Six months later, during the last session of the First Congress, President Washington formally reported Gouverneur Morris' inability to negotiate an improvement in commercial relations with Great Britain. Again Madison saw an opportunity to press for discrimination and retaliation, but the House, anxious to conclude other matters before adjourning, referred the message to a committee dominated by Madison's opponents. The committee in turn referred the matter to Thomas Jefferson, the secretary of state, for consideration in his anticipated report.[9]

Thus the First Congress closed without taking any affirmative action to change Anglo-American trade patterns. Majorities seemingly existed, at least temporarily, in favor of such action on no less than four occasions. The failure to act, ascribed to the pretensions of the pro-British Senate and the sinister influence of Alexander Hamilton, owed much to the pressure of economic interest. New Englanders proved unwilling to tamper with returning prosperity, there was no public outcry for retaliation, and, most important, southern planters refused to approve any proposal that threatened to raise their transportation costs. The minority of delegates who consistently supported discrimination did not unite on other issues, nor did they form an issue-oriented faction that foreshadowed future legislative behavior.

During the latter half of Washington's first term, America's foreign policy continued to favor Great Britain. In addition to the underlying and powerful constant of economic dependence on the former mother country, several temporary factors combined to prevent policy innovation, a situation sought by England. The Harmar and St. Clair failures blunted American aggressiveness on the issue of British forts in the Northwest. Continued hostility in the Southwest raised the spectre of confrontation against two European powers at the same time, a prospect all the nation's policy makers wished to avoid. The formal exchange of ambassadors between Great Britain and the United States offered at least faint hope for improved relations, a development that needed time. Jefferson, who never demonstrated Hamilton's speed and depth in producing written reports, allowed his major statement on commercial relations to gestate for more than two years. During this time Madison could hardly renew the fight for discrimination and retaliation. Finally, the expanding revolution in France not only captured the attention and interest of Americans but also checked policy innovation. When events moved more rapidly than ships, the case for inaction proved overwhelming.

The only foreign policy roll calls recorded in the House during these years dealt with the sending of a rather innocuous note to the King of France congratulating him for his wisdom in accepting a new and republican constitution. This was a matter of little consequence, but the vote on it aroused the wrath of a small but powerful bloc of delegates already alarmed by the revolution. The date, March 10, 1792, is critical in this case, for it preceded publication of the Paine-Burke controversy, the spread of the revolution beyond France, the outbreak of war between France and Great Britain, and regicide. These events obviously expanded and hardened anti-French attitudes in the United States, but the earlier presence of significant and deep hostility against the nation's strongest ally merits attention. Delegates who responded primarily to anti-French feelings injected a complicating dimension into the nation's foreign policy. Acting alone, France could neither halt nor guarantee America's quest for freedom of action in the New World. England could and did do both. The six men most responsible for America's foreign policy—Washington, Adams, Hamilton, Jay, Jefferson, and Madison—disagreed sharply on method, but they united in assigning a primary role to Anglo-American relations. Their vastly different plans concerning France were all designed to use that nation in some measure in the contest against Great Britain for independence, security, and markets. But delegates in the House, somewhat removed from the realities of exercising power, indulged more fully in emotional responses toward France. In doing so, they threatened, often unknowingly, to thwart the nation's primary goals.

Two roll calls mark the first appearance of this threat in the 1790s. After failing in an effort to recommit the entire congratulatory note, nearly one-third of the House, apparently in a pique, voted to strike from the note the hope that "the wisdom . . . displayed in . . . acceptance of the Constitution may be rewarded by the most perfect attainment of its objective, the permanent happiness of so great a people." The note had no effect on anyone, least of all the King of France, but the delegates who contested the matter acted from motives that were of importance later in the decade. Table 44 summarizes the voting behavior of the two blocs that emerged on roll calls dealing with the note. Unlike First Congress voting blocs on discrimination against England, these groups polarized significantly on a variety of issues. Particularly on economic questions and on limiting government authority, administration supporters (who dominated the anti-French bloc) united against a larger group of delegates who refused to act on the basis of their attitude toward France. Thus, the House members most relied upon by the executive on domestic issues could not be counted

Table 44. Cohesion Differences: Early Anti-French Delegates Against All Other Voting Members, Second Congress

	Range of Cohesion Difference			
Issue	*0-34%*	*35-64%*	*65-100%*	*Mean*
	Percent of Roll Calls in Each Range			
Government power	18	55	27	51
Frontier	70	30	0	26
Economic	18	70	12	45
Foreign policy	25	25	50	60
Miscellaneous and personal	50	35	15	35
ALL ROLL CALLS	31	52	17	43

on in making foreign policy. This division became more open after 1796 and severely hampered John Adams' effectiveness in avoiding open confrontation with France, but the break was evident as early as the spring of 1792.[10]

More substantial issues arose during the Third Congress, issues that directly involved the quest for security and wealth. In the spring of 1793, with the legislature adjourned and the president at Mount Vernon, news of France's declaration of war reached Philadelphia. Correspondence from Jefferson and Hamilton convinced Washington that war between England and France would soon follow, a situation that required some response from the United States. Mindful of the advantages of forceful executive action and anxious to avoid lengthy policy discussions in the House, Washington proclaimed America's neutrality. But neutrality meant something more than indifference. Unlike some members of the House, who allowed Francophobia to mold their positions, the cabinet, including Jefferson and Hamilton, grappled with the fundamental policy question of the decade: what actions most enhanced America's security and furthered its expansion of markets. Throughout the year the executive branch followed a pragmatic course aimed at avoiding military conflict with either belligerent while maintaining trade with both. Even the trying experience of Edmond Genet's indiscretions failed to ignite an alteration of policy. France offered only a secondary threat to America's goals, and this made possible a high level of toleration between the two nations. With England the situation differed. Regardless of any bias, no one denied Great Britain's strength in the New World and its naval barrier between America and Europe. Any British action, therefore, immediately and deeply affected the young nation.[11]

Great Britain, seeing its interests threatened by Washington's interpretation of neutrality, took a series of actions calculated to force a change in American policy. In November 1793, a secret order-in-council authorized the seizure of neutral ships trading with the French West Indies. In the four months before word of this order officially reached the United States, Great Britain captured nearly 250 ships. During this time news also arrived of a treaty between Portugal and the Algerian pirates. Supported by England, the treaty effectively sanctioned pirate attacks on American ships trading with France. The full import of British policy seemed clear when news arrived in the spring of 1794 of Lord Dorchester's speech encouraging the Indians of Canada to draw by force a new border between themselves and the United States. The threat to security and markets was now complete.

America's response owed much to the long-awaited report by the secretary of state on American trade. Delivered to the Third Congress in December 1793, it contrasted sharply with Washington's message for war preparations and the need to avoid insult by repelling the Algerian pirates. Both called for sacrifice and greatness, but the military man appealed to strength of arms while the philosopher saw only a need for attention to republican virtues. For more than a year the House weighed fully the merits of the two theories, and in the end it sacrificed each to the other. In the process there emerged two polarized blocs and, most interestingly, a smaller but critical group of delegates unwilling to follow either course.

The bitterness of the contest was evident from the outset, as the House agreed by only two votes to even consider how to pay for measures to provide defense against the Algerian pirates. It was an easy matter to protest British complicity and to cry in anguish over European disregard of America's plight. Strongly worded resolutions calling for more ships with more guns gave the appearance of taking action to protect the nation's honor, but a majority in the House, although only a small one, succeeded in undermining the force of such resolutions by adding to a defense committee's charge the responsibility for devising a way to pay for a navy. Not unexpectedly, the result was to hamstring efforts to provide new ships. Thus, opponents of the administration took the earliest possible opportunity to demonstrate that they would not yield to emotional appeals to patriotism, even from President Washington himself.[12]

The contest continued in earnest when James Madison opened the debate on Jefferson's commerce report with a series of strong resolutions calling for higher tariffs on many manufactured articles, discriminatory tariff and tonnage duties for non-treaty nations, retaliation, and indemnification for seized ships. William L. Smith of South Carolina and Fisher

Ames of Massachusetts, quickly asserting leadership in the fight against the resolutions, asked for and received a ten-day delay to prepare their arguments. Armed with material supplied by Hamilton, Smith produced an all-day speech that exceeded Jefferson's report in length, detail, and emotional force. Madison's response consumed yet another day, but most delegates remained confused and weary. Those who spoke in the weeks that followed generally began with an acknowledgment of their ignorance of commercial affairs and quickly moved on to recitations of colonial history, quotations of the Constitution, claims of personal affronts, and opinions on Hamilton's public credit schemes. Abraham Clark of New Jersey, after seven days of debate, observed that there was "as little prospect of bringing it to a decision as there was at the beginning"; he chided the "passion of members to see their speeches published in the newspapers." The whole business was "a waste of time" as it was "nearly certain that no proselytes would be made either on the one side or the other." He would "pass away the time by listening to some of those gentlemen who seemed so impatient and felt so big with their speeches that they would burst, he feared, should he stand up any longer to prevent their delivery."

Clark was only partially correct. Many delegates did have a great deal to add to the discussion, but he erred in believing that positions were frozen. Although the tedious debate fell on deaf ears, delegates were sharply attuned to developments in the European war, and votes did change with the varying prospects for America's involvement in that struggle. Madison and his supporters, sensing that time might bring news to mitigate the administration's charges that the resolutions would force the country into an unnecessary war against England, successfully postponed further consideration for one month.[13] And news did arrive: ships seized in the West Indies and incitement of Indians on the frontier. At this critical point, late March 1794, the House and Senate reversed previous policy and approved a one-month embargo on all American shipping. Madison and his allies joined administration supporters in securing passage of the embargo. In doing so they had adopted a wait-and-see attitude calculated to avoid war and, though it was hardly Madison's intention, to aid Great Britain. The measure worked its greatest hardship on the French West Indies, which were blockaded by the British navy and already sorely missed the supplies carried in the 250 captured American ships. It also gave precious time for the cooling of popular wrath over British policy and allowed receipt of news of a more generous order-in-council from England.[14]

Upon recovering from fear of being at the precipice of open warfare, the House resumed consideration of purely anti-British measures. In somewhat of a surprise move, Jonathan Dayton of New Jersey, a self-declared independent who always ended up on the administration side, revived Madison's early resolution on compensation for British seizures and added the proviso that payment would come from sequestration of private debts owed by American citizens to British citizens. Dayton was responding primarily to deeply felt indignation over British violation of property rights, but he never intended to upset Anglo-American trade patterns. Sequestration would have meant lengthy court battles and very little compensation. Heated debate over this unrealistic and vindictive proposal caused the House to lose sight of the main issue at hand and once again allowed Madison to deceive himself about the depth of support for his retaliation measures. The House quietly killed sequestration in the Committee of the Whole.[15]

Two weeks slipped by before Congress agreed to consider an embargo directed specifically against Great Britain. Then, even the announcement of John Jay's appointment as special envoy to seek improved relations with England failed to deter the House, which voted to continue debate by a wider margin than ever, 57 to 42. Only three days later a majority approved the prohibition, after November 1, 1794, of all imports of articles grown or manufactured in Great Britain or Ireland. The date was significant; if Jay reported progress, and the majority believed this was likely now that America had demonstrated its will to retaliate, the restrictions would not need to go into effect. This simple resolution cogently expressed the Jefferson-Madison approach to foreign policy: achieve security and wealth by confronting the major threat to these goals with moral supremacy, willingness to sacrifice, and economic retaliation. But the Senate saw no need to assist Jay's efforts in this manner, and an entire session of foreign policy debate produced no permanent action.[16]

In the weeks that followed, large majorities in the House demonstrated their unwillingness to initiate alterations in Anglo-American trade patterns. This majority included not only disciplined supporters of Hamilton but also independents and anti-administration men who believed that (1) the surest path to security was friendship with the greatest threat to security and (2) possible increased prices on imports outweighed any market expansion that might result from retaliation against England. Madison counted on these men, many of them fellow southerners, but he was wrong. Rhetorical appeals to patriotism and threats of future retaliation received support, but action did not. A proposal to double the duty on British tonnage gained only 24 of 79 votes. Revision of the general embargo to have it apply only to trade with the West Indies, Bermuda, and

Nova Scotia lost by 54 to 34. An effort to ban all trade received only 13 of 86 votes cast.[17] Delegates who approved the spirit of Jefferson's report on commerce but who refused to act on it also opposed expensive measures to build a navy and increase the military establishment. Their "middle" position produced a stalemate that left the direction of foreign policy largely to the executive.

In the process of taking no new action, and, consequently, of reaffirming the essentially pro-British posture in effect since 1789, several distinct voting blocs formed in the House. Madison and his supporters comprised the largest, but ultimately the least successful, of these blocs. The forty-one delegates in this group coalesced (97 percent voting in the same way) on the very first roll call of the Third Congress and they remained united on all matters relating to Jefferson's report on commerce.[18] Dominated by representatives from Virginia and North Carolina, the bloc opposed efforts to strengthen the army and navy but actively supported proposals to alter Anglo-American trade patterns. A group of thirty-three delegates, largely from Massachusetts, Connecticut, and New York, took exactly the opposite position with equal consistency.[19] Even if only these two blocs are counted, it is clear that more than three-fourths of the House regularly appeared on the same side on the calling of the roll on foreign policy questions. Legislators at that time and historians since have underestimated the degree of polarization that characterized pre-Jay Treaty voting. Perhaps the most interesting delegates, however, are those who voted with neither of the extreme groups.[20] These men were not obtuse, indifferent, immune from party pressures, or inconsistent. Rather, in debate they outlined a position to which they adhered in voting: approval of Jefferson's sentiments but not Madison's provocative actions, approval of Washington's appeal to patriotism but not the administration's emphasis on military buildup. Sixteen modestly pro-Jefferson delegates and ten modestly pro-administration representatives held the balance of power in the House. Acting together, they alternatively defeated both Madison and the administration.

Table 45 summarizes the interaction of voting records among the four groups that emerged from foreign policy considerations in the Third Congress. The numbers indicate no "melting away" of votes as Madison so often complained, no sinister pressure from Hamilton, and no massive emotional reactions to British depredations. Moderates polarized highly against each other on only one of every ten roll calls; on more than half of all recorded votes they acted as a bloc to prevent action by either of the extreme factions. This pattern of bloc voting by moderates to stalemate

Table 45. Cohesion Differences: Foreign Policy Blocs, Third Congress

Groups[a]	Issue	Range of Cohesion Difference			Mean
		0–34%	35–64%	65–100%	
		Percent of Roll Calls in Each Range			
1 vs. 2	Government power	33	17	50	55
	Frontier	25	25	50	57
	Economic	14	45	41	58
	Foreign policy	11	17	72	69
	Miscellaneous and personal	0	57	43	63
	ALL ROLL CALLS	16	32	52	61
3 vs. 4	Government power	67	17	16	34
	Frontier	44	37	19	42
	Economic	77	23	0	26
	Foreign policy	33	50	17	45
	Miscellaneous and personal	43	57	0	37
	ALL ROLL CALLS	54	36	10	36
1 and 3	Government power	33	17	50	52
vs.	Frontier	31	25	44	54
2 and 4	Economic	18	68	14	49
	Foreign policy	11	22	67	62
	Miscellaneous and personal	28	44	28	48
	ALL ROLL CALLS	22	39	39	55

[a]1 = extreme pro-Jefferson   2 = extreme pro-administration
   3 = moderate pro-Jefferson   4 = moderate pro-administration

House action occurred throughout the 1790s. As a result, the direction of foreign policy devolved increasingly upon the executive branch and the Senate, but always within the broad context of achieving security and markets through a moderately pro-British posture. The Madison-Jefferson alternative failed to gain acceptance because it meant immediate economic loss to planters and merchants, and because it appeared to pose too great a risk to security in the New World for poorly understood future market expansion.

Within this context the Jay Treaty fight in the House exhibits a continuation of voting patterns and policy decisions reached earlier in the decade. The year 1796 remains as appropriate a date as any for the birth of the first American party system, but the treaty itself and reactions to it were hardly new. A brief review of this well-known contest serves to demonstrate certain continuities: (1) formation of two polarized minority blocs, divided over whether to ally with power to achieve the goals sought by both groups; (2) formation of a small but consistent middle group that successfully stalemated legislative action on foreign policy; (3) frequent overestimating by Madison of support for his position; and (4) a shift in emphasis from policy matters to the quest for office.

Whatever the merits of Jay's treaty, the thrust of the document was fully consonant with America's policy towards Great Britain since 1789. The treaty made clear, perhaps too clear, the nation's decision to seek security and markets through a partnership, albeit a strained one, with the primary threat to these goals. The United States gained relatively little but, then again, it gave up nothing of consequence. As Jerald Combs judiciously concludes, "Jay seems to have attained most or all of what Grenville and the British cabinet were willing to concede to America's power."[21] There followed a close but predictable fight in the Senate, during which Hamilton's allies again displayed great acumen, and then a series of political blunders by the administration. The vain attempt to keep the treaty terms secret after Senate ratification displayed a high-handed contempt for the people and unnecessarily raised suspicions about British influence in government circles. Engaging in street debate showed more brashness than wisdom, especially when a crowd greeted Hamilton with stones. Washington's decision to leave the treaty unsigned and to journey to Mount Vernon for a vacation led to misunderstanding and increased uninformed speculation about his ultimate decision. But concern was as shallow as it was volatile, and public tempers cooled greatly by the time the House reconvened in December 1795. The legislature, however, prepared for a full appraisal of the treaty, and only delay in receiving official notification from Great Britain of its ratification postponed House consideration until the following March.

The debate began abruptly with Edward Livingston's call for papers related to the treaty. The resolution primarily raised questions about the loci of government power, and the large majority it received reflected in part the House's frustration over its declining influence, especially on foreign policy matters.[22] Madison believed that the sixty-two supporters of the Livingston Resolution also favored the alteration of Anglo-American trade patterns that would necessarily follow failure to implement the Jay Treaty. He was mistaken. At no time in the 1790s did a majority in the House go beyond empty appeals to patriotism. Indeed, delegates at the time frequently charged that Madison himself was more concerned with politicking than with policy. Historian Stephen Kurtz, the most careful student of these debates, reached a similar conclusion.[23] The motives of Madison, Gallatin, and other Republican leaders cannot be determined with certainty. It is likely that their actions stemmed not only from partisanship and policy aims but also from human error. To put the matter simply, they failed, at times displaying surprising ineptitude in throwing to the wind both principle and party advantage. But intensive investigation of the 1796 debate obscures a most important vantage point for explaining Madison's defeat: for nearly eight years he had lost every foreign policy battle in the House. Even when the Republican interest achieved a majority, the policy of altering Anglo-American trade patterns remained a minority position. In 1789 New England merchants and southern planters combined to defeat Madison. In 1796 economic considerations again melted a majority into a minority.

Madison's followers dwindled from sixty-two on the Livingston Resolution to forty-eight on implementation of the treaty itself. Administration support rose by the same margin, from thirty-eight to fifty-one. Changes in attendance explain part of this reversal of majorities. Four delegates— Gabriel Duvall of Maryland, William Findley of western Pennsylvania, John Patten of Delaware, and John Sherburne of New Hampshire—voted for the Livingston Resolution but were not to be found on the day of the treaty vote. In at least two cases the excuses offered for absence were lame in the extreme. Administration forces lost only one vote due to absence on the treaty roll call, that of Nathaniel Freeman of Massachusetts. Five members who voted on the treaty had been absent for the Livingston Resolution; of these only Daniel Hiester of Pennsylvania opposed Jay's work. The proponents of the treaty, then, gained three net votes between the two roll calls, exactly the number by which they won, due to attendance changes.

No one who opposed the Livingston Resolution subsequently voted against the treaty, and so the remaining gain of eleven for the treaty's proponents had to come from the Madison camp. These eleven are significant not only as individuals but also as representatives of particular areas.

Two crossovers came from the South. William Barry Grove of North Carolina tended to support the administration before and after this Congress; his vote can hardly have been a surprise. The other southern defector, George Hancock of Botetourt County in southwestern Virginia, had established a successful law practice in Fincastle. He never voted consistently with any faction in the House. Hancock represented the lower Shenandoah Valley, which had significant trade connections with Baltimore and Alexandria, and displayed a deep-rooted skepticism about proposals supported by eastern planters. Another factor in Hancock's vote for the treaty was its provision for clearing the Northwest of British fortifications which, it was hoped, would pave the way for settlement by the

more adventurous westerners of his district. These two were the only supporters of the Livingston Resolution south of the Potomac who crossed
over and voted for the Jay Treaty.

The other nine defectors came from the Middle Atlantic region. Aaron
Kitchell of New Jersey, a former blacksmith, accepted the label Republican
when faced with an election fight, but he voted with the administration as
often as not. In earlier Congresses he had supported the nationalist majority on the coin controversy, taxation, and imposition of law and order
in the West, and had never voted for proposals aimed at changing Anglo-
American trade patterns. His state strongly favored the treaty, and his vote
reflected the will of his constituents.

Theodore Bailey and Philip Van Cortlandt, from Westchester and
Dutchess counties respectively, represented the well-to-do of the lower
Hudson Valley estates of New York. Their general adherence to the Re-
publican party reflected local considerations in state politics, where great
families chose sides more because of personal feuds or desire for power
than for reasons of principle. Local ties often held at the national level;
Van Cortlandt consistently supported anti-administration interests in the
House. In a matter of such grave consequence as a treaty that could prevent war with England, however, party took second place. The lower
Hudson Valley had close connections with the merchants of New York
City who formed the base of Hamilton's strength in the state, and both
groups had much to gain from peace with England.

Three Pennsylvanians—John Richards, Frederick Muhlenberg, and
Andrew Gregg—who had voted for the Livingston Resolution turned around
and favored the treaty itself. Richards was a Federalist; possibly his treaty
vote needs less explanation than his earlier support of the Livingston Resolution, an indication of the depth of dissatisfaction with Jay's work. This
dissatisfaction, however, did not extend to completely upsetting the administration's applecart. Muhlenberg, an itinerant minister, had been
Speaker of the House and therefore often did not vote. His acceptance as
Speaker by the pro-administration majorities of the First and Third Congresses, as well as his judiciously impartial handling of the duties of his
office, indicate that he never had been an ardent Republican. He understood the value of compromise. The defection of Andrew Gregg, on the
other hand, was a severe blow to treaty opponents. John Beckley never
forgave the transgression and always afterwards referred to the Pennsylvanian as "trimmer Gregg." Gregg's vote, however, had been forecast a
year earlier when he opposed Madison's effort to implement Jefferson's
report by retaliating against British trade. During his stay in the House,

lasting more than a decade despite Beckley's enmity, Gregg consistently refused to oppose the administration on critical questions when opposition seemed to have a chance of success.

The crossover of three delegates from Maryland—Gabriel Christie, George Dent, and Samuel Smith—resulted from changing economic pressures in the state. Representing the areas of Maryland most affected by the rapidly expanding commercial activity centered around Baltimore, all three gave in to the forces described so clearly by Republican stalwart Smith in the Third Congress, when he had explained his position against restrictions on trade with England. In addition to the rather crass economic factors he cited at that time, Smith now stressed that he would give his consent to the treaty because "it would tend to restore harmony and unanimity to our public measures; a House so nearly divided against itself could never thrive."[24]

And so Madison's majority had melted away. Names and proposals changed over the decade, but a basic pattern repeatedly emerged. Delegates listened graciously and at length, but in the end they calculated gains and losses, usually emphasizing short-term accounts, and, fortified by extremely effective propaganda emanating from Hamilton's offices, defeated attempts to alter Anglo-American trade patterns. Jay's treaty formalized an existing relationship: the United States sought security through friendship with the only nation that seriously threatened its borders and, in exchange, allowed England to set the limits of America's market expansion. The agreement lasted until Madison himself became chief executive, a position he used to implement the alternative he had so long and unsuccessfully sought.

The less happy consequence of the Jay Treaty, of course, was that it brought the nation to the brink of war against France. Again, power was the key consideration. Within the New World France's influence rated a distant third, behind that of the United States and Great Britain. By joining power with power, Jay's treaty directly threatened two major goals of French policy: security for its remaining West Indies possessions and isolation of England. Although the United States clearly was not a world force, it played a preeminent role in these two aspects of French policy. Therefore, a relationship of secondary importance to the United States became primal for France. In its desperate attempt to lure the favor of the United States, France variously tried delay, insult, warlike maneuver, and negotiation. But in reality America had little to gain from Continental Europe, and French efforts came to nought.

The Quasi-War began in earnest in 1795, when Secretary of State

Timothy Pickering reported the capture of more than three hundred American vessels by French cruisers. During the next five years both nations maintained a belligerent posture on the seas, regardless of the state of negotiations between them. The United States entered this contest with truly meager resources; it had no navy. However, signing of the Jay Treaty assured Great Britain that a naval armaments program would be directed elsewhere; consequently, Hamilton's supporters in the House began vigorously to press for such measures in the spring of 1796. The loudest cries always concerned defense against the Algerian pirates, but specific proposals usually concerned large warships, which may have been inappropriate for countering the hit-and-run tactics of pirates but were very impressive floating around the French West Indies.

The Jay Treaty provided an umbrella of security in the New World under which the United States might freely and aggressively seek markets. That is, the conflict between security and markets forced by Great Britain's insistence on trading one for the other no longer existed. Delegates from commercial areas quickly grasped the new situation and pressed hard for naval development. Previously divided and defeated by fear of upsetting Anglo-American trade patterns, they now united to create an innovative program.

Throughout the Fourth Congress a group of twenty-nine representatives led an effort to build frigates.[25] They voted to authorize six frigates instead of three and, when this failed, they successfully pushed for three ships instead of two. They voted to use the very best live oak and red cedar timber for construction of the vessels and favored an authorization to provide crews for the frigates even before they were actually put to sea.[26] The majority of this group of twenty-nine were generally associated with the Federalists, but there were significant exceptions. Six of the group had voted for the Livingston Resolution and four—Dempsey Burges, Edward Livingston, Josiah Parker, and John Swanwick—had opposed the Jay Treaty. Members of the group came from all parts of the country: three from Connecticut, five from Maryland, four from Massachusetts, two from New Hampshire, one from New Jersey, five from New York, one from North Carolina, two from South Carolina, four from Pennsylvania, one from Rhode Island, and one from Virginia. All of these hard core proponents of frigates were directly associated with important commercial interests. Every center of trade stood solidly for the frigates—Boston (represented by Samuel Sewall), Providence (Francis Malbone), New York City (Edward Livingstone), Philadelphia (John Swanwick), Baltimore (Samuel Smith), Norfolk (Josiah Parker), and Charleston (William L.

Smith). Four of these seven urban representatives—Livingston, Swanwick, Samuel Smith, and Parker—were generally associated with the Republican interest. All four favored the Livingston Resolution (Livingston, of course, was its author) and all but Smith voted against the Jay Treaty. The other members of this bloc favoring commercial interests, although not from port cities, represented areas significantly dependent upon trade, such as the Hudson Valley of New York, coastal counties of Massachusetts, Connecticut River Valley towns in New Hampshire, Massachusetts, and Connecticut, and wheat exporting counties in Pennsylvania. These same men, and the districts they represented, stood for the interests of commerce throughout the 1790s. They did so without regard to party label.

Seventeen delegates coalesced to oppose all ten roll calls on the authorization and building of frigates.[27] After an unsuccessful attempt to reduce the proposal from three ships to two, all seventeen voted against building any frigates at all. When this failed, they voted against appropriations to buy timber with which to build the vessels and against provision to provide crews for the ships.[28] Any search for consistencies within the group of seventeen must exclude Joshua Coit, an expert on naval matters who preferred arming merchant ships to building huge frigates. Of the remaining sixteen, all but one had voted for the Livingston Resolution and all but three had opposed the Jay Treaty to the bitter end.[29] Ten of the group were farmers and none represented areas where commerce was the dominant local interest. Half the group came from interior districts in New York and Virginia, but delegates from six other states, as far north as Vermont and as far south as South Carolina, were equally firm in their opposition to frigates.

The blocs that formed on the question of building frigates are typical of the relationship between faction and party. Most opponents of frigates campaigned for Congress using the label Republican and most proponents were Federalists. However, the motivation for their votes on the frigate issue was not party but the extent of commercial interest in their districts. A new and consequential issue brought these motivations to the fore. Edward Livingston's votes provide a useful example of the inadequacy of party label as a conceptual framework for explaining policy outputs and of the inverse relationship between party and faction. There can be no question that Livingston was a Republican: he accepted the label, he participated in partisan politicking, he was an important cog in the party machine. Yet his party label did not always correspond with his voting positions. Livingston opposed the Jay Treaty, but there existed no more ardent advocate of frigates than he. The more significant shortcoming of the two-party approach is its implicit conclusion that party association is in itself a motivation for voting. Too often the reader and, alas, the researcher as well, fail to ask why delegates chose one party rather than the other. Livingston, it is assumed, voted against the Jay Treaty because he was a Republican. Such a conclusion obscures more than it reveals. A variety of factors contributed to Livingston's stand on the treaty: he was feuding, as usual, with John Jay; he objected to the high-handed secretive way in which the Senate had approved the treaty; he wished to embarrass the administration; he favored France over England. In this case, then, party label explains neither positions taken nor reasons for taking them. Factional blocs emerged, though with decreasing frequency later in the decade, to contest policy innovations.

Table 46 summarizes the voting patterns of proponents and opponents of frigates for all roll calls in the Fourth Congress. The percentages indicate blocs caught in the transition from faction to party. Polarity levels were extremely high on questions involving the limits of government authority and on roll calls concerning the frontier. On the other hand, frigate blocs did not unite against each other consistently on economic issues; indeed, they broke apart completely on Gallatin's land tax proposal. If the

Table 46. Cohesion Differences: Proponents Against Opponents of Frigates, Fourth Congress

Issue	Range of Cohesion Difference			Mean
	0–34%	*35–64%*	*65–100%*	
	Percent of Roll Calls in Each Range			
Government power	0	37	63	69
Frontier	10	40	50	62
Economic	61	8	31	38
Foreign policy	8	24	68	68
Partisan politics	20	80	0	44
Miscellaneous and personal	29	42	29	49
ALL ROLL CALLS	20	33	47	58

eight frigate roll calls on which, by definition, the two groups polarized sharply are eliminated from the foreign policy category, levels of cohesion difference on this issue decreased relative to levels on the Jay Treaty fight and on trade restrictions in the preceding Congress. Also significant is the large number of uncommitted delegates—consistent proponents and opponents of frigates comprised less than half the members of the House.

The controversy once again illuminates the relationship between party and faction. The underlying issue involved the timeless conflict between agriculture and commerce, between producer and transporter. A survey of geographically circumscribed economic characteristics clearly shows the strength of such attachments and the readiness of delegates to abandon any conflicting party labels. The innovative nature of the particular proposal at hand, in essence to begin building a "big power" navy, led a majority of delegates to break their steady commitment to one of the two cohesive blocs in the House. The resulting voting pattern might be termed "deviant" or "random" by some historians, or "unpredictable" by the statistician, or the rule of reason over passion by Madison. Within the terminology of the present study, the frigate votes support the conclusion that factional blocs formed to contest innovative policy outputs. They did so early in the decade in the absence of appeals to party. They did so later in the decade only infrequently, in part because of the success of their predecessors, in part because party emphasis on acquiring office dictated against risking the divisiveness that accompanied efforts to forge new programs.

The battle over frigates was but a mild step along the path to war against France. Even as the Fourth Congress ground haltingly to adjournment, President-elect Adams decided to dramatize his efforts to improve relations with France by sending a new negotiating team while calling the legislature into special session to enact war preparation measures. During the years of the Fifth Congress, from the spring of 1797 until the spring of 1799, war was the overriding issue. At the beginning, the mere possibility was critical in the extreme. The political result was a sharp increase in the number of factions operating in the House on any given roll call. As the possibility of war against France drew nearer to reality after disclosure of the XYZ affair, factional behavior attested to the variety of reactions among individual delegates. Some were hardened in their resolve to fight, others were paralyzed by a sense of shock and disbelief at the apparent enmity of an old ally. The result was a sharp break in certain voting patterns and an affirmation of others. By 1799, the threat of war faded rapidly, and further changes in voting behavior occurred. The rise of these groups, and their continuing metamorphoses, show, within a short span of time, political shifts that might otherwise have taken years to develop. These shifts were not random; they can be directly traced to the associations of an individual delegate or, more often, to characteristics of the district he represented. The voting patterns of this Congress, then, present a valuable case study in the reactions of a legislative body attempting to deal with a major problem which it knows is dangerous but for which it cannot agree on a solution.

Desire to acquire and hold office, most frequently expressed through developing party machinery, coexisted with the factional spirit nurtured by the new experience of imminent war. The needs of party, weighing heavily with Federalists and Republicans alike, sharply curtailed legislative output and shaped what little the House did produce. The analysis that follows isolates ten distinct voting factions, but with the caveat that these blocs did not knowingly plan strategy against each other and that the members of a given bloc never thought of themselves as participants in the faction in which the present analysis places them. That is, their votes fell into patterns that they neither saw nor acted upon, patterns useful primarily for analytical purposes. Party, on the other hand, was widely known, understood, and acted upon. We may properly conclude that the explanation of certain pieces of legislation and of many votes lies in knowing party attachment. By the latter part of the decade, then, the impact of party became a variable to be measured in a manner analogous to determining the impact of economic circumstance, or religion, or political theory on legislative output. The focus of the following discussion is not on how Federalists and Republicans voted, but on how the Fifth Congress produced or failed to produce legislation.

The first step in analyzing this process is to define those blocs that arose during the special session called by the president in May 1797. In terms of matters that came before the House, there were four separate requests in Adams' message to Congress. The most widely accepted part of his plan involved coastal defensive operations, which included the outfitting of galleys and the building of port and harbor fortifications. A second part of the plan implied the possible use of the navy as an offensive weapon. The key test on this measure came on an amendment to prohibit the use of frigates as merchant convoys. Adams also recommended reorganization of the militia, the effect of which would have been to bring it more fully under national control. The House rejected all such attempts until after publication of the XYZ dispatches. The last part of the program involved the need to raise additional revenue. In his opening speech, the president did not specify the particular levies he wished, but ultimately four were voted upon. Retail liquor licensing, the stamp tax, and raising the salt tax were straight economic questions. The proposed tax on certificates of naturalization involved more than revenue.

Twelve of the thirty-four roll calls recorded during the first session of the Fifth Congress dealt directly with these four aspects of the Adams program.[30] They are most useful in determining factional groupings because they involved votes on explicit actions. Other roll calls, such as those on a reply to the president's address, are also significant, but they involved words rather than deeds, and it is more accurate to begin with a determination of what action delegates were willing to take. A total of ten factions can be discerned in these roll calls.[31] Similarities existed in the motivations and behavior of several of these ten and, for many purposes, they may be combined. However, in terms of isolating those blocs showing the highest possible levels of internal cohesion, all ten operated as separate entities. The distinctions are even more useful in analyzing the changes in voting behavior that resulted from subsequent changes in the pressure of imminent war. In the votes on these twelve roll calls, then, the following factions are evident.

(1) Delegates who supported all aspects of the Adams program. This group of twenty-seven representatives voted for all phases of the program, including defensive and offensive naval operations, reorganization of the army and all four tax levies.[32] Some members of the group were absent occasionally, but none voted against any part of the program on any of the twelve roll calls involved. The delegates of Connecticut, New Jersey, and New Hampshire were most firmly committed to this position, which was held by 72 percent, 80 percent, and 75 percent of the voting members of their respective delegations. What particular interests these delegates represented is somewhat uncertain. All three states held elections on a statewide, at large basis, and precise electoral districts cannot be determined. It seems, however, that commercial or other economic factors, while contributory in part, do not solely account for the solidarity of these three states.[33] For some positions may have resulted from a deep-rooted Calvinist background that included detestation of an ungodly nation such as France, a strong belief in the sanctity of the American experiment as carried out in New England, and a remarkable willingness to endure sacrifice and hardship in the defense of their cause. As to the Massachusetts delegates who were part of this group, it is apparent that naval preparations favorably affected commercial interests in the state. However, they may also have been motivated by a belief that America had to defend itself immediately against the imminent threats of infidel France.[34] Support of this position also came from two representatives of South Carolina's wealthy class, all three delegates from Maryland's eastern shore counties, Rhode Island, Delaware, aristocratic Rensselaer County in New York, and rich Bucks County in Pennsylvania. Motivated by both ideological and economic considerations, the districts represented by these twenty-seven dedicated proponents of military preparedness generally had supported the administration since the earliest days of the First Congress.

(2) Delegates who supported all aspects of the program except the tax levies.[35] The eight delegates in this category held the same basic position as the group described in (1) above, and they are separated here only because their unwillingness to vote for all taxes indicated that they were not strict Adams men who always supported the administration. In this case they dissented for a variety of reasons. John Reed of Plymouth County, Massachusetts, Harrison Gray Otis of Boston, and George Baer, Jr., and William Craik of the four westernmost counties of Maryland all opposed additional taxation of retail wine and liquor sellers. Robert Goodloe Harper, representing the South Carolina upcountry but tied by marriage and sentiment to Maryland planter interests, opposed the $5 tax on naturalization certificates because he felt that the tax should have been at least $20. The other three members of this group voted to eliminate or limit the duration of the salt tax, which they believed unfairly burdened their constituencies. Two of the three, James Machir and Thomas Evans, were from Virginia. Evans represented the tidewater counties of the lower Chesapeake Bay, whose interests were similar to those of Maryland's solidly Federalist eastern shore planters. Machir represented three of Virginia's northern counties that had always shown strong tendencies to support the administration. The reasons for the particular departures of these delegates from support of the administration are obscure, but the general pattern leads to the conclusion that they were responsive to interests other than those of the administration. During the course of the two years that followed, the voting behavior of these eight independent supporters of Adams was somewhat different from that of the twenty-seven delegates who always voted for the president's proposals.

(3) Delegates who supported all aspects of the program except the Defense of Ports and Harbors Bill. This group of five delegates—David Brooks, James Cochran, Jonathan Freeman, Henry Glen, and John Van Alen—four of whom came from New York, voted against the Defense of Ports and Harbors Bill because they felt it was inadequate and failed to consider the state's own building program. It included only $115,000 for military fortifications, an amount that could hardly provide substantial defense for New York City alone. On all other matters, however, the five supported every effort at preparing for war with France. Their separation from Group 1 was not highly significant during the special session, but it is important in terms of subsequent developments.

(4) Delegates favoring full naval preparedness but opposed to any increase in the army.[36] This group of six delegates represented a diverse range of districts, from commercial Rhode Island to the mountains of western

Virginia. There were no important geographic characteristics common to all six districts: two were in frontier regions, three raised agricultural produce for export, and one was a trading center. Nevertheless, all six had strong Federalist tendencies throughout the decade. The six delegates believed in naval preparation so strongly that they even voted to allow use of frigates as merchant marine convoys.

(5) Delegates favoring partial naval buildup and limited offensive operations but opposed to army revision.[37] The only difference between this group of seventeen representatives and the group discussed in (4) above was their vote on merchant convoys. This faction unanimously rejected the use of frigates to protect commercial shipping as a provocative measure equivalent to open warfare. It also opposed any buildup of the army. However, all its members favored the use of galleys, the Defense of Ports and Harbors Bill, and the Protection of Trade Bill. Delegates holding this position came primarily from Maryland, Virginia, North Carolina, and Kentucky, with scattered additions in Georgia, New York, and Pennsylvania. The group favored a moderate response to France, but it was easily swayed by the pressure of events. Many of the same men and the districts represented in this bloc in previous Congresses had exhibited a tendency to float from faction to faction depending on the issue at hand. This had been particularly true of Dempsey Burges, James Gillespie, William Barry Grove, Josiah Parker, and Samuel Smith, but it would become equally applicable to the remainder of the group.

(6) Delegates favorable toward all coastal operations but opposed to army revision and offensive naval preparations. If moderate is defined as taking a position midway between two extremes, this was the only moderate faction in the House. It consisted of two members, Albert Gallatin and Abraham Baldwin. They were the only delegates to vote for galleys and defense of ports and harbors and against increasing the army and the Protection of Trade Bill. Although he ran in Georgia as a Federalist, Baldwin had been voting for Republican positions ever since the first roll call of the First Congress. With the departure of Madison, Gallatin was presumably the leader of the Republican party in the House.

(7) Delegates favorable toward authorization of galleys for naval defense but opposed to the remainder of the Adams program. This group consisted of only four members—Samuel Cabell and John Clopton of Virginia, Blair McClenachan of Philadelphia, and Thomas Skinner of Massachusetts. Its position is important, however, as an early indication of the trend toward acceptance of purely defensive preparations against France. The resolution that these four accepted authorized the president

to provide galleys, or other vessels, "to defend the seacoast of the United States, and to repel any hostility to their vessels and commerce within their jurisdiction." The group opposed any increase in the army, further increase in the navy, fortification of harbors, and requests for new taxes. It differed from staunch opponents of the administration in that it was willing to consider defensive measures.

(8) Delegates substantially opposed to the Adams program.[38] Each of the seven members of this group voted on one occasion for some aspect of naval preparedness but otherwise opposed the administration. This tendency to stray occasionally, especially after it became certain that a bill would pass anyway, separates these seven from die-hard opponents of the administration. The single break in each of their patterns indicates that they were ideologically opposed to Adams, but that for the sake of political expediency they sometimes voted for his measures. All seven came from areas where opposition to France and dependence upon commerce were widespread. Thus, they usually voted against the wishes of a substantial segment of their constituency but occasionally confused the record by voting for a bill that they knew would pass anyway. On the basis of district characteristics, all seven might have been in the Adams camp, but their personal political philosophy caused them to join the president's opponents. The districts involved were western Vermont, upcountry South Carolina, the western Chesapeake counties of Maryland, the Pamlico Sound area of North Carolina, parts of tidewater Virginia, and the Cape Cod–Nantucket area of Massachusetts. These were all areas of shifting political views and sharp conflict between diametrically opposed interests. All seven districts elected men who called themselves Federalists at some time during the decade. In viewing the movement of this faction in the next two sessions of the Fifth Congress, it must be remembered that their position was based on personal convictions that conflicted with much of the sentiment in the districts they represented.

(9) Delegates who opposed all aspects of the program except the tax levies.[39] This group included seven delegates of whom two, Joshua Coit and John Chapman, voted for all four tax levies. Coit's position against all naval preparations and against increasing the army is surprising. He had previously been counted as an orthodox Federalist; he had explained away his opposition to frigates during the Fourth Congress on purely practical grounds. A noted historian of this period classified Coit as a moderate Federalist, but he also classified John Adams as a moderate Federalist.[40] Coit voted against every proposal by the president to increase military preparedness. Some of Adams' supporters de-emphasized the navy on the

assumption that the English navy could be relied upon to hold off the French, but these men were all proponents of building up the army, a position Coit opposed. Rather than attempting to find a convenient label for Coit, it is best to note simply that at this time he, along with a number of other delegates, opposed all attempts to prepare for war with France. Five of the members of this group voted only for certain taxes, probably in the hope of avoiding the imposition of even more odious levies. The relationship of this group to delegates opposed to the entire Adams program (Group 10) is similar to that which existed between unanimous supporters of the president (Group 1) and the eight independents who nearly always voted for his program (Group 2).

(10) Delegates who opposed all aspects of the Adams program. There were ten members in this group, which unanimously opposed every part of the president's plan as reflected on all twelve roll calls under consideration.[41] These men simply did not believe that France wanted war. They maintained that the whole scare was a Federalist scheme designed to gain support for their party, and under no circumstances were they willing to irritate an old ally by making provocative military gestures. All ten members of the group had previously served in the House and had generally adhered to the Republican positions on issues such as opposition to the Jay Treaty, refusal to condemn Democratic Societies in connection with the Whiskey Rebellion, and opposition to increasing the military establishment.[42] The group represented sparsely populated areas having insignificant commercial interests and carrying on farming for subsistence rather than export. Their districts included the south-central region of Virginia, the westernmost two districts of North Carolina, and the remote districts of Pennsylvania west of York County and east of Pittsburgh. They had no use for the navy and had always viewed the federal army as an instrument of domestic tyranny rather than as a shield against enemies. They saw no justification for burdening farmers with even higher taxes.

Several members are not included in any of the ten factions above. Eleven delegates who served in the second or third sessions of the Fifth Congress were mid-term replacements not present at the first session and therefore they are not classified. Seven representatives elected to the Congress did not vote often enough during the first session to allow an accurate judgment about their positions. Six delegates voted in such a way that they do not fall into any of the above ten categories.[43]

Table 47 summarizes, by state, the factions that arose during voting on the twelve roll calls dealing directly with the Adams program for military preparedness. Intrastate divisiveness was widespread. Virginia and Massa-

Table 47. Geographic Distribution of Factions Emerging on the Adams Program, Fifth Congress

State	1	2	3	4	5	6	7	8	9	10	U	TOTAL
Connecticut	5								1		3	9
Delaware	1											1
Georgia					1	1						2
Kentucky				2								2
Maryland	3	2			2			1				8
Massachusetts	6	2		1			1	1	1		3	15
New Hampshire	3		1								1	5
New Jersey	4										1	5
New York	1		4	1	1					1	2	10
North Carolina					4			2	1	3	1	11
Pennsylvania	1	1		2	2	1	1		2	1	5	16
Rhode Island	1			1							1	3
South Carolina	2	1						1	1		2	7
Tennessee											1	1
Vermont								1			1	2
Virginia		2		1	5		2	1	1	5	3	20
TOTAL[b]	27	8	5	6	17	2	4	7	7	10	24	117

[a]The numbers at the top of each column refer to the numbered groups in the text. "U" indicates unclassified delegates.

[b]The total exceeds the 106 seats in the House because of the eleven mid-term replacements that occurred.

chusetts, respective bastions of the Republican and Federalist parties, had delegates in more than half the factional groups shown. Pennsylvania, New York, Maryland, and South Carolina were also sharply divided. The response to President Adams, then, followed neither strict party lines nor firm sectional commitments.

A total of thirty-four roll calls were recorded during this session. Twelve of these, which dealt directly with the Adams program, were used to identify factions. Table 48 summarizes the voting of these ten blocs on the other roll calls of the special session. A casual visual inspection of the table reveals the major point to be made about legislative response to Adams: delegates tended to take extreme, polarized positions. With the few exceptions discussed below, members of the House came to Philadelphia with firm commitments for or against the president's policies. Debate certainly raised no compelling arguments, and news of French actions was not forthcoming. Within the resulting legislative stalemate, however, several factions acted in ways that merit closer examination.

Table 48. Voting of Ten Factions Emerging on the Adams Program, Fifth Congress, First Session

Roll Call[c]	Range of Adams Support[a] by Group[b]				
	0-20%	*21-40%*	*41-60%*	*61-80%*	*81-100%*
1	5-10, B				1-4, A
2	5-8, 10, B	9			1-4, A
3	5-10, B				1-4, A
4			6, 7, 9, 10, B	5, 8	1-4, A
5	4-8, 10, B	9	2	A	1, 3
6	5-8, 10, B	9			1-4, A
7	8, 10	7, 9, B	5		1-4, 6, A
8				7, 10	1-6, 8, 9, A, B
10	3, 9		1, 2, 5, 7, 8, 10, A, B	4	6
11	7-10, B	5	6		1-4, A
14			2, 3, 6-9, A	1, 4, 5, 10, B	
15	6-10, B	5			1-4, A
16	5-10, B			4	1-3, A
18	4-10, B	2	1, A		3
19	5-10, B			4	1-3, A
20	9		10	6, 7, 8, B	1-5, A
21	6-10, B	5	4	2	1, 3, A
25	5, 7-10, B		6		1-4, A
26	5-10, B				1-4, A
28			3	5, 7, 9, 10	1, 2, 4, 6, 8, A, B
29				1, 2, 3, A	4-10, B
30	5-10, B				1-4, A

[a]Adams support is defined as the position taken by the majority of delegates in Group 1.

[b]Groups 1-10 as numbered and defined in the text; Group A combines groups 1 through 4; Group B combines groups 5 through 10.

[c]See Appendix I, Roll Call Descriptions.

The faction unanimously supporting the Adams program (Group 1) had a cohesion level of 90 percent or higher on all but five roll calls. It is apparent, therefore, that this faction was highly consistent throughout the session. The five breaks in pattern reveal more information about the group. A minor split occurred on an amendment to the House's reply to the president that expressed "utmost satisfaction" at the fresh attempt to negotiate peacefully with France (roll call 5). On this occasion four delegates—Christopher Champlin, Samuel Dana, John Rutledge, Jr., and James Schureman—voted for the amendment, but the other twenty-three members of the group opposed it. Negotiations were at this time as much a part of Adams' approach as military preparations, and the objection of so large a portion of the president's supporters to this harmless amendment reflected the extent to which administration support came from representatives who then favored a more aggressive stance than the president himself had taken. The differing extent to which members of the group were prepared for sharp action against France accounted for two other breaks in the cohesion of the group. The first occasion was on a vote to eliminate from the expatriation bill the section prohibiting anyone who renounced American citizenship to join a foreign army or navy for a period of one year (roll call 14). Nine extremists in Group 1 voted for removal of the clause so as to make the bill so objectionable that it could not pass at all.[44] They opposed any measure that gave legal sanction to the right of expatriation. A segment of the group that was slightly less committed to naval armament is shown by the break on providing for the building of nine new twenty-gun vessels (roll call 18). Eleven delegates joined the overwhelming majority against such provision.[45] The sharp drop in cohesion on roll call 29 shows the influence of a "moneyed interest" within the group. Eight of its members favored exemption from the stamp tax for all bank notes.[46] It is of note that the proposed exemption was defeated by a resounding 76 to 11. The only other substantial split occurred on a matter of purely local interest involving money owed by New York to the federal government (roll call 10). The lack of cohesion on this matter shows that the *raison d'être* of this group was its attitude toward France rather than any local or sectional interest.

The faction generally supporting Adams, but showing some independence by voting against certain taxes (Group 2), had a slightly less cohesive voting pattern than the unanimous Adams supporters in Group 1. Nevertheless, there was substantial similarity between the records of the two groups. Breaks among the independent Adams supporters were sharper, but they occurred on the same roll calls and for the same reasons that brought about significant cohesion changes among the unanimous Adams men.

The small interest group that voted for all aspects of the administration program except the Defense of Ports and Harbors Bill (Group 3) was the most cohesive of all factions that supported Adams. It split only on the expatriation bill, exemptions from the stamp tax, and the matter relating to New York's debt. This division on New York's debt (roll call 10) reflected local considerations; the split on expatriation (roll call 14) occurred because of the differing degree of opposition to France among the five members of the faction. The lack of cohesion on the stamp tax exemptions (roll calls 28 and 29) once again revealed the presence of moneyed interests among Adams supporters. At this time, then, Groups 1,

2, and 3 acted in unison, but the minor differences noted earlier foreshadowed major changes in subsequent sessions of Congress.

Delegates favoring full naval preparedness but opposed to additions to the army (Group 4) had the most inconsistent voting pattern of any of the ten factions. The districts represented by the six delegates in the group all exhibited Federalist tendencies, but they did not have significant socioeconomic characteristics in common. In sharp contrast to other groups supporting the administration, over 80 percent voted for the amendment expressing satisfaction at the president's attempt to negotiate with France (roll call 5). One-third of the group favored adjournment at a time when much important business remained (roll call 16), and opposed authorizing the president to use cutters wherever he deemed necessary (roll call 19). Half voted to limit the duration of the Protection of Trade Bill to one year (roll call 21) and over 80 percent opposed the building of new twenty-gun vessels. In general, the group consisted of lukewarm supporters of the administration whose votes could not be counted upon with certainty.

Representatives opposed to all aspects of the Adams program (Group 10) not surprisingly exhibited a pattern virtually opposite from that of any of the factions discussed thus far. There were only five breaks in Group 10's voting on the twenty-two roll calls shown in Table 48.[47] One occurred on the New York debt question (roll call 10), again showing that factions were cohesive only on issues on which they had a substantial interest. The restriction on joining foreign armies in the expatriation bill (roll call 14) was another source of division within the group. Nearly one-third of the faction voted to eliminate the restriction because they opposed any limitation on the right to renounce citizenship. Thus, the extreme wing of this group joined the extreme element of the unanimous Adams supporters, though for opposite reasons. The other three breaks did not occur on the same roll calls that resulted in divisiveness among their opponents. Half the group voted against the amendment to the reply to the president that requested France to compensate for "injuries done to our neutral rights" (roll call 4). Thus, the handful of Adams supporters who had opposed any attempt to negotiate with France were counterbalanced by a small band who refused even to concede that the French had violated America's neutral rights.[48] The other two sharp drops in cohesion also resulted from the action of extreme opponents of the administration, who voted against a ban on shipping arms and ammunition (roll call 8)[49] and against authorization of the use of existing cutters for coastal defense (roll call 20).[50]

Delegates who opposed all aspects of the Adams program except the tax levies (Group 9) had a somewhat less cohesive, but nonetheless similar, voting pattern as the extreme opponents of the administration. One of the major differences between the two factions occurred over the reply to the president's address (roll calls 1 through 7) during which the Group 9 delegates were substantially more moderate than those in Group 10. Their divisiveness on roll calls involving words disappeared, however, on questions of real substance. They unanimously opposed any authorization for using cutters for coastal defense (roll call 20), whereas less than half the unanimous opponents of the administration had taken such a radical position.

Delegates substantially opposed to the Adams program (Group 8) and delegates favoring only limited use of galleys (Group 7) had similar voting patterns. Representatives in Group 8, it will be recalled, appeared to be voting from personal convictions that conflicted with powerful interests in their home districts. Members of Group 7, on the other hand, came from districts having strong Republican tendencies. While this distinction became important later on, it did not affect voting patterns during this session.

The voting patterns of the two groups favoring moderate naval preparedness but opposed to building up the army (Groups 5 and 6) resembled those of other opponents of the administration. Generally moderate on response to the president's address, they unanimously favored using cutters for coastal defense. Their positions on other matters did not differ substantially from those taken by other factions opposed to the administration. In the later sessions of the Fifth Congress, these two groups followed widely differing paths.

Voting patterns in the first session of the Fifth Congress present, in miniature, several significant general characteristics of factions and parties. The first is that parties (Groups A and B in Table 48), even when polarized against each other, were composed of numerous smaller factions that were discernible on key roll calls and that coalesced without losing their separate identities. The falling away of one or more of these factions was often responsible for what appeared to be lack of party unity. A second characteristic is that factions were heavily influenced by news from abroad and by the nature of the issue at hand. They disintegrated entirely on matters of purely local concern or when conflicting pressures were brought to bear. This phenomenon leads to the conclusion that voting was motivated not only by party attachment but simultaneously by adherence to interests. Parties, concerned primarily with acquisition of power, avoided divisive issues; the party line became an average from which deviance was normal. Republican and Federalist parties coexisted with factional blocs, from which deviance was not normal but, rather, indicative of conflicting interests. Although a particular interest was usually more fully represented in one party than in the other, it was the interest rather than the party that motivated voting. Because it lasted only two months, during which time the possibility of war against France neither increased nor decreased, the effects of the pressure of external events on factional groupings is not apparent from analysis of this session. However, the changes that occurred in the next two sessions of the Fifth Congress are highly illuminating in this regard.

When John Adams delivered his opening address to the second session of the Fifth Congress on November 23, 1797, the danger of war with France seemed no nearer than it had five months earlier when the House had refused all but the most moderate measures for building up the country's defenses. Accounts of depredations by the French upon United States shipping continued to fill the newspapers but, as long as the negotiators were in Paris, hopes for peace remained. Adams' message asked for essentially the same preparations he had requested at the beginning of the special session of the preceding May: a naval force sufficient to protect the nation's commerce, an increase in the standing army, legislation to establish a provisional army, and new tax revenues to pay for these defensive measures.

Despite the similarities between the circumstances of May and November, a certain change had taken place among some members of the House. In May they had taken a wait-and-see attitude in the hope that the situation would just go away or that France would see the error in her treatment of an old ally. They had argued that momentous decisions possibly leading to war ought not to be taken in haste. By November, however, delegates had sufficient time to consider all the consequences of a military buildup, and the continuing French policy of attacking and confiscating American shipping made it clear that the danger of war would not pass away by itself and that France's unfriendly policy was not soon likely to change. Negotiation might ultimately be successful, but pragmatic wisdom dictated military preparedness for the other possibilities that lay ahead. This change in attitude, from opposition to support of the Adams program, resulted from the pressure exerted by the months during which commercial depredations continued and hopes for peace faded. A much greater shift of delegates occurred when negotiations virtually collapsed in the aftermath of the XYZ affair.

The objective of the following analysis is to measure the effects of these pressures on the factions that appeared during the first session of the Fifth

Congress. However, any such effects must exclude changes that resulted from mid-session replacements. William Edmond replaced James Davenport of Connecticut, and Bailey Bartlett succeeded Theophilus Bradbury of Massachusetts. All four were consistent supporters of the Adams program; therefore, no change in voting patterns resulted. In the case of two other replacements, that of Jeremiah Smith by Peleg Sprague in New Hampshire and that of William L. Smith by Thomas Pinckney of Charleston, South Carolina, voting patterns were affected. All four were Adams supporters but the two Smiths had been very regular in their attendance and voting, whereas Sprague and Pinckney were absent more often than not. Pro-administration forces also lost the votes of two moderates, George Ege of Pennsylvania and Elisha Potter of Rhode Island. In normal times Potter's replacement, Thomas Tillinghast, might have been classified as a Republican, but the pressure of the French war scare made this an impossibility in 1798. He ultimately joined the Adams forces wholeheartedly, but during the second session he voted against the pro-Adams position on about 35 percent of all recorded roll calls; he cannot be assigned to any of the ten factions isolated during the special session. Joseph Hiester, who succeeded Ege, voted with the faction that favored defensive naval preparations but opposed the administration on all other matters (Group 5).

Several members had been absent too often or voted too inconsistently to be assigned to any of the factions that arose during the first session. Based on voting during the second session, some of them can be assigned to particular factions, although they might not have been part of the same groups during the first session. Isaac Parker of Massachusetts and Roger Griswold of Connecticut consistently voted with the faction that unanimously supported the Adams program. Lemuel Benton of South Carolina and Philip Van Cortlandt of New York were equally cohesive in joining the group opposed to every administration proposal. William Claiborne of Tennessee voted most nearly in accord with the faction that supported defensive naval operations but opposed any other war preparations. Stephen Bullock of Massachusetts, who opposed the administration but represented a district with substantial commercial interests, voted in the same unclassifiable way as Tillinghast of Rhode Island. Both were in the predicament of effectively misrepresenting the wishes of their districts. Although they have been described as "moderates," such a label inadequately explains the peculiar positions of these two delegates.[51] Both ultimately became highly cohesive administration supporters. Eight representatives not previously classified continued to be absent so often that they cannot be assigned properly to any faction.[52]

With the exceptions noted above, all groups identified during the first session have been continued into the second session for analytic purposes. Before examining these small blocs in detail, however, some measure may be made of general trends in legislative behavior during the winter and spring of 1798. Of the seventy-five roll calls recorded during the second session of the Fifth Congress, forty-four saw House members polarize into two cohesive blocs. Administration supporters (Groups 1 through 4) outnumbered their opponents (Groups 5 through 10) by only one potential vote, and good health, attention to duty, and pressure against deviants meant the difference between success and failure. But delegates assigned more power to themselves than they in fact exercised. Direction of the undeclared war against France remained largely with President Adams and the Senate, in part at least because the very close strength of the two sides in the House led to stalemate and inaction. To be sure, bills were passed, but often only by narrow margins after lengthy debate and much parliamentary stumbling. As a result, Congress followed or was dragged along paths set by others, by John Adams and by France.

A brief survey of the roll calls on which the House divided into two sharply polarized blocs indicates the futility that characterized many of its actions. Six of the forty-four roll calls dealt with the possibility of expelling Matthew Lyon, a fiery Vermonter, for the "gross indecency" of spitting upon Roger Griswold of Connecticut. The issue became clouded when Griswold took matters into his own hands and smashed Lyon with a fireplace utensil. In the end, both gentlemen retained their seats. Four roll calls dealt with minor salary questions and two with troublesome spectators in the House gallery who were recording debates illegally. Four other highly polarized votes arose from unsuccessful efforts to curb executive or Senate power, and four more resulted in elimination of the recently passed stamp duty. Five roll calls dealt with the highly partisan alien and sedition legislation and four with patriotic but ineffective resolutions condemning France. Although some of these issues attracted great interest, they did not confront the war situation directly.

Only thirteen of the forty-four roll calls on which administration supporters and opponents polarized sharply against each other directly involved France. Of these, two resulted in rejection of legislation providing bounties for the capture of armed French vessels, two rejected restrictions on the number and sailing range of American naval ships, and one established a Department of the Navy. The remaining eight roll calls dealt with the army: to limit the duration and amount of regular army buildup, to use state militia rather than new volunteers for the provisional army, to force volunteers to purchase their weapons, to allow the president to begin appointing officers for the provisional army, and to pay for the army. The military question, along with alien and sedition legislation, occasioned the most bitter debate of the Fifth Congress. Opponents of the administration, aware of the political gains involved in standing firmly for a free press and for the local militia, needed only to expand slightly upon the threat to domestic freedom implicit in the administration's program. The possibility that the army might be used to suppress the legitimate opposition of American citizens to their government seemed very real to ardent Republicans. Federalists, thoroughly alarmed by French subversion on the Continent, were equally certain that only a large army could save the nation. Yet even this critical issue gave rise to factional divisions that crossed party lines.

Table 49 summarizes the thirty-one roll calls of the second session of the Fifth Congress on which either or both of the two major blocs in the House divided internally. On these votes the significance of factional attachment and the changing pressures of imminent war were apparent. The issues involved ranged from such trifling questions as the amount of an annuity for the daughters of the deceased Count de Grasse to the critical matter of authorizing full naval war against France. The sources of divisions that occurred in the session can best be understood by returning to an analysis using the ten factions initially isolated during the May 1797 session.

The cohesiveness of the faction that had unanimously supported the Adams program (Group 1) dropped below 81 percent on thirteen occasions, usually because moderates in the group refused to approve extremely belligerent actions. Several rolls calls serve to isolate moderating tendencies within Group 1. Six members of the faction opposed Robert Goodloe Harper's radical amendment allowing merchant vessels to "attack, take, or destroy" any vessel that had captured an American ship (roll call 83), and seven voted against Peleg Sprague's angry proposal to authorize the capture of unarmed French vessels (roll call 97). A total of eleven different delegates opposed one or both of these attempts to put the country on a full war footing with France.[53] It is not surprising, then, that an attempt to declare war never came to a vote; 40 percent of the president's most consistent supporters recoiled at amendments that led in the direction of full-scale war.

Adams' firmest allies were also divided over the role of the provisional army. A majority of the delegates in Group 1 approved the restriction that the provisional army could be called out only in the event that a foreign power declared war on the United States or that a landed invasion appeared

Table 49. Voting of Ten Factions Emerging on the Adams Program, Fifth Congress, Second Session, Divisive Roll Calls

Roll Call[c]	Range of Adams Support[a] by Group[b]				
	0–20%	21–40%	41–60%	61–80%	81–100%
Adams Supporters Divided					
37	4-10, B	2	3, A	1	
41	3, 5-10, B			1, 2, 4, A	
58	5-10, B	2		1, 3, 4, A	
61	5-7, 9, 10, B	4, 8		A	1-3
64	6-8, 10, B	5, 9	2, 4	A	1, 3
67	5-10, B	2, 4		A	1, 3
68	5-10, B	4	1, A	2	3
69	5-10, B		4	1, A	2, 3
83	5-10, B	2		1, 3, A	4
85	4-8, 10, B	3, 9	A	1	2
97	5-10, B			1, 2, A	3, 4
104			1, 3	4, A	2, 5-10, B
107	3, 5, 7, 8, B	4, 9, 10	2, 6, A	1	
109	5, 6, 8-10, B	2, 4	7	1, 3, A	
Adams Opponents Divided					
39	8		5, 7, 9, 10, B	4	1-3, 6, A
45	6, 7	5, 8, 10, B	9		1-4, A
59	6, 7, 10	5, 8, B	9		1-4, A
73	6-8, 10	9, B	5		1-4, A
76	7	8, 10	6, B	5	1-4, 9, A
78	6, 7, 10	9, B	5	8	1-4, A
82	7	10	6, 8, 9, B	3, 4, 5	1, 2, A
84			7, 8, 10, B	5, 9	1-4, 6, A
93	7	8, 10	5, 6, 9, B		1-4, A
95	6	8	7, 10, B	5, 9	1-4, A
98	6-8, 10	5, B	9		1-4, A
102	7, 8, 10	5, B	6, 9		1-4, A
103	7		9, 10	8, B	1-6, A
Both Groups Divided					
38	8	5, 9, 10, B	2, 4, 6, 7	1, 3, A	
48			2	4, 5, 8, A, B	1, 3, 6, 7, 9, 10
55	3		5, 8	1, 2, 4, 10, A, B	6, 7, 9
92	6, 7, 8	10, B	5, 9	2, 3, A	1, 4

[a]Adams support is defined as the position taken by the majority of delegates in Group 1.

[b]Groups 1-10 as numbered and defined in the text; Group A combines groups 1 through 4; Group B combines groups 5 through 10.

[c]See Appendix I, Roll Call Descriptions.

imminent (roll call 68). Resolutions of this kind played into the hands of the president's opponents by admitting the threat to domestic freedom implicit in expansion of the military establishment. Yet many Federalists broke ranks to support this Republican measure, an indication that fear of the army cut across party lines. Further expression of concern lest the military grow too powerful came on a successful vote to decrease the provisional army from 20,000 to 10,000 men (roll call 69). One in four delegates in Group 1 voted for the cut. Less than a month later, in June 1798 when war fever still ran high, nine of twenty-three Adams supporters voting agreed to provide arms for state militia units (roll call 85). Reliance on the militia rather than on a federal army was of course a basic Republican alternative for facing the threat of war against France.[54] These breakdowns in factional cohesion constitute a pattern that goes beyond isolated or random deviation from normal voting behavior. Only nine of twenty-nine voting delegates in Group 1 failed to support curtailment of the army on at least one of the three roll calls.[55] Those who have studied this period carefully, notably Alexander DeConde, Manning Dauer, and Stephen Kurtz, correctly point out Adams' own doubts about expanding the army too greatly. To these doubts must be added the unwillingness of the president's supporters in the House to provide for a grandiose military establishment, even when caution provided ammunition for the Republican opposition.

The only other major division within Group 1 occurred on the question of calling for papers related to the XYZ affair (roll call 58). Eight members of this faction joined the call (led by the president's opponents) for the papers. They are all included in the group designated by historian Manning Dauer as "High Federalists." Their motivations, he argued, included the stirring up of public sentiment in favor of the war.[56] In terms of cohesive roll call voting, however, the category High Federalists does not exist, although certain Adams supporters were more willing to go to war than others. All eight members of Group 1 who called for the papers had on occasion voted to limit war preparations; half opposed extending naval combat (roll calls 83 and 97) and all supported at least some restrictions on the army.[57] There were Federalists who took neither of these positions, but they opposed calling for the XYZ papers. Evidence from the debates and from correspondence with Hamilton indicates that John Allen and Peleg Wadsworth probably did join the call for papers for the purpose of stirring up the flames of war, but the other six appear to have acted from a genuine desire to examine all facets of such an important question before taking any decisive action. Certainly they voted cautiously on other matters.

This intensive analysis of the voting behavior of the president's strongest supporters in the House leads to the conclusion that their moderate tendencies were instrumental in blocking the declaration of war that many believed was sure to come in the spring of 1798. Emphasis on Adams' subsequent quest for peace and on the rhetoric of so-called High Federalists should not obscure the crucial role this faction played in resisting the "black cockade fever" that raged during these months. But not all blocs moved in the same direction.

Delegates previously characterized by independent support of the administration (Group 2) changed considerably under the increased pressure of war. During the preceding session their voting pattern had been remarkably similar to that of the unanimous Adams supporters, but after the call for the XYZ dispatches on April 2, 1798, the two groups diverged. The cohesion of the independent Adams supporters dropped sharply on a number of significant roll calls. Some of them opposed all-out war against France and others voted against repressive policies at home, but in no case did they do so as a cohesive group. Under the pressure of domestic opposition to the proposed alien and sedition legislation and fear of disastrous involvement in Europe's war, the faction simply ceased to operate as a faction. The individual members, who had previously arrived independently on the same side on most roll calls, now went their separate ways. Harrison Gray Otis of Boston, William Craik of western Maryland, and Thomas Hartley of York County, Pennsylvania, all supported the president without exception. On the other hand, George Baer, Jr., turned against the Adams group on taxation (roll calls 53 and 92), unrestricted naval warfare (roll calls 83 and 97), arresting Matthew Lyon (roll call 41), and warlike resolutions against France (roll call 81). He supported the administration, however, on army expansion and on alien and sedition legislation. Robert Goodloe Harper was as ready for war as any man in the House, but he voted to moderate the most odious features of the Sedition Act (roll call 105). James Machir of western Virginia was absent a great deal, but his vote to recommit the Alien Enemies Bill (roll call 75) indicated his opposition to the domestic policy of the Adams camp. Thomas Evans, representing parts of tidewater Virginia, voted against the direct land tax (roll call 92), against nullification of treaty ties with France (roll call 101), and with Harper to moderate the Sedition Act. He also opposed unrestricted naval warfare. John Reed of Plymouth, Massachusetts, voted to cut the provisional army in half (roll call 69), to recommit the Alien Enemies Bill, to restrict naval warfare, and against increasing the standing army. No general statement can encompass the effects of pressure on the delegates in this group except that they were completely scattered.

During the special May session, a small group of delegates had supported the administration on everything but the Defense of Ports and Harbors Bill, which they opposed only because they wanted an even stronger and more expensive measure (Group 3). The bloc had formed the most cohesive of all factions supporting Adams, and it continued to do so during the second session, when it divided on only eight occasions. The effect on this faction of the increased danger of war was to solidify its members even further in their support for preparedness.

A dramatic increase in cohesiveness occurred in the faction that had favored full naval preparedness but had opposed additions to the army (Group 4). Its members had been highly independent in their voting during the special session, and lack of cohesion continued to characterize them during the early roll calls of the second session, until the full impact of the XYZ papers brought about a complete change in the group. Yielding to the pressure of impending war, it voted to increase the standing army by 12,000 instead of 8,000 (roll calls 99 and 102), thereby unanimously reversing its earlier position against any increase in the army. The faction was equally firm in its support of naval preparations and suppression of dissension at home. The voting pattern of this group demonstrates one of the more important effects of pressure upon a faction: temporary unity not grounded in the socio-economic characteristics of its members' districts.

Groups that generally had opposed the administration during the special session also underwent change as the apparent danger of war increased. But on balance the changes did not result in greater support for the president. Indeed, delegates previously willing to approve modest defensive measures often turned to total opposition to anything proposed by Adams' supporters. The two issues falling outside this pattern—the direct tax (roll calls 82, 84, 93, 94, and 95) and provision for increasing the standing army (roll calls 102 and 103)—arose under special circumstances. A direct tax on land, buildings, and slaves had initially provoked sharp divisiveness when proposed by Gallatin two years earlier. Although by 1798 the tax was a war measure, he and many other administration opponents supported it, for considerations of principle and partisanship. The levy might lessen dependence on commercial connections with England and its passage could now be blamed on the Federalists. Provision to increase the regular army by twelve regiments ultimately passed by a margin of fifty-one votes. Administration opponents joined the majority, which in any event was unassailable, partly because they desired to mitigate the need for a large provisional army. All other breakdowns in the cohesion levels of factions opposed to Adams occurred on relatively minor matters.

Within this general pattern, the behavior of specific blocs merits further attention. Delegates previously classified as staunch opponents of all aspects of the Adams program (Group 10) unanimously joined the call for the XYZ papers. Subsequently, they denied the apparent proof of France's malice contained in the documents and pressed even harder than before with positive alternatives to administration policy. They successfully limited the size and mandate of the provisional army, turned the alien and sedition debate into a fatal victory for the Federalists, and proposed that Elbridge Gerry continue negotiating in Paris. With only rare exceptions, the faction stood firmly against all appeals for escalating hostilities, even opposing essentially defensive measures.[58]

The actions of the bloc generally opposed to Adams (Group 8) were less consistent than those of staunch opponents. Since all the delegates in the former group represented districts that had substantial Federalist tendencies, they were subjected to pressure from their constituents as well as from the increasing danger of war. Nathaniel Freeman of Nantucket, Massachusetts, yielded early; from the outset of the session until he stopped voting immediately after the XYZ call, he supported the administration. Others voted to suspend trade with France (roll call 78), against letting Gerry continue talks in Paris (roll call 98), and for the provisional army (roll call 88). But against these votes must be balanced the highly cohesive opposition of the bloc to most aspects of administration policy and its unanimous refusal to consider offensive war measures. Allowing Freeman as an exception, the voting pattern of this faction was about the same during the second session as it had been during the first: its members generally opposed the war, but occasionally voted for a proposal that was sure to pass anyway. The ability of these delegates to resist the movement toward war owed much to their long experience at resisting the pressure of constituents against whose wishes they so often voted.

Pro-administration forces hardly anticipated much support from delegates in the two opposition groups discussed thus far, but they were dismayed by the action of representatives who formerly had approved modest defensive preparations (Groups 6 and 7). The two blocs, though small in numbers, constituted a critical swing vote that, as the danger of war grew nearer, moved sharply against the president. Led by Albert Gallatin, these moderates solidified and shifted from a middle position to one at the extreme opposite end from the pressure that faced them. By joining the growing resistance to both offensive and defensive operations, they forced a stalemate in the House and consequently provided a check against the momentum toward war that swept the nation in the spring of 1798.

The actions of two blocs previously included among the president's opponents (Groups 5 and 9), however, offset heightened resistance by Groups 6, 7, 8, and 10. The bloc that had opposed all aspects of the Adams plan except the tax levies (Group 9) ceased to operate as a cohesive faction. Joshua Coit and John Chapman broke with the group at the very outset of the second session and never returned. Both represented heavily Federalist areas, Connecticut and Philadelphia, respectively, where leading citizens had exerted great pressure on them during the months between the two sessions. Coit in particular suffered bitter attacks from the local Federalist press and, even worse, received gleeful praise from Republican propagandists for his opposition to the administration during the May session. Five months of bombardment at home plus continued depredations by the French convinced both delegates that their earlier caution had been a mistake; they reversed themselves and wholeheartedly supported the war effort. The other members of Group 9 held firm until disclosure of the XYZ affair, at which point they broke apart and failed to vote in a cohesive or even predictable way.

Changes in the voting behavior of delegates who had supported only a partial naval buildup (Group 5) demonstrate a significant long-range factor in legislative behavior on foreign policy issues. This bloc now consisted of nineteen delegates, mostly from Virginia, Maryland, Kentucky, and North Carolina, and generally calling themselves Republicans. The faction opposed the administration unanimously on alien and sedition legislation, but on questions of preparation for war it usually divided. Four members of the group voted for establishment of a Department of the Navy (roll call 63), five for the Provisional Army Bill (roll call 72), three for increased defense of harbors (roll call 77), six against reliance on state militias, eight for suspension of commerce with France (roll call 78), and five against allowing Gerry to continue negotiations (roll call 98). Several favored increasing the regular army by twelve regiments instead of eight (roll calls 99 and 102) and all ultimately voted for final passage of the bill (roll call 103). Although the group had little interest in protecting commerce, its members were fully prepared to defend the country against the encroachments of any European nation, including France. Western representatives in the group, such as Claiborne of Tennessee and Davis and Fowler of Kentucky, may also have been motivated by the possibility that war would lead to further expansion in the West and securing of trade connections with New Orleans. It is more than coincidental that the delegates in this faction, which favored a belligerent policy toward France while opposing the administration on domestic matters, represented the same areas that most strongly advocated war with England in 1812. The districts involved were the only areas of the country that favored both war preparation in 1798 and war itself fourteen years later. The particular enemy involved was not of great consequence to this group, nor was the surface reason for going to war, protection of commerce, a primary consideration. The pressure of war seemed to bring out the instinct to fight cultivated by the recent frontier experience of most of the group. If we may take them at their word, when faced with a dangerous enemy, be it nature or Indians or Frenchmen, their reaction was in the direction of a frontal assault.

When the second session finally adjourned in July 1798, it looked back on a mixed record. Passed during the crucible of seemingly imminent invasion and fear of treachery at home, the Alien and Sedition Acts stood as a testament to the danger that liberty faces in time of crisis. Such legislation would have been an impossibility in 1797, and it was nearly repealed by the same men who initially voted for it. Only the pressure of war accounted for these changes in the behavior of the House. Yet it would be unjust to base an appraisal of the Fifth Congress solely on those unfortunate laws. One must also give this Congress substantial credit for keeping the country from a senseless war against France in the critical spring of 1798. Provision for a defensive quasi-war was made, as several factions in the House yielded to the momentum of events. However, at a time when President Adams considered asking for a formal declaration of war, and the people clamored their readiness, the House stubbornly refused to take the final step. The president's own allies recoiled at offensive war preparations and, with moderates moving rapidly in the direction of peace, the House arrived at a stalemate situation. Historians have been generous in heeding Adams' request that he be remembered for bringing peace with France, but his actions did not come until the fall of 1798 and then only in response to favorable gestures by Talleyrand. The House, albeit with some waverings, stood, in defiance of partisan considerations, against war in the critical months following the insult of X, Y, and Z.

Congress had moved to the very brink of declaring war upon its old ally, only to be held back by the moderation of a number of Adams supporters. Even without formal declaration, engagements with the enemy took place on the high seas and full-scale war seemed only to await France's next move. It was with matters in this precarious state that Congress adjourned and hurriedly abandoned Philadelphia to the heat and to the yellow fever. As President Adams journeyed back to Quincy, tumultuous crowds greeted him everywhere. The country was ready for war, even if some congressmen were not. In the five months before the House reconvened for its last session, however, a basic change in attitude occurred.

Adams began receiving reports from his son, John Quincy, and from William Vans Murray at the Hague, indicating that Talleyrand and the Directory did not want war and still sought peace through negotiation of differences with the United States. France quickly recognized that its belligerent policy neither secured its West Indies possessions nor isolated England. Quaker George Logan, acting as a private citizen, assisted in easing tensions by securing the release of American prisoners in France. Those who clamored for war denounced Logan as a traitor, but their disbelief and horror at his success could not hide the fact that the French Directory was changing its attitude and that a fresh attempt at peaceful settlement might work. Elbridge Gerry finally returned in October and convinced his old friend John Adams that armed conflict was not inevitable. But news of these peaceful overtures did not reduce the fever pitch of war cries that filled the Federalist press. The prospect of French invasion remained "imminent," and news columns devoted more and more space to army matters. This brink of disaster propaganda, however, worked in some measure against its purveyors, as many readers reached the state of total exhaustion and disbelief that followed too long a wait for an expected catastrophe that did not happen.

When Congress assembled in December of 1798, therefore, pressures were not the same as they had been six months earlier. Although no definite peace feelers could be cited publicly, negotiation again seemed a possibility. The mere fact that France had not declared war during the preceding summer and fall cast doubt upon the dire predictions of certain Federalists. As the threat of war subsided, opposition to repressive measures at home, particularly to the Sedition Act, increased. For the most part the third session of the Fifth Congress found delegates filling in or defending their earlier legislative record, but they did not move in any new directions.

Patterns of legislative behavior reflected this new situation. Previously, the House's commitment to peace had been essentially negative; it had refused to approve a variety of proposals aimed at shifting the war effort from defense to offense. During the third session it moved to place positive restraints on the president's war powers. Commercial interests joined administration opponents in successfully limiting executive authority to suspend trade with ports that aided France, first by excluding New Orleans and then by denying the right to embargo any Spanish or Dutch ports.[59] Later, without the support of commercial interests, a majority formed to deny bounties for capture of armed French vessels, to predicate increases in the size of the army upon the actual outbreak of war, and to allow army volunteers to refuse service outside their states of residence.[60] This last provision could have produced a military disaster in the event of an invasion that did not occur simultaneously and equally in all the states. In reality, it was a warning by opponents of the administration not to use the enlarged army to infringe upon the rights of citizens in the states.

A survey of the roll calls on which the factions (initially identified by their response during the special session of 1797) failed to polarize sharply against each other further illuminates the new attitude in the House.[61] Analysis of internal factional divisions during the critical second session reveals three major voting patterns: (1) refusal by pro-Adams delegates to alter the defensive character of the war, (2) intense and consistent opposition to war preparations by representatives formerly only moderately opposed to the administration, and (3) increasing support for offensive measures by Republicans of the upper South. During the third session, as the pressure of imminent war waned, these three trends were reversed as delegates returned to earlier positions. Table 50 summarizes the thirteen roll calls of the third session of the Fifth Congress on which either of the two major blocs in the House divided internally.[62] Of the thirteen, four concerned George Logan's usurpation of executive authority,[63] four dealt with restrictions on commerce, and four involved relatively minor procedural matters. Only one of the thirteen, a vote to vest severely limited powers of retaliation in the president, occurred on an issue bearing directly upon the war. In the previous session divisiveness had characterized the consideration of most critical war issues; now internal divisions usually occurred on less consequential matters. During this lame duck session, partisan advantage reasserted its influence over the nature of issues debated as well as over the pattern of roll call voting.

During the two years that followed, some members of the House continued to pursue positive steps toward establishing peace, only to be checked in their quest by party considerations. The new Congress that assembled in December 1799 accomplished very little; it neither agreed on new foreign policy legislation nor did it repeal or extend old provisions due to expire. With both presidential aspirants moving to blur policy differences between themselves, Republicans and Federalists alike sought to avoid too close an association with war or peace. Devoting most of its time to such matters as the Jonathan Robbins episode, John Randolph's breach of privilege petition, and the crude rulings of Speaker Theodore Sedgwick, the House avoided innovative action on the war. Although greater numerical strength ultimately assured victory for those who sought to limit legislative

Table 50. Voting of Ten Factions Emerging on the Adams Program, Fifth Congress, Third Session, Divisive Roll Calls

Roll Call[c]	Range of Adams Support[a] by Group[b]				
	0-20%	21-40%	41-60%	61-80%	81-100%
Adams Supporters Divided					
115				1, 2, A	3-10, B
120	6, 8-10, B	5, 7	4	2, 3, A	1
121	5-10, B		1-4, A		
124	3, 5-10, B		2	1, 4, A	
126	5-7, 9, 10, B	2, 8		4, A	1, 3
128	5-10, B		2	1, 3, 4, A	
129	5-10, B		2, 4	1, 3, A	
130		3	1	2, A	4-10, B
133	2, 5-10, B	3	1, 4, A		
136	5-10, B	2		1, 3, A	4
Adams Opponents Divided					
116	10	7, 8, B	5, 6	9	1-4, A
149			5, 6	8, 10, B	1-4, 7, 9, A
153	6-8, 10	B	5, 9		1-4, A

[a]Adams support is defined as the position taken by the majority of delegates in Group 1.

[b]Groups 1–10 as numbered and defined in the text; Group A combines groups 1 through 4; Group B combines groups 5 through 10.

[c]See Appendix I, Roll Call Descriptions.

action to acquiescence in President Adams' cautious retreat from war, advocates of peace put constant pressure on the House to restore friendly relations with France.

Hard core proponents of peace emerged most clearly in opposing passage of a bill, early in 1800, to continue the embargo on trade with France.[64] All twenty-eight delegates who took this position subsequently voted for Jefferson in his House contest against Aaron Burr.[65] They unanimously supported reduction of the regular army, discharge of the new army, and repeal of the sedition law. In addition to trying regularly to embarrass the administration (which all Republicans did during the Sixth Congress), they attempted to forge a positive foreign policy program. In so doing they were joined only partially and belatedly by those in their party who gave greater weight to partisan considerations, and therefore demurred at reopening trade with France.

Efforts to reduce the military establishment attracted an additional seventeen delegates.[66] Republican propaganda, warning that the army might become an instrument to suppress freedom at home, made such a position attractive to administration opponents both on the grounds of policy and party. Only by the narrow margin of four votes did Federalists turn back a move to completely dismantle the new army.[67] Even more cautious in their support for moves toward peace were delegates who finally conceded, in February of 1801, that the time had come to set naval appropriations at a peacetime level.[68] An additional thirty-one delegates, including a number of Federalists, may be assigned to this group.[69] Finally, thirty-six delegates never voted for a proposition calculated to bring peace with France.[70]

Table 51 portrays the voting behavior of these four groups for all roll calls in the Sixth Congress. The table includes a comparison with votes in the Jefferson-Burr House election in order to highlight the partisan nature of

Table 51. Cohesion Differences Among Foreign Policy Blocs, Sixth Congress

Groups[a]	Range of Cohesion Difference			Mean
	0-34%	*35-64%*	*65-100%*	
	Percent of Roll Calls in Each Range			
1 vs. 2	97	2	1	15
1 vs. 3	12	13	75	70
1 vs. 4	8	11	81	73
1 vs. 5	99	1	0	12
1 vs. 6	8	13	79	68
2 vs. 3	14	20	66	60
2 vs. 4	13	9	78	71
2 vs. 5	99	1	0	19
2 vs. 6	13	14	73	74
3 vs. 4	98	0	2	16
3 vs. 5	12	21	67	63
3 vs. 6	98	2	0	11
4 vs. 5	9	13	78	77
4 vs. 6	98	2	0	21
5 vs. 6[b]	9	14	77	82

[a]1 = hard core for repeal of war measures
2 = moderately for repeal of war measures
3 = moderately against repeal of war measures
4 = hard core against repeal of war measures
5 = voted for Jefferson in House election
6 = voted for Burr in House election

[b]*Annals of Congress*, 6th Cong. 2d sess., pp. 1023–1032, reports the balloting by delegates as leaked to the *National Intelligencer*. The designations in this table refer to Burr strength as demonstrated on the thirty-five ballots preceding abstention by pro-Burr delegates from Maryland and Vermont.

these foreign policy groupings. The minor shades of cohesion difference in 1 vs. 2 and 3 vs. 4 are insignificant; indeed, the lack of difference largely accounts for the stalemate situation in the House. The country moved toward peace with France and toward the election of Jefferson, but Republicans in Congress, concentrating on the election, did little about the peace.

*   *   *   *   *

Legislative behavior in the 1790s on foreign policy questions differed substantially from actions on domestic affairs. Congress, together with the executive, proved unable to achieve security and markets. The House had rejected Madison's visionary appeal for alteration of Anglo-American trade patterns, but he received another chance as president and exploited it fully. The Jay Treaty had provided security against England, but only at the cost of open hostility with France. The "war" with France had been resolved through negotiation, but America's relationship with Continental Europe remained uncertain. A variety of new markets were opened, but the nation had not gained control over the distribution of its produce. Foreign policy questions remained the most important source of divisiveness in national politics until at least 1815, and the situation as of 1801 was highly transitory. The nation's search for security and markets had not failed, but, at best, it had barely managed to muddle along. Foreign policy outputs lacked the permanence and wide acceptance of answers forged by Congress on the issues of limits of government authority, acquisition of landed abundance, and development of a strong national economy. But the process of reaching foreign policy decisions did stabilize in the 1790s; patterns of division proved durable, even though particular decisions did not.

Among the most significant of these patterns was the negative role played by the legislature. The bicameral structure of Congress, the inevitable presence of confirmed obstructionists, the impossibility of maintaining secrecy, and the difficulty in translating an understanding into a law, all combined to prevent speedy and forceful House action, no matter what the particular issue at hand. Madison's efforts were defeated, at least in part because of growing reliance on committees and the independence of the Senate. Jefferson's report on commerce to the Third Congress, even after delegates understood its full import, could not be translated into legislation. In responding to the Quasi-War, the House consistently moved more slowly than the president, at first refusing to prepare for war, then restraining the call for full war, then lagging behind in the return to peace. The pattern of the 1790s, in which Congress acted as a check on the executive rather than as a positive and innovative force, continues to the present day.

The significance of economic interest in determining foreign policy outputs also became evident in the 1790s. Because delegates in the House represented small geographic areas, often containing a narrow range of economic activities, debate and voting more frequently and openly revealed a confluence between differences in property and differences in foreign policy. Two issues stand out in this regard: the opposition of southern planters, anxious to keep down transportation costs, to any change in Anglo-American trade patterns; and the unanimous support, regardless of party affiliation, of urban representatives for the building of frigates to protect American commerce. Although the strength of economic interest is most easily demonstrated in instances when it conflicted with party attachment, its presence was hardly limited to these cases.

The mutual antagonism between security and markets that has plagued America's foreign policy makers also emerged from House deliberations during the decade. Madison's predictions of war with England if southern planters continued their dependence on the former mother country, met the problem squarely. Ultimately, John Jay accepted Great Britain's offer of security in the New World, but the price was market freedom. Albert Gallatin, in debate over the Logan Act, commented perceptively on the causal relationship between mercantile activity and war. But the House, and the nation, proved unable to resist the lure of markets. The cost was fulfillment of John Jay's assertion that "nations in general will make war whenever they have a prospect of getting anything by it."

Lastly, legislative behavior revealed the role of factions in reaching foreign policy outputs. Neither party discipline nor lack of it defeated James Madison for eight years on discrimination, retaliation, Jefferson's report, and the Jay Treaty. On each of these matters, issue-oriented factions coalesced to preserve and strengthen America's decision to ally with strength in the New World. Similarly, the actions of the Federalist party, especially its "High" wing, fail to explain the crucial role of the House in preventing President Adams from declaring war against France in 1798. Instead, one must examine the several factions in Congress and the variance in their responses to an ever-increasing threat of war to see that moderates, in both parties, turned toward peace at the very time that the country clamored for war. When party allegiance finally did rule supreme in the Sixth Congress, the legislature produced no new policies, even abandoning the quest for peace to John Adams.

THE TRIUMPH OF PARTY

In reviewing the failure of national government under the Articles of Confederation, James Madison, in Number 50 of *The Federalist*, had lamented the division of the legislature "into two fixed and violent parties . . ." "In all questions, however unimportant in themselves or unconnected with each other," he wrote, "the same names stand invariably contrasted on the opposite columns." Eight years later, in his memorable final words to the nation, President Washington had warned "against the baneful effects of the spirit of party," a spirit of "greatest rankness" in republican governments and "truly their worst enemy." Yet only five years later, in 1801, in his inaugural address, Thomas Jefferson assured his fellow citizens that "every difference of opinion is not a difference of principle. We have called by different names brethren of the same principle. We are all Republicans, we are all Federalists."

Imbued with sentiments so well expressed by Madison and Washington, dismayed Republicans and temporarily relieved Federalists misunderstood Jefferson's words, for his actions soon revealed that he paid great attention to party labels in the filling, vacating, and abolishing of offices. But the words were not mere rhetorical flourish. They accurately summarized the administration's aim: to maintain control of the regime while continuing (indeed, by continuing) to stand on the policy outputs of the Federalist decade.

The preceding chapters have analyzed in detail the factional behavior that by 1795 had produced acceptable answers to the four major problems confronting the new nation, and the shift after that date from consideration of policy alternatives to the quest for power. Analysis of factions provided an essentially negative measure of the influence of party on legislative behavior. The decline of factional voting, however, is not the only way to view the impact of electoral politics on policy outputs in the 1790s. In addition, we may employ a positive measure of the significance of the first American party system as it developed during the decade.

Before turning to the statistical analysis, it is worthwhile to repeat the problem of definition involved in use of the term party. Dismissing Madison's prejudiced attack on party as the "rule of passion," as one definition of party we may adopt his idea of names appearing on the same side at the calling of the roll. In this instance, party is purely a descriptive term applied to a particular voting pattern. It is a measure of what position delegates took, but not of why they did so. If we define Republicans as those who voted against the Jay Treaty and Federalists as those who supported legislation against sedition, we cannot then conclude that party attachment motivated these positions. But the term party, as used in this study and in the work of most students of American politics, designates a multi-dimensional organization that seeks a regular, predictable, and successful means of achieving office. Employing this latter definition, Noble Cunningham and David Fischer have written outstanding accounts of electoral politics in the early national period. Less clear, however, is the impact of party on legislative behavior. The needs of this organization may motivate its members who serve in the legislature to adopt one policy position rather than another, to provoke discussion of new alternatives, or to avoid completely innovative propositions. Conversely, the action of the legislature—its success in framing laws to meet demands placed on the regime—may alter the machinery and composition of power-seeking parties as well as shape their competitive patterns. How, then, are votes to be used to separate the two definitions of party, to determine the impact of party as organization on policy outputs, and to analyze the effects of legislative action on party structure?

The first step in such a procedure involves briefly setting forth a model of the relationship between party and faction. Within the legislature, attachments to both necessarily exist within the same persons (delegates); therefore, they must either compete with or complement each other in producing expressions (votes). Further, on any roll call the respective pressures of party and factional attachments may range from total congruence to complete disharmony. For the 1790s one may usefully draw a mental picture of two growing circles, labeled respectively "Federalist" and "Republican," floating in a House along with a variety of smaller and generally contracting circles, the factions analyzed in the preceding chapters. The dimensions of the two large and growing circles, their intersections, and their success in producing laws are given in quantitative terms in Tables 52 and 53.

The most obvious conclusion to be drawn from the data is that the first American party system increasingly affected legislative behavior. In the First and Second Congresses the two parties polarized against each

Table 52. Cohesion Differences: Republicans Against Federalists, 1789–1801[a]

Issue	Pct. Range of Cohesion Difference	Congress					
		1st	2d	3d	4th	5th	6th
		Percent of Roll Calls in Each Range					
ALL	0–34	69	56	28	29	9	10
ROLL	35–64	28	43	43	34	23	13
CALLS	65–100	3	1	29	37	68	77
	MEAN	28	31	48	53	72	72
Govt.	0–34	45	64	33	12	3	9
Power	35–64	45	36	17	0	24	0
	65–100	10	0	50	88	73	91
	MEAN	38	30	59	84	78	80
Frontier	0–34	100	92	38	17	0	12
	35–64	0	8	37	32	0	25
	65–100	0	0	25	51	100	63
	MEAN	16	18	47	60	83	69
Economic	0–34	54	24	23	69	8	0
	35–64	46	73	68	8	29	16
	65–100	0	3	9	23	63	84
	MEAN	31	41	46	35	69	75
Foreign	0–34	100	50	17	8	10	10
Policy	35–64	0	50	22	52	20	15
	65–100	0	0	61	40	70	75
	MEAN	28	29	58	57	74	66

[a]All delegates for all years were assigned to one of two parties. Initially, assignments were made on the basis of available biographic materials, local studies, newspapers, and correspondence. There remained a substantial number of delegates whose party association was dubious or non-existent. In these instances voting records in the House were used to assign representatives to the bloc of "party" men with which they voted most frequently. This procedure created a bias towards maximizing the influence of party since the data to be tested, votes, were used to assure that the results would show party solidarity. To do otherwise, that is, to leave out of the calculation delegates without strong partisan attachment, would have obscured the changing influence of electoral politics during the decade by isolating only hard core Federalists and Republicans. Comparisons over the decade, then, involve a substantial number of delegates with weak organizational attachments in the earlier years against representatives with strong and certain party labels in the later years. Thus, the calculations provide a picture of the maximum number of votes that may potentially be "explained" by party. Further, the data allow some measure of party as defined by Madison, which existed in the earlier years, and party as a power-seeking organization in the later Congresses. Universal inclusion of delegates maximizes the explanatory power of party (under either definition), a bias chosen because it is in the opposite direction from the conclusions reached in the present study. Appendix II lists party designations for all delegates.

other on less than half of all recorded roll calls (see Table 52). During Washington's second term, however, Republicans and Federalists opposed each other sharply on almost seven of every ten votes. Finally, in the last four years of the Federalist era, parties polarized on over 90 percent of all roll calls. Every deep division in the Fifth and Sixth Congresses was in substantial measure a party division. Extreme cohesion differences, the 65 to 100 percent range, also occurred with increasing frequency through the decade.

These changes took place in four-year cycles, an indication that midterm congressional elections and external events only slightly modified the tempo of legislative behavior set in harmony with the presidential contest. A polarized response greeted Washington at the very outset of his second term and remained fairly constant until his retirement. The Adams years again saw the early establishment of polarity levels that remained unchanged until 1801. Richard P. McCormick's work emphasizes the crucial role of the presidential contest in spurring party development. Apparently, the relationship extended to legislative behavior as well, even before the advent of extensive partisan machinery.[1]

Table 53, on the other hand, reveals patterns and forces that did not increase steadily over time with the rhythm of the presidential contest. While polarization (and, hence, levels of cohesion difference) changed in four-year cycles, success ratios for the two parties did not do so. The position of the majority of Federalists, however small that majority, also became the position of the entire House on 79 percent of all roll calls recorded in the First Congress. Never again did the party forge policy so successfully although, except in the Fourth Congress, Republicans did not achieve legislative victory as frequently as did their opponents. To state the matter in another way, increasing polarization by both parties led to decreasing success for *both* parties. This strange phenomenon occurred because of the decreasing frequency of roll calls on which majorities in both parties united to produce policy.

Levels of high polarization were about the same for both parties with the important exception of Federalists in the Third Congress, who coalesced strongly on 72 percent of all roll calls against a corresponding figure of only 44 percent for Republicans. This dramatic increase for Federalists, the largest for either party for any Congress, occurred before the development of effective electoral machinery. Although it is but a solitary instance, the figure supports the claim of administration opponents that they were forced to resort to partisan politicking in order to counterbalance solidification by the party in power. Certainly, cohesive voting preceded party discipline.

Table 53. Success Patterns: Federalists and Republicans, 1789–1801

Party	Issue	Pattern[a]	1st	2d	3d	4th	5th	6th	Mean
FED	Govt. power	Successful	75	50	67	0	76	82	58
		Polarized	35	7	100	100	79	100	70
		Polarized Success	100	100	67	0	85	82	72
		Divided Success	62	46	–	–	43	–	50
	Frontier	Successful	100	85	63	28	100	37	69
		Polarized	33	31	75	67	100	75	64
		Polarized Success	100	100	67	25	100	49	74
		Divided Success	100	78	52	33	–	0	53
	Economic	Successful	85	77	96	69	75	70	79
		Polarized	40	34	82	53	100	85	66
		Polarized Success	100	100	100	72	75	82	88
		Divided Success	75	65	78	67	–	0	57
	Foreign policy	Successful	100	75	44	64	59	80	70
		Polarized	0	25	61	64	77	70	50
		Polarized Success	–	100	54	75	70	93	78
		Divided Success	100	100	72	44	26	50	65
	Location of capital (1st Cong.) and party politics (4th-6th Cong.)	Successful	64	–	–	80	50	80	70[b]
		Polarized	14	–	–	100	92	80	91
		Polarized Success	100	–	–	80	54	93	76
		Divided Success	58	–	–	–	0	30	15
	ALL ROLL CALLS	Successful	79	72	68	56	66	76	70
		Polarized	28	26	72	70	83	82	60
		Polarized Success	100	100	76	57	74	87	82
		Divided Success	71	62	46	53	30	28	48
REP	Govt. power	Successful	55	80	67	100	33	27	60
		Polarized	25	40	83	100	91	100	73
		Polarized Success	80	100	81	100	33	27	70
		Divided Success	47	67	0	–	33	–	37
	Frontier	Successful	67	69	69	89	0	77	62
		Polarized	0	15	44	83	100	75	53
		Polarized Success	–	100	89	94	0	84	73
		Divided Success	67	63	56	65	–	52	61
	Economic	Successful	51	37	23	77	46	38	45
		Polarized	29	29	18	31	79	85	45
		Polarized Success	68	68	78	100	42	36	65
		Divided Success	44	24	11	67	62	46	42
	Foreign policy	Successful	50	75	61	68	56	45	59
		Polarized	50	100	67	68	85	95	78
		Polarized Success	100	75	84	76	54	48	73
		Divided Success	0	–	15	50	67	0	26

Table 53. (Continued)

Party	Issue	Pattern[a]	Congress						Mean
			1st	2d	3d	4th	5th	6th	
	Location of capital	Successful	64	–	–	40	67	29	45[b]
	(1st Cong.) and	Polarized	23	–	–	20	100	94	71
	party politics	Polarized Success	100	–	–	100	67	28	65
	(4th-6th Cong.)	Divided Success	53	–	–	25	–	50	38
	ALL ROLL	Successful	58	64	53	76	49	39	57
	CALLS	Polarized	26	34	44	60	84	92	57
		Polarized Success	81	85	86	90	48	38	71
		Divided Success	50	53	27	55	50	50	48

[a]For calculation of patterns, see note (a) of Table 10, Chapter 2, p. 29.

[b]*Mean* applies only to party politics issues in the Fourth, Fifth, and Sixth Congresses.

The data in Table 53 also shed light on how Republicans and Federalists achieved victory. Until 1797 for the Republicans and except during the Fourth Congress for the Federalists, polarization meant success. This was possible only because unified action by one party did not spur the other to unite against it. Roll calls that generated solidarity in one party gained enough support in the other to assure victory. The polarized success ratio of the minority Republican party through 1797 exceeded that of their numerically superior opponents. In the later years, however, polarization led consistently to victory only for the majority party. Herein lies one of the important effects of partisan politicking on legislative behavior.

Further conclusions may be drawn from "divided success" ratios. This measure of how frequently the position of a small majority (51 to 75 percent) in each group also became the position of the entire House indicates cross-party (or non-party) voting. Republicans, with the exception of a dismal showing in the Third Congress (when, it will be recalled, the Federalists' solidarity increased dramatically) consistently won about half the battles in which their own forces were divided. An even chance of successfully forging policy, despite a dissident minority of substantial size in its own ranks, undermined the cogency of the Republican leaders' appeals for unity. Federalists, on the other hand, slipped consistently from very high divided success ratios of 71 and 62 percent in the First and Second Congresses, respectively, to extremely low figures of 30 and 28 percent during the Adams years. For Federalists, internal division came to mean defeat. Party leaders recognized the problem but turned, fatally, toward partisan politicking and away from the factional activity that had brought them such success, even while divided, earlier in the decade.

The above figures indicate the inadequacy of the traditional view that parties developed around 1795 to carry on the policy and personal battles of the First and Second Congresses, and that in so doing they brought order out of legislative chaos, clarified the issues for the general public, and set the stage for the triumph of Jeffersonian democracy. As we have seen, voting patterns, while complex, were consistent and purposeful in the absence of party discipline. The resort to newpapers and other publicity devices for partisan ends obscured the Federalist policy base upon which Jefferson built an organization highly successful in retaining control of the regime but unable to initiate new policies. For a generation his party failed to act on potentially divisive national problems—slavery, protection for manufacturers, internal improvements—left unsolved in the 1790s. Consideration of these issues by factional groupings between 1815 and 1828 brought a swift end to the Republican machine by eroding its one vulnerable point, the policy base on which it rested.

Returning to the data at hand, Table 53 outlines the degree of congruence between party attachment and the categories of issues that generated distinctive voting patterns during the 1790s. Federalists polarized most frequently on roll calls involving narrowly political matters (91 percent), but since these all occurred after 1795 the figure cannot be compared directly against polarization levels on other issues. Interestingly, Republicans, supposedly members of the party more advanced in the development of partisan machinery, united on only 71 percent of the same roll calls. Apparently, the greater propensity of Federalists to unite extended even to questions of a partisan nature. Foreign policy issues and roll calls involving the limits of government power generated greater unity among Republicans than among their opponents. With regard to government power, however, it is of note that neither party polarized frequently until after Washington's response to the Whiskey Rebellion effectively closed the issue and cleared the way for rhetoric aimed at acquiring and holding office rather than for policy alternatives. The difference in polarization levels on foreign policy issues reflects the early commitment of Madison and his followers to an alteration of Anglo-American trade patterns, at a time when the administration's policy was somewhat fluid and uncertain, and also shows the divided response of Federalists in the face of seemingly imminent war against France. During the Adams years foreign policy questions were paramount. The Federalists, who had the votes to forge policy outputs, yielded to factional pressures more frequently on this than on other issues and more frequently than the opposition party. Consideration of frontier policy, the general area in which factions had produced legislation with least success, generated relatively low levels of polarization in both parties. Finally, and very significantly, economic issues gave rise to only moderate cohesion among Federalists (66 percent) and to the lowest level of polarization among Republicans for any issue (45 percent).

Contrary to the widely accepted view that controversy over economic policy, particularly Hamilton's funding and assumption plans, provided the most direct and powerful stimulus to the development of the first American party system, the above data suggest that the causes of cohesion among Federalists lay equally in non-economic policy directions. Moreover, they suggest that Republicans, even if they successfully unified yeoman farmers and artisans against merchants and speculators at the electoral level, never polarized to produce, or even to attempt, an alternative to Hamiltonian finance. The cogency and clarity of the secretary's reports made them an easy target for partisan rhetoric. Other issues, especially the limits of government power, were too amorphous and complex to make effective newspaper propaganda. Attacks in this area ran headlong into Washington's personal popularity and later into charges of treason and seditious libel. Similarly, Madison's call for change in Anglo-American trade patterns involved too great a short-term sacrifice; it did not find favor with the electorate except briefly when cloaked in reaction against the administration's clumsy handling of the Jay Treaty.

Recognizing Federalist success in creating policy in the early years—a success pattern that often cut across party lines—Republicans turned to partisan machinery aimed at acquiring office. The effort required support from the general electorate and from actual and potential office-holders. The most attractive appeal proved to be the traditional one: attack the King's closest minister by charging him with favoritism and improper handling of public monies. But Republicans did not represent an economic interest that had suffered at government hands. They wanted the minister's position but they had no innovative policy to implement. Indeed, when offered the politically unpalatable alternative of a land tax, the party divided sharply and ultimately placed acquisition of office ahead of a chance to reverse Hamiltonian finance.

Finally, the figures tend to refute the hypothesis that parties represented coalitions of factions. They suggest, rather, that although party and faction necessarily coexisted, their goals were more often contradictory than complementary. Federalists were most successful on economic issues (79 percent), but they controlled policy more consistently in the First and Second Congresses (before they had polarized and with the aid, of course, of future Republicans) than they did in the later years. Republicans wrote and spoke most about economic issues, but they polarized least on such questions (45 percent) and with least success (45 percent). Federalists complained most loudly about the opposition's efforts to undermine effective government and its favoritism toward France. Yet it was division in the Federalist party that held the nation back from war in the spring of 1798 and Republican support that forged a national government limited only by its own volition. As partisan politicking increased—until by 1800 at least some Federalists believed literally that Jefferson was God's chosen instrument to punish national wickedness and many Republicans thought John Adams to be a monocrat—concern with policy decreased. Whereas the First Congress achieved a legislative record unexcelled in American history, the Sixth and last Congress of the Federalist era must rank at the bottom of any list that emphasizes policy outputs. The two trends accurately reflected the conflicting goals of party and faction and each produced a notable accomplishment consistent with its goals: factions forged policies that guided the nation for decades. The Sixth Congress elected a president who built the most successful party in the annals of American politics.

The preceding analysis necessarily merges somewhat the two definitions of party introduced at the outset of this chapter. We have seen that cohesion differences between Federalists and Republicans exceeded 34 percent on nine of every ten roll calls in the Fifth and Sixth Congresses, but in this instance party is a descriptive term of measurement. It explains what positions delegates took but not necessarily why they did so. "Federalist" and "Republican," used as descriptive terms, lack the precision and accuracy of the issue-oriented factional groupings discussed in earlier chapters. Particularly for the years before 1795, but also for an understanding of legislative response to the Quasi-War, a two-party framework has led to the incomplete conclusions that voting resulted from the "ramblings of individual views and shifting relationships [that] were only occasionally joined into blocs representing particular interests"[2] and that John Adams resisted a war-hungry Congress and brought peace with France.

Even when party as defined by votes proves to be an accurate descriptive term, it simultaneously over- and underestimates the impact of "party as organization" on policy outputs. It is mere chance if the errors turn out to compensate for each other. The sources of underestimation lie primarily in aspects of party that, deservedly, have received much attention from scholars but are not the subject of the present study: choosing of candidates for office, mobilization of public opinion on current issues, use of patronage and similar rewards to generate loyalty, and establishment of extra-constitutional mechanisms to mold divergent views into a relatively coherent program. Overestimating results from *assuming* that correlations between voting position and party label are causal rather than casual.[3]

For the 1790s historical fact aids the effort to determine the impact of party as organization on policy outputs. Students of the Federalist era unanimously agree that the beginning point for national party machinery was the Jay Treaty contest. Before the Fourth Congress, then, correlations between party label and voting position may be taken as measures of the "legislative" party action so feared by Madison. Cohesion differences for the Third Congress (see Table 52)—significant polarization on 72 percent of all recorded roll calls—represent the highwater mark, in the absence of party machinery, of cohesive response to the Washington-Hamilton program for establishing a powerful and energetic government. Against this figure may be placed the sharper and more frequent polarization that occurred in the Sixth Congress, one concerned from the outset and ultimately dramatically involved in the presidential contest and in a variety of lesser job-creating and -filling activities. Between the legislative parties of 1794 and the organizational parties of 1800, there were increases of 25 percent in the frequency of significant polarization (above 34 percent) and 165 percent in the frequency of extreme polarity (above 64 percent). Of course, the latter parties were not totally organizational in nature, but the figures do indicate the maximum influence of office-seeking organization on legislative behavior.

The figures, together with the trends outlined in Table 53, suggest several conclusions. In the First and Second Congresses, delegates successfully formed policies to meet the critical problems facing the young nation. Although behavior at this time was largely factional, occasions of party unity usually brought legislative victory over a divided opposition. In the Third Congress, in the absence of party discipline and clear organizational goals, delegates polarized frequently and consistently into two definable voting blocs. Two years of steady defeat led representatives who opposed the administration to turn to electoral politics in order, they claimed with some justice, to counteract the successful legislative party that Federalists had become. Results of this effort became apparent as early as the Fourth Congress: unity brought victory only for the majority party, a condition that fostered avoidance of divisive policy questions by the majority and inclined the minority toward irresponsibility, since its efforts seemed doomed at the outset. Division led to defeat, especially for the majority party, and spurred efforts to find and hold to a consensus policy, a situation achieved most easily by standing firm on existing legislative output. The majority party emphasized holding the allegiance of its own members, while the minority, recognizing that innovative propositions might further weaken and divide its own ranks without offering any assurance of new recruits, claimed that fundamental differences of principle no longer existed, a claim that by its very assertion became reality. A high frequency of bi-polar voting in the Third Congress provided a milieu conducive to the development of office-seeking machinery. Thereafter, party attachment greatly increased the depth and intensity of polarization, a situation that perpetuated and reinforced acceptance of policy outputs reached before 1795.

Students of the subject discern cycles in American politics. Voter turn-out, primary and secondary response to issues, ethnocultural forces, generational gaps, business cycles, and alterations in party machinery have all been used to try to explain why America's political system establishes norms of party success and policy positions that remain quite stable, usually for about thirty years, only to shift suddenly and quickly to a different set of norms that again produce stability. Walter Dean Burnham combines policy and party considerations in outlining five basic periods in American politics: the experimental system, 1789–1820; the democratizing system, 1828–1854/1860; the Civil War system, 1860–1893; the industrial system, 1894–1932; and the New Deal system, 1932–?. The present study of a portion of the "experimental" system suggests the need for closer examination of legislative behavior and its impact on political cycles. In the 1790s highly cohesive issue-oriented factions created an energetic, positive government. Delegates in the House accepted the policy agreements of the early decade and increasingly devoted their talents to the battle for control of the now powerful and secure regime. Republicans emerged from the contest with a victory that held at the national level for twenty-four years. Their success has not been equalled in American political history. But the price of victory, one that later successful parties also paid, was the avoidance of potentially divisive policy changes for so long that the system, relying on outmoded agreements, failed to promote the general welfare and encouraged violent reactions against its continued existence.

APPENDIX I :
ROLL CALL DESCRIPTIONS

First Congress

ROLL CALL	SOURCE	DATE	AFFIRMATIVE	NEGATIVE
001	Annals, 365	May 16, 1789	41	8

To limit the duration of a bill laying duties on imports

002	Annals, 408	May 22, 1789	36	1

To seat William L. Smith though he had not been a citizen for seven years

003	Annals, 580	June 22, 1789	30	18

To allow the president to remove appointees without Senate approval

004	Annals, 585	June 22, 1789	31	19

To eliminate specific wording "removable by the President" since the Constitution implied this right

005	Annals, 591	June 24, 1789	29	22

Passage of Department of Foreign Affairs Bill

006	Annals, 618	July 1, 1789	31	19

To accept Senate's elimination of discriminatory duties against England

007	Annals, 688	August 10, 1789	30	16

Bill to pay members of the House and Senate

008	Annals, 703	August 12, 1789	28	23

To appropriate $40,000 for negotiation of Indian treaties

First Congress

ROLL CALL	SOURCE	DATE	AFFIRMATIVE	NEGATIVE
009	Annals, 759	August 18, 1789	16	34

To consider all proposed constitutional amendments

010	Annals, 768	August 21, 1789	17	32

In what became the Tenth Amendment to insert the word "expressly" before delegated

011	Annals, 772	August 21, 1789	23	28

To prohibit Congress from interfering with time, place, and manner of elections

012	Annals, 777	August 22, 1789	9	39

To prohibit laying of direct taxes by the federal government

013	Annals, 796	August 29, 1789	27	16

Bill to establish salaries for the executive branch

014	Annals, 881	September 7, 1789	21	29

Permanent capital on the north side of the Potomac in Maryland

015	Annals, 882	September 7, 1789	19	32

Temporary capital at Wilmington, Delaware

016	Annals, 883	September 7, 1789	23	28

Permanent capital on the Potomac, Delaware, or Susquehanna rivers

017	Annals, 883	September 7, 1789	4	46

Permanent capital on the Delaware River

018	Annals, 884	September 7, 1789	26	26

Permanent capital on the Susquehanna in Pennsylvania

019	Annals, 884	September 7, 1789	25	26

Permanent capital on the Susquehanna in Maryland

First Congress

ROLL CALL	SOURCE	DATE	AFFIRMATIVE	NEGATIVE
020	Annals, 884	September 7, 1789	21	30
	Temporary capital at Wilmington instead of New York City			
021	Annals, 885	September 7, 1789	22	29
	Temporary capital at Philadelphia			
022	Annals, 886	September 7, 1789	24	25
	Establishment of any sort of capital on the Susquehanna only if Pennsylvania and Maryland made it navigable to its mouth			
023	Annals, 886	September 7, 1789	28	21
	Permanent capital on the east bank of the Susquehanna in Pennsylvania			
024	Annals, 889	September 10, 1789	24	29
	To limit duration of bill establishing differential pay rates for senators			
025	Annals, 891	September 11, 1789	29	25
	Adherence to Senate amendment giving senators higher pay			
026	Annals, 891	September 11, 1789	28	26
	Same as number 024			
027	Journal, 111	September 15, 1789	20	23
	To place federal court in Chestertown, Maryland, instead of Eastown, Maryland			
028	Annals, 911	September 22, 1789	31	17
	Third reading of bill for permanent capital on east bank of Susquehanna			
029	Annals, 913	September 24, 1789	37	14
	"Speedy and public trial by jury" amendment			

First Congress

ROLL CALL	SOURCE	DATE	AFFIRMATIVE	NEGATIVE
030	Annals, 914	September 24, 1789	25	18

Writs to be issued in name of United States rather than name of the president

| 031 | Annals, 923 | September 26, 1789 | 28 | 22 |

Adherence to Senate's insistence on writs with the president's name

| 032 | Annals, 923 | September 26, 1789 | 25 | 29 |

To postpone adherence to Senate amendments to capital location bill

| 033 | Annals, 926 | September 28, 1789 | 31 | 24 |

To adhere to Senate's bill locating capital one mile north of Philadelphia

| 034 | Annals, 927 | September 28, 1789 | 26 | 25 |

To adhere to Senate's removal of navigation clearance provisions in capital location bill

| 035 | Annals, 927 | September 28, 1789 | 16 | 25 |

To adhere to Senate's amendment allowing executive to issue general militia call

| 036 | Annals, 1205 | February 12, 1790 | 43 | 11 |

To commit Friends of Philadelphia memorial against slavery

| 037 | Journal, 390 | February 24, 1791 | 53 | 2 |

Refusal to alter the system for funding public debt

| 038 | Annals, 1473 | March 23, 1790 | 29 | 25 |

Inclusion of the debate on the Quaker Petition in the House Journal

| 039 | Annals, 1530 | April 15, 1790 | 33 | 23 |

To consider Hamilton's report on means of supporting public credit

First Congress

ROLL CALL	SOURCE	DATE	AFFIRMATIVE	NEGATIVE
040	Annals, 1545	April 26, 1790	32	18

To exclude consideration of assumption of state debts for the present time

041	Annals, 1556	May 7, 1790	28	21

To lower Baron von Steuben's annuity from $2,706 to $1,500

042	Annals, 1556	May 10, 1790	25	30

To allow the Baron an annuity of $2,700

043	Annals, 1557	May 10, 1790	34	21

To allow the Baron an annuity of $2,000

044	Annals, 1619	May 26, 1790	31	25

To fund old continental money at a ratio of one hundred to one

045	Annals, 1619	May 26, 1790	15	42

To pay back interest on funded continental money

046	Annals, 1620	May 27, 1790	18	38

To adhere to Senate amendment appropriating a lump sum for payment of officers

047	Annals, 1621	May 28, 1790	32	25

To allow the Baron an annuity of $2,500 but eliminate lump payment of $7,000

048	Journal, 227	May 28, 1790	16	37

Adherence to a Senate amendment to the foreign intercourse bill

049	Annals, 1623	May 31, 1790	32	27

To consider holding the next session of Congress at Philadelphia

First Congress

ROLL CALL	SOURCE	DATE	AFFIRMATIVE	NEGATIVE
050	Annals, 1624	May 31, 1790	29	30
	Permanent and temporary capital on the Delaware River at a convenient place			
051	Annals, 1625	May 31, 1790	25	25
	The next session to remain in New York City			
052	Annals, 1626	May 31, 1790	22	38
	The next session to be held at Philadelphia or Baltimore			
053	Annals, 1626	May 31, 1790	38	22
	The next session to be held at Philadelphia			
054	Annals, 1634	June 10, 1790	32	29
	Same as number 053			
055	Annals, 1635	June 10, 1790	28	33
	To convene as Committee of the Whole on location of capital issue			
056	Annals, 1636	June 11, 1790	26	31
	To remove duties on spirits and promote agriculture to pay the public debt			
057	Annals, 1637	June 11, 1790	31	28
	To hold the next session at Baltimore			
058	Annals, 1637	June 11, 1790	53	6
	Same as number 057			
059	Annals, 1639	June 14, 1790	30	24
	To consider payment of public debt though the Senate had not yet done so			
060	Annals, 1642	June 18, 1790	19	35
	To eliminate all excise taxes from the bill to raise money to pay the public debt			

First Congress

ROLL CALL	SOURCE	DATE	AFFIRMATIVE	NEGATIVE
061	Annals, 1644	June 21, 1790	23	35

To engross a bill repealing duties on foreign spirits

062	Annals, 1645	June 21, 1790	10	45

To strike out proposal that state debts be apportioned in the same manner as for representation and taxation

063	Annals, 1646	June 22, 1790	26	27

Elimination of an appropriation to trade with and bribe Indians

064	Annals, 1678	July 9, 1790	22	39

Permanent capital on the Delaware River

065	Annals, 1678	July 9, 1790	22	39

Permanent capital in Germantown, Pennsylvania

066	Annals, 1678	July 9, 1790	25	26

Permanent capital between the Potomac and Susquehanna rivers

067	Annals, 1678	July 9, 1790	26	34

Permanent capital at Baltimore

068	Annals, 1678	July 9, 1790	26	35

Buildings in the new capital had to be donated

069	Journal, 261	July 9, 1790	26	33

Buildings in the new capital to be purchased only with consent of the president

070	Journal, 262	July 9, 1790	25	32

To limit amount to be spent for buildings for the new capital

071	Journal, 263	July 9, 1790	28	33

To hold the next session at Philadelphia

First Congress

ROLL CALL	SOURCE	DATE	AFFIRMATIVE	NEGATIVE
072	Journal, 263	July 9, 1790	28	32

Next session in New York City but Second Congress to meet in Philadelphia

| 073 | Journal, 264 | July 9, 1790 | 28 | 33 |

Same as number 072

| 074 | Journal, 265 | July 9, 1790 | 26 | 33 |

To postpone consideration of location for next session

| 075 | Journal, 266 | July 9, 1790 | 32 | 29 |

Establishment of a permanent capital on the Potomac

| 076 | Journal, 266 | July 9, 1790 | 13 | 48 |

Let president decide when to move to permanent capital

| 077 | Annals, 1684 | July 19, 1790 | 40 | 15 |

Third reading of the engrossed bill to fund the national debt

| 078 | Annals, 1686 | July 22, 1790 | 35 | 20 |

To refuse to adhere to Senate's amendment allowing postmaster to establish cross postroads

| 079 | Annals, 1710 | July 24, 1790 | 29 | 32 |

To reject assumption of state debts

| 080 | Annals, 1711 | July 26, 1790 | 15 | 45 |

Original holders to have six months to claim their certificates

| 081 | Annals, 1712 | July 26, 1790 | 13 | 47 |

To eliminate provision to pay interest to the states if the full amount of debt was not subscribed to within a time limit to be determined

| 082 | Annals, 1712 | July 26, 1790 | 34 | 28 |

To assume state debts

First Congress

ROLL CALL	SOURCE	DATE	AFFIRMATIVE	NEGATIVE
083	Annals, 1716	July 29, 1790	33	27

To defer interest on new stock for ten years instead of seven

084	Annals, 1716	July 29, 1790	33	27

To pay 3-percent interest on indents instead of 4 percent

085	Journal, 288	August 4, 1790	36	19

To add two commissioners to board established to settle accounts between the United States and the individual states

086	Annals, 1720	August 5, 1790	23	35

To reconsider movement of the temporary capital from New York City to Philadelphia

087	Journal, 292	August 6, 1790	28	30

To lower the salt duty from twelve to nine cents

088	Annals, 1837	December 29, 1790	8	43

To consider a militia bill

089	Annals, 1870	January 17, 1791	16	36

To eliminate the proposed tax on spirits

090	Annals, 1878	January 21, 1791	21	37

Amendment to prevent revenue inspectors from interfering with elections

091	Annals, 1882	January 24, 1791	19	39

To limit the duration of the revenue bill

092	Annals, 1883	January 25, 1791	35	20

To engross the revenue bill for third reading

093	Annals, 1884	January 27, 1791	35	21

Passage of the revenue bill

First Congress

ROLL CALL	SOURCE	DATE	AFFIRMATIVE	NEGATIVE
094	Annals, 1894	February 1, 1791	23	34
	To recommit the bill establishing a national bank			
095	Annals, 1902	February 3, 1791	21	38
	To recommit the bank bill			
096	Journal, 372	February 8, 1791	38	20
	To vote on the bank bill			
097	Annals, 1960	February 8, 1791	39	20
	Passage of the bank bill			
098	Annals, 1964	February 15, 1791	34	21
	To allow land purchases with any certificate of funded debt			
099	Annals, 1965	February 18, 1791	35	21
	To strengthen enforcement of collection provisions in the revenue bill			
100	Annals, 1966	February 19, 1791	34	20
	To raise compensation for whiskey tax collectors from 5 percent to 7 percent of collections			
101	Journal, 386	February 22, 1791	36	24
	To insist, after Senate rejection, to limit compensation provision to two years			
102	Journal, 391	February 25, 1791	30	29
	To limit total annual allocation for compensation for tax collectors to $45,000			
103	Journal, 395	February 28, 1791	23	27
	Minor amendment to bill compensating the Commissioners of Loans			
104	Journal, 396	March 1, 1791	30	23
	Payment of court officers, clerks, jurors, and witnesses			

First Congress

ROLL CALL	SOURCE	DATE	AFFIRMATIVE	NEGATIVE
105	Journal, 397	March 1, 1791	39	18

Permanent capital on the Potomac and temporary site in Philadelphia

106	Journal, 401	March 2, 1791	33	14

Passage of bill to compensate George Gibson

107	Journal, 402	March 3, 1791	25	21

Passage of a bill to establish a mint

108	Journal, 403	March 3, 1791	20	22

To give extra compensation for loan commissioners of Massachusetts, New York, Pennsylvania, and Virginia

109	Journal, 403	March 3, 1791	23	20

To recede from amendment in 108

Second Congress

ROLL CALL	SOURCE	DATE	AFFIRMATIVE	NEGATIVE
001	Annals, 191	November 15, 1791	35	23

To apportion one representative to the House for each 30,000 people

002	Annals, 208	November 23, 1791	21	38

To apportion one representative for each 34,000 people

003	Annals, 210	November 24, 1791	43	12

Third reading of one for 30,000 ratio

004	Journal, 473	December 14, 1791	23	37

To apportion as follows: N.H. 5, Mass. 16, Conn. 8, R.I. 2, Vt. 3, N.Y. 11, N.J. 6, Penn. 14, Del. 2, Md. 9, Va. 21, Ky. 2, N.C. 12, Ga. 2, and S.C. uncertain

Second Congress

ROLL CALL	SOURCE	DATE	AFFIRMATIVE	NEGATIVE
005	Annals, 251	December 14, 1791	29	31

To apportion as follows: N.H. 4, Mass. 14, Conn. 7, R.I. 2, Vt. 2, N.Y. 10, N.J. 5, Penn. 13, Del. 1, Md. 8, Va. 19, Ky. 2, N.C. 10, Ga. 2, and S.C. uncertain

006	Annals, 274	December 19, 1791	27	33

Reconsideration of 005 after Senate refused to adopt 004

007	Annals, 274	December 19, 1791	32	27

To adhere to refusal to accept Senate version (1:34,000 formula)

008	Annals, 302	January 2, 1792	24	27

To place Speaker of the House after vice-president for succession to presidency

009	Annals, 303	January 2, 1792	26	25

To place president of Senate pro tempore after vice-president for succession

010	Annals, 311	January 5, 1792	14	43

To continue state licenses of stage coach routes over federal post roads

011	Annals, 311	January 5, 1792	25	33

To allow carriages conveying mail to receive passengers

012	Annals, 335	January 24, 1792	22	36

To strike out expiration date of March 3, 1797, from apportionment bill

013	Annals, 336	January 24, 1792	33	26

To strike out 1:30,000 limit applicable to apportionment after 1797

014	Annals, 354	January 30, 1792	18	34

To add to frontier defense three regiments of infantry

Second Congress

ROLL CALL	SOURCE	DATE	AFFIRMATIVE	NEGATIVE
015	Annals, 355	February 1, 1792	29	19

Third reading of frontier protection bill

016	Annals, 401	February 9, 1792	38	21

Third reading of bill to encourage and regulate cod fishermen

017	Annals, 402	February 10, 1792	32	22

To eliminate House Speaker and Senate president pro tempore from succession

018	Journal, 508	February 14, 1792	29	21

Presidential electors to be equal to number of congressmen at time of inauguration

019	Annals, 415	February 20, 1792	23	26

To eliminate taking a new census for 1797 reapportionment

020	Annals, 415	February 20, 1792	25	26

To eliminate reference to 1:30,000 apportionment ratio after 1797

021	Annals, 416	February 20, 1792	29	22

To reapportion in 1797 at 1:30,000

022	Annals, 417	February 21, 1792	31	24

To recede from placing secretary of state next in line of succession after vice-president

023	Annals, 418	February 21, 1792	34	16

Passage of apportionment bill using 1:34,000 until 1797 and then 1:30,000

024	Annals, 425	February 23, 1792	31	27

Request that Hamilton list balances owed to the United States before 1789

Second Congress

ROLL CALL	SOURCE	DATE	AFFIRMATIVE	NEGATIVE
025	Annals, 430	February 28, 1792	43	9

To allow the president limited authority to make appointments to the army

026	Annals, 435	March 6, 1792	31	27

Engrossing of a bill to defend the frontier

027	Annals, 452	March 8, 1792	31	27

Request that Hamilton report on means of raising additional supplies for army

028	Annals, 456	March 10, 1792	17	35

To recommit a congratulatory note to the King of France

029	Annals, 457	March 10, 1792	50	2

On sending a portion of the note voted on in number 028

030	Annals, 457	March 10, 1792	35	16

To add to the note several words of praise for France and its revolution

031	Annals, 471	March 14, 1792	20	41

To accept evidence on local corruption in seating of Anthony Wayne case

032	Journal, 537	March 16, 1792	58	0

To deny Anthony Wayne his seat

033	Annals, 473	March 17, 1792	29	31

To limit the number of members in the House to 120

034	Annals, 479	March 21, 1792	29	30

To allow James Jackson to take the seat denied to Anthony Wayne

Second Congress

ROLL CALL	SOURCE	DATE	AFFIRMATIVE	NEGATIVE
035	Annals, 482	March 23, 1792	31	29

To recede from remaining differences with Senate over apportionment bill

| 036 | Annals, 485 | March 24, 1792 | 26 | 22 |

To not place the name G WASHINGTON on coins

| 037 | Annals, 485 | March 24, 1792 | 42 | 6 |

To place on coins, instead of G WASHINGTON, the word LIBERTY

| 038 | Annals, 486 | March 26, 1792 | 32 | 22 |

Passage of a bill establishing a mint

| 039 | Annals, 489 | March 26, 1792 | 24 | 32 |

To place G WASHINGTON on the coins instead of LIBERTY

| 040 | Annals, 493 | March 27, 1792 | 21 | 35 |

To request the president to inquire into the defeat of General St. Clair

| 041 | Annals, 493 | March 27, 1792 | 44 | 10 |

To set up a House committee to investigate St. Clair's defeat

| 042 | Annals, 533 | April 2, 1792 | 27 | 30 |

To repay a maximum of 8 percent per year on funded debt not yet subscribed

| 043 | Annals, 534 | April 3, 1792 | 22 | 30 |

To extend assumption of state debts to debts already discharged by the states

| 044 | Annals, 535 | April 3, 1792 | 26 | 29 |

To consider the resolution in number 043

Second Congress

ROLL CALL	SOURCE	DATE	AFFIRMATIVE	NEGATIVE
045	Annals, 537	April 4, 1792	29	26
	To indemnify General Nathaniel Greene's estate for expenses incurred during Revolution			
046	Annals, 540	April 6, 1792	17	45
	To commit for three months the bill to indemnify Greene's estate			
047	Annals, 541	April 6, 1792	28	33
	To pass apportionment bill over the president's veto			
048	Annals, 548	April 9, 1792	34	30
	To apportion for 1793 at 1:33,000			
049	Annals, 550	April 10, 1792	37	23
	To allow third reading of bill to indemnify Greene's estate			
050	Annals, 551	April 11, 1792	33	24
	Passage of bill to indemnify Greene's estate			
051	Annals, 552	April 12, 1792	37	20
	To allow president to call out the militia while Congress was not in session			
052	Annals, 555	April 12, 1792	24	37
	To allow the president to call out the militia at any time			
053	Annals, 562	April 19, 1792	32	32
	To impose a duty on imported cotton			
054	Annals, 572	April 21, 1792	37	20
	Passage of bill for defense of frontiers (and aid to fisheries)			
055	Annals, 588	April 30, 1792	26	27
	To tax whiskey at eight cents per gallon (opposition wanted lower rate)			

Second Congress

ROLL CALL	SOURCE	DATE	AFFIRMATIVE	NEGATIVE
056	Annals, 590	May 2, 1792	25	27

To accept referees' decision on amounts owed to Revolutionary War suppliers

| 057 | Annals, 591 | May 3, 1792 | 18 | 38 |

To invalidate insolvency laws passed by the states on Revolutionary War debts

| 058 | Annals, 594 | May 5, 1792 | 30 | 23 |

Third reading of bill to settle claims of Anthony Walton White

| 059 | Annals, 596 | May 5, 1792 | 24 | 35 |

To consider assumption of remaining state debts

| 060 | Annals, 598 | May 7, 1792 | 23 | 22 |

Third reading of bill to settle claims of John Brown Cutting

| 061 | Annals, 599 | May 7, 1792 | 30 | 17 |

To adhere to refusal expressed in number 057

| 062 | Annals, 710 | November 21, 1792 | 6 | 50 |

To repeal provisions for providing arms for the militia

| 063 | Annals, 722 | November 21, 1792 | 25 | 32 |

To withdraw request that Hamilton report a plan for redemption of public debt

| 064 | Annals, 736 | December 4, 1792 | 24 | 25 |

To allow $12,000 for negotiations with the Creek Indians

| 065 | Annals, 736 | December 5, 1792 | 20 | 21 |

To allow $900 for negotiations with the Creek Indians

| 066 | Annals, 749 | December 18, 1792 | 21 | 27 |

To allow the president to use militia for offensive operations against Indians

Second Congress

ROLL CALL	SOURCE	DATE	AFFIRMATIVE	NEGATIVE
067	Annals, 760	December 26, 1792	18	35

To eliminate authorization for a loan of $2 million at 5 percent to repay another loan

| 068 | Annals, 760 | December 26, 1792 | 27 | 27 |

To allow a maximum of $200,000 for payment of this loan

| 069 | Annals, 802 | January 8, 1793 | 26 | 32 |

To reduce the military establishment and increase ratio of privates to officers

| 070 | Annals, 802 | January 8, 1793 | 20 | 36 |

To reduce the military establishment

| 071 | Annals, 803 | January 9, 1793 | 40 | 20 |

To disallow pensions for veterans not on the rolls as of March 23, 1792, and not covered under legislation to provide for widows and orphans

| 072 | Annals, 804 | January 10, 1793 | 36 | 13 |

Passage of bill to provide pensions for invalid veterans

| 073 | Annals, 810 | January 12, 1793 | 38 | 23 |

To give state legislatures veto power over loans from general settlement of accounts

| 074 | Annals, 810 | January 12, 1793 | 34 | 28 |

To continue processing of the general settlement of accounts

| 075 | Annals, 823 | January 15, 1793 | 30 | 24 |

To consider Charleston merchant petition asking for financial relief

| 076 | Annals, 824 | January 15, 1793 | 24 | 30 |

To refer the Charleston merchants' petition to Committee of the Whole

Second Congress

ROLL CALL	SOURCE	DATE	AFFIRMATIVE	NEGATIVE
077	Annals, 826	January 16, 1793	43	10

To reject a series of memorials from Revolutionary War veterans

| 078 | Annals, 842 | January 24, 1793 | 30 | 33 |

To allow only original holders to subscribe to loans under the general settlement

| 079 | Annals, 842 | January 24, 1793 | 29 | 30 |

To allow loans under the general settlement only for Revolutionary War debts

| 080 | Annals, 843 | January 25, 1793 | 22 | 24 |

To grant further compensation to receivers of continental taxes

| 081 | Annals, 843 | January 25, 1793 | 39 | 20 |

To open loan offices for the general settlement of accounts effective January 1, 1794

| 082 | Annals, 844 | January 25, 1793 | 33 | 32 |

Third reading of bill to establish loan offices for general settlement

| 083 | Annals, 850 | January 28, 1793 | 33 | 31 |

To consider passage of a bill establishing loan offices

| 084 | Annals, 851 | January 28, 1793 | 33 | 32 |

Passage of a bill establishing loan offices

| 085 | Annals, 861 | February 5, 1793 | 48 | 7 |

Passage of a bill providing for recovery of fugitive slaves

| 086 | Annals, 866 | February 7, 1793 | 27 | 33 |

To limit duration of bill providing salaries for the president and vice-president

Second Congress

ROLL CALL	SOURCE	DATE	AFFIRMATIVE	NEGATIVE
087	Annals, 882	February 19, 1793	30	31

To ask public debt commissioners to give the House their resolves approved by the president (in essence a resolution questioning Hamilton's integrity)

088	Annals, 882	February 19, 1793	18	43

To lessen the implicit condemnation of Hamilton in the investigation of public debt

089	Annals, 883	February 19, 1793	39	22

To investigate the public debt handling question

090	Annals, 887	February 21, 1793	17	39

To strike out the same clause attempted in number 087

091	Journal, 713	February 22, 1793	41	18

To adjourn for one-half hour

092	Annals, 890	February 22, 1793	30	31

To allocate a lump sum rather than an itemized appropriation for War Department

093	Annals, 891	February 23, 1793	39	17

To extend the time limit for concluding the general settlement of accounts

094	Annals, 892	February 23, 1793	34	25

To limit installment payments on debt due the Bank of the United States to $50,000

095	Annals, 955	March 1, 1793	40	12

To disagree with resolution that Hamilton violated the law in repaying interest

Second Congress

ROLL CALL	SOURCE	DATE	AFFIRMATIVE	NEGATIVE
096	Annals, 956	March 1, 1793	39	12

To disagree with resolution that Hamilton deviated from Washington's instructions

ROLL CALL	SOURCE	DATE	AFFIRMATIVE	NEGATIVE
097	Annals, 958	March 1, 1793	33	15

To disagree with resolution that Hamilton failed to discharge essential duties

098	Annals, 959	March 1, 1793	33	8

To disagree with resolution that Hamilton acted without Washington's permission

099	Annals, 959	March 1, 1793	33	8

To disagree with resolution that Hamilton failed to consult the public interest

100	Annals, 963	March 1, 1793	34	7

To disagree with resolution that Hamilton was guilty of "indecorum" to the House

101	Annals, 964	March 2, 1793	24	17

To raise the salaries of the auditor of the treasury and the commissioner of revenue

102	Annals, 965	March 2, 1793	17	24

Passage of a bill for the relief of Simeon Thayer

Third Congress

ROLL CALL	SOURCE	DATE	AFFIRMATIVE	NEGATIVE
001	Annals, 154	January 2, 1794	46	44

To consider defense measures against pirates

002	Annals, 166	January 8, 1794	50	42

To alter the flag of the United States

Third Congress

ROLL CALL	SOURCE	DATE	AFFIRMATIVE	NEGATIVE
003	Annals, 254	January 21, 1794	64	24
	To eliminate proposed pay raise for commissioned officers			
004	Annals, 255	January 21, 1794	54	32
	To provide pensions to widows and orphans of officers killed in action			
005	Annals, 431	February 5, 1794	51	47
	To delay for one month consideration of Jefferson's report on commerce			
006	Annals, 454	February 14, 1794	57	31
	To assign seat denied to John Patton of Delaware to Henry Latimer			
007	Annals, 459	February 21, 1794	43	41
	To provide a naval force of four ships of 44 guns and two ships of 20 guns			
008	Annals, 476	March 4, 1794	8	77
	To allow state courts to hear suits against them by foreigners or residents of another state			
009	Annals, 477	March 4, 1794	81	9
	To prohibit federal courts from hearing such suits			
010	Annals, 497	March 10, 1794	50	39
	Passage of naval armament bill			
011	Annals, 563	April 8, 1794	39	56
	To investigate procedures used in general settlement of accounts			
012	Annals, 596	April 15, 1794	53	44
	To consider prohibition of all trade with Great Britain			
013	Annals, 600	April 18, 1794	57	42
	To consider the embargo despite John Jay's mission			

Third Congress

ROLL CALL	SOURCE	DATE	AFFIRMATIVE	NEGATIVE
014	Annals, 602	April 21, 1794	58	38

To prohibit all trade with Great Britain in British goods after November 1, 1794

015	Annals, 604	April 24, 1794	57	34

To engross the bill voted on in number 014

016	Annals, 605	April 25, 1794	58	34

Passage of the bill voted on in number 014

017	Annals, 656	May 7, 1794	34	53

To eliminate a proposed carriage tax

018	Annals, 666	May 8, 1794	35	58

To eliminate a proposed stamp tax

019	Annals, 666	May 8, 1794	64	23

To impose stamp duties only on documents involved in federal court proceedings

020	Annals, 667	May 8, 1794	41	45

To eliminate a proposed duty on tobacco

021	Annals, 670	May 9, 1794	50	37

To eliminate a proposed duty of six cents per ton on U.S. ships in foreign trade

022	Annals, 670	May 9, 1794	25	61

To double the proposed duty on foreign tonnage

023	Annals, 672	May 10, 1794	24	55

To double the proposed duty for British tonnage only

024	Annals, 672	May 10, 1794	30	44

To eliminate a proposed stamp tax on deeds

Third Congress

ROLL CALL	SOURCE	DATE	AFFIRMATIVE	NEGATIVE
025	Annals, 682	May 12, 1794	34	52
	To continue the embargo only on ships bound for the West Indies, Bermuda, or Nova Scotia			
026	Annals, 683	May 12, 1794	13	73
	To continue the embargo only on British trade			
027	Annals, 685	May 14, 1794	23	58
	To relinquish all balances owed to the United States by the several states			
028	Annals, 685	May 14, 1794	27	60
	To make no further payment on state debts after 1798			
029	Annals, 686	May 14, 1794	52	37
	To consider a bill to pay creditor states in the general settlement of accounts			
030	Annals, 686	May 14, 1794	51	36
	To engross the bill considered in number 029			
031	Annals, 687	May 14, 1794	33	53
	To postpone for three months third reading of the bill in number 029			
032	Annals, 694	May 15, 1794	57	31
	To consider linking indemnity for spoliations with sequestration of British debts			
033	Annals, 696	May 16, 1794	52	33
	Passage of bill for paying interest on balances due to the states			
034	Annals, 699	May 16, 1794	39	45
	To increase the duty on American tonnage by six cents			

Third Congress

ROLL CALL	SOURCE	DATE	AFFIRMATIVE	NEGATIVE
035	Annals, 707	May 19, 1794	31	56
	To reject bill for laying duties on tobacco and refined sugar			
036	Annals, 709	May 19, 1794	30	50
	To raise an additional provisional military force			
037	Annals, 711	May 20, 1794	25	55
	To deny compensation to Arthur St. Clair for his treaty negotiation efforts			
038	Annals, 711	May 21, 1794	50	27
	Passage of a bill to compensate St. Clair			
039	Annals, 712	May 21, 1794	37	40
	Third reading of pension bill for widow and children of Robert Forsyth			
040	Annals, 716	May 23, 1794	24	46
	To discontinue consideration of restrictions on commerce with Great Britain			
041	Annals, 723	May 26, 1794	44	35
	To engross a bill laying duties on stamped vellum and paper			
042	Annals, 726	May 27, 1794	32	50
	Passage of the stamp tax			
043	Annals, 730	May 29, 1794	49	22
	Passage of a carriage tax			
044	Annals, 738	May 30, 1794	50	32
	To reject a bill to increase the military establishment			
045	Annals, 740	May 31, 1794	53	23
	Passage of retail wine and liquor sales tax			

Third Congress

ROLL CALL	SOURCE	DATE	AFFIRMATIVE	NEGATIVE
046	Annals, 741	May 31, 1794	55	23
	Passage of bill paying debts owed to the French Republic			
047	Annals, 741	May 31, 1794	55	27
	Passage of bill laying duties on property sold at auction			
048	Annals, 744	May 31, 1794	49	32
	To consider legislation against privateers attacking British commerce			
049	Annals, 757	June 2, 1794	48	38
	To prohibit sale of goods captured from nations not at war against the United States			
050	Annals, 759	June 3, 1794	46	26
	To grant further compensation to Robert Forsyth, Marshal of Georgia			
051	Annals, 765	June 4, 1794	42	32
	To allow the president to purchase as many as ten galleys for naval service			
052	Annals, 767	June 5, 1794	43	32
	To raise pay of clerks in the Departments of State, Treasury, and War			
053	Annals, 779	June 6, 1794	26	42
	To concur with Senate in establishing a standing army of 1,140 men in Southwest			
054	Annals, 781	June 7, 1794	30	28
	To adhere to rejection voted on in number 053			
055	Annals, 943	November 27, 1794	47	45
	To condemn self-created societies for their role in the Whiskey Rebellion			

Third Congress

ROLL CALL	SOURCE	DATE	AFFIRMATIVE	NEGATIVE
056	Annals, 944	November 27, 1794	47	46

To condemn societies only in the four western counties of Pennsylvania

| 057 | Annals, 944 | November 27, 1794 | 42 | 50 |

To add that self-created societies elsewhere countenanced the insurrection

| 058 | Annals, 965 | December 4, 1794 | 52 | 38 |

Resolution of thanks to Major General Wayne and his gallant volunteers

| 059 | Annals, 977 | December 15, 1794 | 50 | 29 |

To reject pay reduction for officers in the militia

| 060 | Annals, 1000 | December 19, 1794 | 52 | 31 |

To request Washington to ascertain property losses incurred in Whiskey Rebellion

| 061 | Annals, 1057 | January 2, 1795 | 28 | 63 |

To prohibit immigrants from bringing slaves with them

| 062 | Annals, 1057 | January 2, 1795 | 59 | 32 |

To require immigrants to renounce any foreign titles they might have

| 063 | Annals, 1161 | January 30, 1795 | 14 | 56 |

To reimburse original purchasers of land ceded by North Carolina to the United States

| 064 | Annals, 1222 | February 13, 1795 | 25 | 58 |

To reduce the military establishment in the event of peace with the Indians

Third Congress

ROLL CALL	SOURCE	DATE	AFFIRMATIVE	NEGATIVE
065	Annals, 1222	February 13, 1795	36	44

Resolution that the sole purpose of the military was protection from foreign invasion and Indians

066	Annals, 1243	February 21, 1795	39	49

To eliminate stringent repayment provisions from public credit bill

067	Annals, 1256	February 27, 1795	43	37

To reject bill to prevent depredations on Indians south of the Ohio River

068	Annals, 1269	February 28, 1795	40	46

To allow persons in pursuit of hostile Indians to bear arms while on Indian lands

069	Annals, 1280	March 2, 1795	41	24

Passage of bill authorizing purchase of certain lands from Georgia

Fourth Congress

ROLL CALL	SOURCE	DATE	AFFIRMATIVE	NEGATIVE
001	Journal, 405	January 6, 1796	78	17

To charge Robert Randall with contempt for attempting to bribe certain House members

002	Journal, 407	January 7, 1796	52	30

To discharge Charles Whitnes to allow him time to prepare a defense against Representative Buck's charges of a bribe attempt

003	Annals, 759	March 24, 1796	62	37

The Livingston Resolution calling for the Jay Treaty papers

004	Annals, 820	March 28, 1796	23	68

To recommit a bill for relief and protection of American seamen

Fourth Congress

ROLL CALL	SOURCE	DATE	AFFIRMATIVE	NEGATIVE
005	Annals, 820	March 28, 1796	77	13

Passage of a bill for the relief and protection of American seamen

006	Annals, 768	March 30, 1796	55	37

To meet in Committee of the Whole to consider Washington's refusal to furnish Jay Treaty papers

007	Annals, 840	March 31, 1796	72	21

To lend the city of Washington up to $300,000 at 6 percent per annum

008	Journal, 495	April 5, 1796	40	45

To subdivide land northwest of the Ohio River into 320-acre lots

009	Journal, 496	April 5, 1796	45	42

To subdivide into 160-acre tracts

010	Annals, 771	April 6, 1796	57	36

To meet in Committee of the Whole on Washington's response to Livingston Resolution

011	Annals, 782	April 7, 1796	54	37

To consider resolution that House had right to consider the Jay Treaty

012	Annals, 782	April 7, 1796	57	35

Passage of resolution voted on in number 011

013	Annals, 783	April 7, 1796	57	35

Resolution that the House need not furnish the reason for its request for papers

014	Annals, 886	April 8, 1796	55	36

To increase the number of frigates to be outfitted

Fourth Congress

ROLL CALL	SOURCE	DATE	AFFIRMATIVE	NEGATIVE
015	Annals, 891	April 8, 1796	25	57
	To outfit two frigates instead of three			
016	Annals, 893	April 9, 1796	62	23
	To outfit three frigates			
017	Annals, 905	April 11, 1796	36	47
	To strike out provision for forfeiture of Indian land settled by whites			
018	Journal, 513	April 14, 1796	90	0
	Passage of resolution approving the Pinckney Treaty			
019	Annals, 974	April 14, 1796	37	55
	To commit resolution against the Jay Treaty			
020	Annals, 1289	April 30, 1796	49	50
	To approve the Jay Treaty while calling it "highly objectionable"			
021	Annals, 1291	April 30, 1796	51	48
	Resolution to carry the Jay Treaty into effect			
022	Annals, 1328	May 6, 1796	43	30
	To admit the Territory of Tennessee as a state			
023	Annals, 1337	May 9, 1796	51	34
	To raise pay of the secretaries of state, treasury, and war			
024	Annals, 1373	May 13, 1796	14	64
	To continue consideration of fortifications for New York City harbor			
025	Annals, 1384	May 16, 1796	49	30
	Passage of the bill voted on in number 023			

Fourth Congress

ROLL CALL	SOURCE	DATE	AFFIRMATIVE	NEGATIVE
026	Annals, 1416	May 20, 1796	19	50

To raise the salary of the accountant of the War Department from $1,600 to $1,900

027	Annals, 1419	May 21, 1796	22	58

To accept Senate proposal to retain all light dragoons currently in the army

028	Annals, 1422	May 21, 1796	34	49

To retain the post of major general

029	Annals, 1426	May 23, 1796	56	26

To further indemnify the widow of General Greene

030	Annals, 1429	May 23, 1796	25	51

To reconsider number 027

031	Annals, 1430	May 23, 1796	37	45

To reconsider number 028

032	Journal, 576	May 25, 1796	33	49

To require 25-percent payment in advance on sales of government land

033	Journal, 577	May 25, 1796	45	35

To sell government shares of stock in the Bank of the United States

034	Journal, 578	May 25, 1796	55	24

Passage of a bill to indemnify the widow of General Greene

035	Annals, 1464	May 27, 1796	40	35

To postpone consideration of adding an agent to the treasury for foreign expenses

Fourth Congress

ROLL CALL	SOURCE	DATE	AFFIRMATIVE	NEGATIVE
036	Annals, 1472	May 28, 1796	45	35

To allow government debt shares bearing 6-percent interest to sell below par

037	Annals, 1473	May 28, 1796	48	30

To admit Tennessee without first taking a census

038	Journal, 588	May 28, 1796	5	62

To assign Tennessee two representatives rather than one

039	Journal 589	May 28, 1796	41	29

To assign Tennessee one representative rather than none

040	Annals, 1496	May 31, 1796	39	25

To appropriate $20,000 for spoliation claims in connection with Pinckney Treaty

041	Annals, 1489	May 31, 1796	40	34

To postpone consideration of a bill prohibiting the sale of prizes

042	Annals, 1497	May 31, 1796	28	41

To unseat Israel Smith in favor of Matthew Lyon

043	Annals, 1666	December 15, 1796	30	49

To add to the response to Washington's last annual address an assurance that the citizens would remember the "character and dignity of our Government"

044	Annals, 1667	December 15, 1796	24	54

To strike from the response words indicating hope that posterity would follow Washington's example

045	Annals, 1667	December 15, 1796	67	12

To consent to the response to the president

Fourth Congress

ROLL CALL	SOURCE	DATE	AFFIRMATIVE	NEGATIVE
046	Annals, 1727	December 28, 1796	55	24

To reject relief for Savannah after its major fire

047	Annals, 1810	January 5, 1797	57	26

Request for payment by the states of debts incurred prior to 1789

048	Annals, 1812	January 5, 1797	23	62

To refuse payment on assumed state debts until debtor states paid the federal government what they owed under the general settlement of accounts

049	Journal, 748	January 17, 1797	53	36

To print confidential reports on the situation with Algiers

050	Annals, 1933	January 20, 1797	48	39

To impose a land tax

051	Annals, 1941	January 20, 1797	68	23

To include a tax on slaves

052	Annals, 1941	January 20, 1797	49	39

To agree to resolutions in numbers 050 and 051 as one main motion

053	Annals, 1981	January 24, 1797	44	39

To reduce the army from four regiments to three

054	Annals, 1982	January 24, 1797	18	64

To restore the dragoons

055	Annals, 1984	January 25, 1797	44	28

To reject a petition against Joseph Varnum's election

056	Annals, 2010	January 27, 1797	39	49

To raise by $500 the salaries of the secretary of war and the attorney general

Fourth Congress

ROLL CALL	SOURCE	DATE	AFFIRMATIVE	NEGATIVE
057	Annals, 2010	January 27, 1797	51	39

To deny a permanent raise to the secretary of war

058	Annals, 2012	January 27, 1797	57	32

To give raises, for 1797 only, to all cabinet members

059	Annals, 2013	January 27, 1797	60	27

To give loan officers of Massachusetts and New York a bonus, for 1797 only, of $375

060	Annals, 2079	February 2, 1797	49	37

To disallow any further claims for lost loan office certificates

061	Annals, 2094	February 7, 1797	50	44

To reduce the present four regiments to three

062	Annals, 2105	February 9, 1797	58	38

To reject a bill raising the salaries of the president and the vice-president

063	Annals, 2148	February 11, 1797	63	28

To repeal prior acts concerning the outfitting of naval vessels

064	Annals, 2149	February 11, 1797	69	21

To build three frigates

065	Annals, 2150	February 11, 1797	62	29

To reject use of live-oak and red cedar timber for naval purposes

066	Annals, 2150	February 11, 1797	38	47

To bring in only one bill to implement authorization for three frigates

067	Annals, 2153	February 13, 1797	63	25

To bring in a bill, or bills, to build three frigates

Fourth Congress

ROLL CALL	SOURCE	DATE	AFFIRMATIVE	NEGATIVE
068	Annals, 2162	February 15, 1797	57	19

To repeal duties on distilled spirits and to lay them instead on capacity of stills

069	Annals, 2208	February 18, 1797	59	25

To add appropriations to build three frigates to the naval appropriations bill

070	Annals, 2235	February 21, 1797	19	65

To remove secrecy injunction from reports on situation with Algiers

071	Journal, 711	February 21, 1797	50	36

To remove secrecy injunction from president's message on the matter

072	Annals, 2246	February 22, 1797	63	19

To authorize money for negotiations and payment for the Dey and Regency of Algiers

073	Annals, 2280	February 24, 1797	30	60

To increase duties not only on cotton goods but on other cloths as well

074	Annals, 2289	February 25, 1797	66	21

To engross a bill laying additional duties on certain imports

075	Annals, 2292	February 25, 1797	50	34

To allow remission of fines in certain tax cases

076	Annals, 2310	February 27, 1797	54	27

To authorize funds to prosecute claims for property captured by belligerent powers

077	Annals, 2319	February 27, 1797	63	27

To allow President Adams to spend up to $14,000 on furnishings

Fourth Congress

ROLL CALL	SOURCE	DATE	AFFIRMATIVE	NEGATIVE
078	Annals, 2332	March 1, 1797	55	36
	To override Washington's veto of bill reducing the military establishment			
079	Annals, 2351	March 2, 1797	45	47
	To finish only the hulls of the three frigates			
080	Annals, 2351	March 2, 1797	58	32
	Passage of bill to finish the whole of the three frigates			
081	Annals, 2351	March 2, 1797	39	31
	To require newsprint to be sufficiently dried before delivery by mail			
082	Journal, 738	March 3, 1797	54	15
	To move the district court of North Carolina to Newbern			
083	Annals, 2361	March 3, 1797	36	52
	To increase executive flexibility in expending appropriations			

Fifth Congress

ROLL CALL	SOURCE	DATE	AFFIRMATIVE	NEGATIVE
001	Annals, 210	June 1, 1797	48	46
	Resolution implying that the people had full confidence in the new administration			
002	Annals, 216	June 1, 1797	49	50
	Resolution to place France in the position of an outlaw			
003	Annals, 230	June 2, 1797	51	48
	To require compensation from France for injury done to America's neutral rights			

Fifth Congress

ROLL CALL	SOURCE	DATE	AFFIRMATIVE	NEGATIVE
004	Annals, 230	June 2, 1797	78	21

To approve the sentiments in number 003 as a resolution

005	Annals, 231	June 2, 1797	58	41

Resolution expressing satisfaction with Adams' attempt to negotiate with France

006	Annals, 233	June 2, 1797	45	53

To recommit the reply to the president that included above provisions

007	Annals, 233	June 2, 1797	62	36

Passage of reply to the president

008	Annals, 267	June 8, 1797	74	8

Consideration of a bill to prevent exportation of arms and ammunition

009	Annals, 297	June 10, 1797	68	21

Resolution authorizing Adams to use galleys for coastal defense

010	Annals, 319	June 15, 1797	50	44

To allow New York to deduct fortification expenses from its debt to federal government

011	Annals, 323	June 15, 1797	48	41

Allocation of $115,000 for military fortifications on federal property

012	Annals, 324	June 16, 1797	54	35

Passage of the Act for Defense of Ports and Harbors

013	Annals, 347	June 20, 1797	57	39

To reject Senate bill for raising an additional corps of artillery and engineers

Fifth Congress

ROLL CALL	SOURCE	DATE	AFFIRMATIVE	NEGATIVE
014	Annals, 355	June 21, 1797	34	57

To reject prosecution for treason of expatriates joining a foreign army or navy

015	Annals, 356	June 21, 1797	52	44

To postpone for five months consideration of the expatriation bill

016	Annals, 358	June 22, 1797	51	47

To adjourn on June 28, 1797

017	Annals, 374	June 23, 1797	50	48

To prevent use of frigates as merchant marine convoys

018	Annals, 374	June 23, 1797	72	25

To eliminate provision for nine additional twenty-gun vessels

019	Annals, 375	June 23, 1797	46	52

To sharply restrict use of cutters to coastal operations only

020	Annals, 375	June 23, 1797	82	14

To authorize use of cutters for coastal defense

021	Annals, 376	June 23, 1797	53	43

To limit the duration of the protection of trade bill to one year

022	Annals, 385	June 24, 1797	70	25

Passage of the protection of trade bill

023	Annals, 391	June 27, 1797	56	27

Passage of a bill laying additional duties on wines and spirits

024	Annals, 392	June 27, 1797	29	61

To postpone for five months consideration of the protection of trade bill

Fifth Congress

ROLL CALL	SOURCE	DATE	AFFIRMATIVE	NEGATIVE
025	Annals, 392	June 27, 1797	46	50

To adhere to prohibition on use of frigates as merchant convoys

026	Annals, 409	June 29, 1797	51	47

To recede from prohibition on use of frigates as merchant convoys

027	Annals, 430	July 1, 1797	46	42

To impose a tax of $5 on certificates of naturalization

028	Annals, 431	July 1, 1797	71	12

To exempt patents for military lands from the stamp tax

029	Annals, 432	July 1, 1797	76	11

To strike out the exemption of bank notes from the stamp tax

030	Annals, 432	July 1, 1797	37	40

To allow courts to receive in evidence papers not legally stamped

031	Annals, 433	July 3, 1797	47	41

Passage of the stamp tax

032	Annals, 443	July 4, 1797	47	41

To impose a duty of eight cents per bushel on salt

033	Annals, 446	July 5, 1797	47	43

To limit the duration of the salt tax to two years

034	Annals, 446	July 5, 1797	45	40

Passage of the salt tax

035	Annals, 637	November 24, 1797	57	20

To reply to the president's speech in writing

036	Annals, 700	December 11, 1797	45	45

To consider a bill for protection of commerce and defense of the country

Fifth Congress

ROLL CALL	SOURCE	DATE	AFFIRMATIVE	NEGATIVE
037	Annals, 756	December 20, 1797	68	25

To engross a bill to discourage circulation of foreign currency

| 038 | Annals, 808 | January 5, 1798 | 40 | 43 |

To allow the daughters of Count de Grasse an annuity

| 039 | Annals, 808 | January 5, 1798 | 55 | 25 |

Passage of an annuity of $400 for each of the Count's four daughters

| 040 | Annals, 955 | January 30, 1798 | 49 | 44 |

To consider expulsion of Matthew Lyon (for spitting at Roger Griswold)

| 041 | Annals, 956 | January 30, 1798 | 29 | 62 |

To place Lyon in the custody of the Sergeant-at-Arms until further notice

| 042 | Journal, 161 | February 5, 1798 | 88 | 4 |

To consider all evidence against Lyon in Committee of the Whole

| 043 | Journal, 177 | February 12, 1798 | 44 | 52 |

To censure Lyon

| 044 | Annals, 1008 | February 12, 1798 | 52 | 44 |

To expel Lyon (two-thirds vote required)

| 045 | Annals, 1047 | February 19, 1798 | 35 | 55 |

To set aside the act of limitation on the claims of Amy Dardin

| 046 | Annals, 1060 | February 21, 1798 | 46 | 48 |

To commit federal government to paying compensation to holders of land in Indian territory

| 047 | Annals, 1063 | February 23, 1798 | 38 | 53 |

To postpone Griswold-Lyon case for one year (Griswold had hit Lyon with a poker)

Fifth Congress

ROLL CALL	SOURCE	DATE	AFFIRMATIVE	NEGATIVE
048	Annals, 1066	February 23, 1798	73	21
	To oppose a resolution expelling both Griswold and Lyon			
049	Annals, 1067	February 23, 1797	47	48
	To reprimand both Griswold and Lyon			
050	Annals, 1080	February 26, 1798	41	52
	To postpone consideration of stamp duties for three weeks			
051	Journal, 205	February 26, 1798	44	49
	To postpone consideration of stamp duties for one week			
052	Annals, 1083	February 26, 1798	52	36
	To bring in a bill to repeal the stamp tax			
053	Annals, 1098	February 28, 1798	51	42
	Third reading of repeal of stamp duties			
054	Journal, 213	March 5, 1798	48	52
	To limit salaries of special envoys			
055	Annals, 1267	March 15, 1798	29	58
	To provide for trial of matters involving two states			
056	Annals, 1295	March 21, 1798	44	44
	To postpone consideration of action on spectators recording House debates			
057	Annals, 1295	March 21, 1798	50	36
	To reject providing a special place for those recording House debates			
058	Annals, 1371	April 2, 1798	65	27
	To request papers related to the XYZ affair			
059	Journal, 258	April 11, 1798	32	54
	To specify by place appropriations for defense of ports and harbors			

Fifth Congress

ROLL CALL	SOURCE	DATE	AFFIRMATIVE	NEGATIVE
060	Journal, 262	April 16, 1798	36	45
	To limit the duration of a bill to increase the regular army			
061	Journal, 267	April 20, 1798	45	37
	To outfit twelve ships instead of sixteen			
062	Journal, 268	April 20, 1798	32	50
	To limit narrowly to defensive operations the vessels approved in number 061			
063	Journal, 272	April 25, 1798	47	41
	To engross a bill to establish a Navy Department			
064	Journal, 273	April 25, 1798	39	31
	To raise the salary of the Clerk of the House			
065	Journal, 285	May 4, 1798	49	37
	To reject allowing Thomas Pinckney to receive presents from Great Britain and Spain			
066	Journal, 294	May 15, 1798	46	43
	To refer to Committee of the Whole a petition against recent government actions			
067	Journal, 296	May 17, 1798	53	35
	To limit the president's power to call out the provisional army			
068	Journal, 297	May 17, 1798	64	26
	To call out the provisional army only after declaration of war, invasion, or imminent invasion			
069	Journal, 298	May 17, 1798	56	35
	To cut the provisional army from 20,000 men to 10,000 men			
070	Journal, 299	May 17, 1798	39	51
	To use state militia rather than new volunteers for the provisional army			

Fifth Congress

ROLL CALL	SOURCE	DATE	AFFIRMATIVE	NEGATIVE
071	Journal, 300	May 17, 1798	40	50

To reduce from three years to six months the time for recruiting the provisional army

072	Journal, 301	May 18, 1798	51	40

Passage of the bill to add to the provisional army

073	Journal, 307	May 22, 1798	26	45

To pay federal marshals through fees for service rather than salary

074	Journal, 308	May 22, 1798	35	45

Same as number 073

075	Journal, 309	May 23, 1798	46	44

To recommit the alien enemies bill

076	Journal, 313	May 26, 1798	20	70

To apply defense provisions not only against France but also all other nations

077	Journal, 315	May 26, 1798	50	40

Third reading of a bill to defend harbors

078	Journal, 321	June 1, 1798	55	25

Passage of a bill to suspend commerce with France

079	Journal, 326	June 7, 1798	46	34

To increase flexibility in spending of military appropriations

080	Journal, 327	June 7, 1798	49	32

Passage of a bill to regulate pay of internal revenue collectors

081	Journal, 329	June 8, 1798	41	42

To consider resolutions that (1) treaty with France no longer obligatory, (2) reprisals should apply to all French ships, and (3) bounties for captured ships

Fifth Congress

ROLL CALL	SOURCE	DATE	AFFIRMATIVE	NEGATIVE
082	Journal, 332	June 11, 1798	22	59

Proposed land tax should apply to all property taxed by the respective states

| 083 | Annals, 1916 | June 12, 1798 | 28 | 47 |

To allow merchant vessels to "attack, take, or destroy" any hostile vessel

| 084 | Annals, 1925 | June 13, 1798 | 69 | 19 |

Passage of the direct tax bill

| 085 | Annals, 1938 | June 15, 1798 | 55 | 17 |

To provide arms for militia throughout the country

| 086 | Annals, 1950 | June 15, 1798 | 42 | 39 |

To expand president's power to appoint officers to the provisional army

| 087 | Annals, 1953 | June 15, 1798 | 35 | 46 |

To force army volunteers to purchase their own hand weapons

| 088 | Annals, 1954 | June 16, 1798 | 42 | 30 |

Passage of the supplementary provisional army bill

| 089 | Annals, 2028 | June 21, 1798 | 46 | 40 |

Passage of alien enemies bill

| 090 | Annals, 2042 | June 25, 1798 | 37 | 38 |

To limit the amount of executive borrowing for public service to $5 million

| 091 | Annals, 2048 | June 25, 1798 | 34 | 48 |

To limit the amount of interest that could be paid on the loan in number 090

Fifth Congress

ROLL CALL	SOURCE	DATE	AFFIRMATIVE	NEGATIVE
092	Annals, 2059	June 29, 1798	32	46
	To make the direct tax equal on houses, land, and other improvements			
093	Annals, 2059	June 29, 1798	24	54
	To tax slaves at fifty cents each			
094	Annals, 2060	June 29, 1798	38	39
	To tax lands at the same rate as the lowest rate of tax on buildings			
095	Annals, 2066	July 2, 1798	62	18
	Passage of direct tax bill			
096	Annals, 2082	July 2, 1798	39	43
	To disallow outfitting privateers to cruise against French vessels			
097	Annals, 2082	July 2, 1798	31	52
	To authorize attacks on all French vessels, including unarmed merchant marine			
098	Annals, 2086	July 3, 1798	30	51
	That the president should instruct Elbridge Gerry to continue negotiations in Paris			
099	Annals, 2092	July 5, 1798	40	40
	To authorize twelve new regiments instead of eight			
100	Annals, 2113	July 5, 1798	36	47
	To reject the Sedition Act			
101	Annals, 2127	July 6, 1798	47	37
	Passage of a bill invalidating the treaty with France			
102	Annals, 2131	July 7, 1798	29	43
	To authorize eight regiments instead of twelve			

Fifth Congress

ROLL CALL	SOURCE	DATE	AFFIRMATIVE	NEGATIVE
103	Annals, 2132	July 9, 1798	60	11
	Passage of a bill increasing the size of the regular army			
104	Annals, 2137	July 9, 1798	67	15
	To allow juries to determine the law and the fact in sedition cases			
105	Annals, 2138	July 9, 1798	43	39
	To make action rather than advocacy punishable under the sedition law			
106	Annals, 2171	July 10, 1798	44	41
	Passage of the Sedition Act			
107	Annals, 2176	July 13, 1798	45	28
	To allow debtor states credits for their expenditures for defense fortifications			
108	Annals, 2178	July 13, 1798	34	36
	Passage of bill granting bounties for capture of armed French ships			
109	Annals, 2179	July 13, 1798	29	43
	To allow merchants to sign an oath rather than post a bond to guarantee compliance with embargo on trade with France			
110	Annals, 2181	July 14, 1798	40	41
	To bring in a bill to provide bounties for capture of armed French vessels			
111	Annals, 2453	December 14, 1798	35	41
	To print copies of the Constitution along with copies of the Alien and Sedition Acts			
112	Journal, 412	December 14, 1798	29	47
	To print those parts of the Constitution related to the Alien and Sedition Acts			

Fifth Congress

ROLL CALL	SOURCE	DATE	AFFIRMATIVE	NEGATIVE
113	Annals, 2454	December 14, 1798	32	45
	To print copies of the Bill of Rights			
114	Annals, 2455	December 14, 1798	34	45
	To print the Alien and Sedition Acts for general distribution			
115	Annals, 2485	December 21, 1798	11	69
	To delay impeachment proceedings against William Blount			
116	Annals, 2545	December 28, 1798	65	23
	Resolution to prepare a bill to outlaw usurpation of executive authority			
117	Annals, 2590	January 9, 1799	35	51
	Amendment to usurpation bill to allow prosecution under existing treason laws			
118	Annals, 2599	January 9, 1799	37	48
	To exclude from usurpation bill persons seeking release of seamen or restoration of property or debts			
119	Annals, 2648	January 11, 1799	49	44
	To recommit the bill on executive usurpation			
120	Annals, 2676	January 15, 1799	44	47
	Passage of the usurpation of executive authority bill			
121	Annals, 2679	January 16, 1799	69	27
	To exclude from usurpation bill persons seeking redress for personal injury or loss			
122	Annals, 2680	January 16, 1799	41	56
	To limit the duration of the usurpation bill to one year			
123	Annals, 2680	January 16, 1799	39	57
	To include consideration of intent in usurpation bill			

Fifth Congress

ROLL CALL	SOURCE	DATE	AFFIRMATIVE	NEGATIVE
124	Annals, 2681	January 16, 1799	61	35

To disallow unauthorized negotiations by government officials

125	Annals, 2721	January 17, 1799	58	36

Passage of the usurpation of executive authority bill

126	Journal, 442	January 18, 1799	54	33

To take the census in May 1799 rather than April 1800

127	Annals, 2789	January 25, 1799	36	53

To restrict the president's power to suspend trade with France's allies

128	Annals, 2790	January 25, 1799	57	32

To limit duration of president's power to suspend commerce to March 3, 1800

129	Annals, 2790	January 25, 1799	55	34

To exclude Mississippi River trade from power allowed in numbers 127 and 128

130	Annals, 2791	January 28, 1799	18	74

To reconsider the amendment passed in number 129

131	Annals, 2791	January 28, 1799	55	37

Passage of bill allowing president to suspend trade with hostile ports

132	Annals, 2792	January 28, 1799	53	33

To consider pay raises for officers in the executive branch

133	Annals, 2802	January 30, 1799	73	20

To refer to committee a petition against the alien and sedition laws

134	Annals, 2814	January 31, 1799	49	40

To allow stamp tax collectors a compensation of 4 percent of amount collected

Fifth Congress

ROLL CALL	SOURCE	DATE	AFFIRMATIVE	NEGATIVE
135	Annals, 2819	February 1, 1799	47	45

To reject pay increase for collectors of the direct tax

136	Annals, 2822	February 7, 1799	59	32

To exclude from president's power to suspend commerce all Spanish and Dutch ports

137	Annals, 2856	February 8, 1799	40	54

To eliminate provision for building six ships of seventy-four guns each

138	Annals, 2883	February 11, 1799	54	42

Passage of a bill to augment the navy

139	Annals, 2905	February 12, 1799	51	48

To refer to committee memorials against the act concerning aliens

140	Annals, 2915	February 14, 1799	52	38

To call for information from Adams about peaceful overtures by France

141	Annals, 2953	February 20, 1799	52	48

To eliminate a proposed bounty for capture of armed French vessels

142	Annals, 2973	February 23, 1799	49	45

To expel Matthew Lyon (two-thirds vote required)

143	Annals, 2974	February 23, 1799	57	36

To raise the pay of tax assessors from $1.50 to $2 per day

144	Journal 493	February 25, 1799	52	48

Resolution that it is inexpedient to repeal the Alien Enemies Act

145	Journal, 494	February 25, 1799	52	48

Resolution that it is inexpedient to repeal the sedition laws

Fifth Congress

ROLL CALL	SOURCE	DATE	AFFIRMATIVE	NEGATIVE
146	Annals, 3016	February 25, 1799	52	48

Resolution that it is inexpedient to repeal any laws concerning army, navy, or revenue

147	Annals, 3018	February 26, 1799	52	45

To increase the army only if war actually broke out

148	Annals, 3019	February 27, 1799	52	43

To increase the salaries of certain executive officers

149	Journal, 505	March 1, 1799	56	15

Passage of a bill for the relief of Comfort Sands

150	Annals, 3042	March 1, 1799	51	44

Army volunteers could not be compelled to serve out of their state of residence

151	Annals, 3043	March 1, 1799	39	56

To deny the president the power to appoint officers for proposed new regiments

152	Annals, 3044	March 1, 1799	54	41

Passage of a bill authorizing twenty-four more army regiments

153	Annals, 3052	March 2, 1799	56	30

To vest power of retaliation, in certain cases, in the president

Sixth Congress

ROLL CALL	SOURCE	DATE	AFFIRMATIVE	NEGATIVE
001	Annals, 222	December 30, 1799	39	45

To eliminate secretary of state from responsibility for the census

002	Annals, 244	January 3, 1800	84	1

To reject petition from Absalom Jones and other free blacks for emancipation

003	Annals, 369	January 10, 1800	60	39

To reject a resolution calling for reduction of the army

004	Annals, 403	January 23, 1800	10	82

To postpone consideration of army reduction until the next session

005	Annals, 403	January 23, 1800	38	57

To discontinue further enlistments for the new army

006	Annals, 419	January 23, 1800	50	48

To repeal the sedition law

007	Annals, 423	January 23, 1800	51	47

To make crimes just repealed punishable under common law

008	Annals, 425	January 23, 1800	11	87

To approve the combination imposed by passage of numbers 006 and 007

009	Annals, 502	January 28, 1800	43	50

To recommit the unfavorable report of the committee to which John Randolph's petition to the president on a breach of privilege had been committed

010	Annals, 505	January 29, 1800	42	56

To insert in the report a condemnation of the conduct of Randolph's attackers

Sixth Congress

ROLL CALL	SOURCE	DATE	AFFIRMATIVE	NEGATIVE
011	Annals, 505	January 29, 1800	61	39

To insert a statement that their conduct had been improper

012	Annals, 507	January 29, 1800	49	51

To agree that Randolph's case lacked sufficient evidence for further action

013	Annals, 506	January 29, 1800	56	42

To disallow a vote on the resolve disapproving the conduct of Randolph's attackers

014	Annals, 508	January 31, 1800	41	56

To consider a uniform bankruptcy law

015	Annals, 521	February 12, 1800	43	51

To eliminate exemption given to army enlistees from imprisonment for debt

016	Annals, 530	February 19, 1800	39	56

To prohibit trade by neutrals between the United States and France

017	Annals, 530	February 19, 1800	50	46

To disallow shippers from the West Indies and Canada from trading between France and the United States

018	Annals, 531	February 20, 1800	68	28

Passage of a bill to continue suspension of trade with France

019	Annals, 534	February 21, 1800	48	48

To postpone consideration of the uniform bankruptcy bill

020	Annals, 557	February 26, 1800	14	76

To discontinue consideration in Committee of the Whole of the Jonathan Robbins case

Sixth Congress

ROLL CALL	SOURCE	DATE	AFFIRMATIVE	NEGATIVE
021	Annals, 577	February 27, 1800	32	63

To postpone calling for South Carolina Court records on the Robbins case

022	Annals 578	February 27, 1800	44	51

To ask Adams to furnish South Carolina Court records on the Robbins case

023	Annals, 587	March 4, 1800	46	54

To ask Adams to furnish related papers on the William Brigstock case

024	Annals, 594	March 5, 1800	46	46

Same as number 023 following a parliamentary maneuver

025	Annals, 595	March 6, 1800	59	38

To continue consideration of the Robbins case

026	Annals, 619	March 8, 1800	61	35

To disagree with resolutions critical of Adams' interference in the Robbins case

027	Annals, 621	March 10, 1800	62	35

To approve Adams' handling of the Robbins case

028	Annals, 623	March 12, 1800	47	44

To revoke commission of any Marine Corps officer refusing to deliver a subordinate to civil authority

029	Annals, 632	March 18, 1800	54	37

To disallow right of a territorial governor to prorogue the legislature

030	Annals, 633	March 18, 1800	52	39

Passage of a bill allowing the president to borrow money for public service

Sixth Congress

ROLL CALL	SOURCE	DATE	AFFIRMATIVE	NEGATIVE
031	Annals, 642	March 24, 1800	87	4

To give Captain Thomas Truxton a gold medal for his capture of the *Vengence*

| 032 | Annals, 643 | March 24, 1800 | 41 | 41 |

Passage of a bill to relieve the trustees of Rhode Island College

| 033 | Annals, 644 | March 25, 1800 | 44 | 50 |

To postpone until the next session consideration of federal court revision

| 034 | Annals, 648 | March 28, 1800 | 46 | 52 |

Same as number 033

| 035 | Annals, 658 | April 7, 1800 | 30 | 57 |

To postpone a bill authorizing acceptance of Connecticut's cession of Western Reserve

| 036 | Annals, 659 | April 7, 1800 | 36 | 54 |

To postpone a bill to continue aid to fisheries

| 037 | Annals, 662 | April 9, 1800 | 54 | 36 |

To authorize Adams to accept the Western Reserve cession

| 038 | Annals, 666 | April 14, 1800 | 48 | 46 |

Same as number 033

| 039 | Annals, 667 | April 14, 1800 | 54 | 38 |

To continue the added salt duty passed by the Fifth Congress

| 040 | Annals, 674 | April 18, 1800 | 48 | 52 |

To postpone consideration of a mode for deciding disputed presidential elections

| 041 | Annals, 675 | April 18, 1800 | 44 | 50 |

To continue the added salt duty for two years rather than ten years

Sixth Congress

ROLL CALL	SOURCE	DATE	AFFIRMATIVE	NEGATIVE
042	Annals, 677	April 21, 1800	44	45

To postpone appointment of a vice admiral and four rear admirals to the navy

043	Annals, 682	April 23, 1800	42	49

To concur with Senate in allowing a territorial governor to prorogue the legislature

044	Annals, 685	April 25, 1800	46	34

To reject authorization of commissioners to settle land claims in Mississippi

045	Annals, 690	April 28, 1800	64	23

To postpone consideration of a bill to establish a military academy

046	Annals, 694	May 1, 1800	41	47

To reject joint House-Senate committee to examine presidential election disputes

047	Annals, 695	May 1, 1800	43	46

To amend the disputed elections bill to allow combined House-Senate vote to decide any irregularities

048	Annals, 697	May 1, 1800	52	37

Passage of the disputed elections bill

049	Annals, 699	May 3, 1800	67	5

To consider prohibiting the slave trade with foreign countries

050	Annals, 705	May 7, 1800	54	28

To lay an additional levy on sugar

051	Annals, 710	May 9, 1800	15	73

To "admit" rather than "reject" disputed presidential votes

Sixth Congress

ROLL CALL	SOURCE	DATE	AFFIRMATIVE	NEGATIVE
052	Annals, 712	May 10, 1800	54	19

To erect a mausoleum in Washington in George Washington's honor

| 053 | Annals, 714 | May 10, 1800 | 38 | 42 |

To authorize the president to discharge the new army immediately

| 054 | Annals, 714 | May 10, 1800 | 47 | 27 |

To give dischargees of the new army a bonus of one month's pay

| 055 | Annals, 791 | November 26, 1800 | 36 | 32 |

Passage of the reply to the president's address

| 056 | Annals, 816 | December 9, 1800 | 46 | 45 |

To limit the admission of stenographers to the galleries

| 057 | Annals, 836 | December 17, 1800 | 39 | 46 |

To reduce the second regiment of artillery from four to three battalions

| 058 | Annals, 853 | December 22, 1800 | 70 | 11 |

To inquire into the conduct of Governor Winthrop Sargent of Mississippi Territory

| 059 | Annals, 864 | December 23, 1800 | 44 | 40 |

Engrossing of a bill authorizing a mausoleum for George Washington

| 060 | Annals, 875 | January 1, 1801 | 45 | 37 |

Passage of a bill authorizing a mausoleum for George Washington

| 061 | Annals, 877 | January 2, 1801 | 47 | 33 |

To consider continuation of the sedition law in Committee of the Whole

| 062 | Annals, 889 | January 6, 1801 | 58 | 30 |

To take no action to redress the grievance of Sergeant-at-Arms Joseph Wheaton

| 063 | Annals, 889 | January 6, 1801 | 45 | 42 |

To reconsider number 062

Sixth Congress

ROLL CALL	SOURCE	DATE	AFFIRMATIVE	NEGATIVE
064	Annals, 890	January 6, 1801	50	38
	To take no action for Wheaton but to note that he had properly carried out his duty			
065	Annals, 906	January 12, 1801	49	42
	To modify the lines of the federal court of the Western District of Virginia			
066	Annals, 907	January 13, 1801	71	18
	To limit the privilege of appeal in civil suits to cases involving more than $400			
067	Annals, 908	January 13, 1801	36	53
	To allow circuit courts to hear suits for recovery of notes and bonds payable to assigns			
068	Annals, 909	January 13, 1801	55	35
	To disallow circuit courts from hearing suits for recovery of notes to assigns			
069	Annals, 910	January 15, 1801	41	47
	To place a two-year limit on tax on licenses for selling retail liquor			
070	Annals, 911	January 16, 1801	46	31
	To continue taxes on carriages, retail liquor licenses, and goods sold at auction			
071	Annals, 915	January 20, 1801	51	43
	Passage of bill to restructure the judiciary			
072	Annals, 975	January 23, 1801	49	48
	To continue in force the sedition law			
073	Annals, 978	January 27, 1801	67	13
	To release Samuel Lewis from prison			
074	Annals, 989	January 29, 1801	50	44
	To incorporate the Mine and Metal Company			

Sixth Congress

ROLL CALL	SOURCE	DATE	AFFIRMATIVE	NEGATIVE
075	Annals, 1008	February 9, 1801	47	53

To prevent adjournment of the House until completion of presidential balloting

076	Annals, 1009	February 9, 1801	45	54

To ballot for president behind closed doors

077	Annals, 1019	February 10, 1801	40	59

To postpone consideration of a bill to continue the embargo against France

078	Annals, 1019	February 10, 1801	57	37

To reject the bill continuing the embargo on trade with France

079	Annals, 1021	February 10, 1801	36	59

To ballot for president using tickets with pre-printed names

080	Annals, 1038	February 19, 1801	50	50

To reject a bill continuing the sedition law

081	Annals, 1042	February 20, 1801	48	54

To castigate Speaker Theodore Sedgwick for having expelled Samuel H. Smith from the galleries since he had in no way been disorderly

082	Annals, 1042	February 20, 1801	60	42

Same as number 081 except that a negative vote was for castigation

083	Annals, 1043	February 20, 1801	50	53

Same as number 081

084	Annals, 1049	February 21, 1801	49	53

To engross a bill continuing the sedition law

085	Annals, 1052	February 24, 1801	56	36

Passage of a bill to govern the District of Columbia

Sixth Congress

ROLL CALL	SOURCE	DATE	AFFIRMATIVE	NEGATIVE
086	Annals, 1057	February 26, 1801	48	49

To eliminate lifetime half-pay when unemployed guarantee for naval officers

087	Annals, 1057	February 26, 1801	53	40

To authorize discharge of men in marine corps not needed for naval service

088	Annals, 1058	February 26, 1801	70	27

To engross a bill reducing the navy

089	Annals, 1061	February 27, 1801	49	42

Third reading of uniform bankruptcy bill

090	Annals, 1061	February 27, 1801	69	18

Third reading of naval peace establishment bill

091	Annals, 1065	February 28, 1801	50	42

To reconsider allowing forced entry and arrest of persons in bankruptcy

092	Annals, 1071	March 2, 1801	34	49

To make the base of the mausoleum for Washington 100 square feet instead of 50 square feet

093	Annals, 1072	March 2, 1801	46	33

To concur with Senate on some minor details about the mausoleum

094	Annals, 1074	March 3, 1801	39	28

To pay the doorkeepers and Sergeant-at-Arms $200 extra for services during Jefferson-Burr election

095	Annals, 1074	March 3, 1801	38	40

To discontinue proceedings against Winthrop Sargent

096	Annals, 1079	March 3, 1801	40	35

To thank Theodore Sedgwick for his conduct as Speaker

APPENDIX II :
PARTY DESIGNATIONS

First Congress, Pro-administration (39)

Connecticut—Benjamin Huntington, Roger Sherman, Jonathan Sturges,
 Jonathan Trumbull, and Jeremiah Wadsworth
Delaware—John Vining
Maryland—Daniel Carroll, Benjamin Contee, George Gale, Joshua Seney,
 William Smith, and Michael Stone
Massachusetts—Fisher Ames, Benjamin Goodhue, George Leonard, George
 Partridge, Theodore Sedgwick, and George Thacher
New Hampshire—Abiel Foster and Nicholas Gilman
New Jersey—Elias Boudinot, Lambert Cadwallader, James Schureman, and
 Thomas Sinnickson
New York—Egbert Benson, John Hathorn, John Laurance, and Peter Sil-
 vester
North Carolina—John Steele and Hugh Williamson
Pennsylvania—George Clymer, Thomas Fitzsimons, Thomas Hartley, Fred-
 erick Muhlenberg, and Henry Wynkoop
Rhode Island—Benjamin Bourn
South Carolina—William Smith
Virginia—Richard Lee and Alexander White

First Congress, Anti-administration (27)

Georgia—Abraham Baldwin, James Jackson, and George Matthews
Massachusetts—Elbridge Gerry and Jonathan Grout
New Hampshire—Samuel Livermore
New York—William Floyd and Jeremiah Van Rensselaer
North Carolina—John Ashe, Timothy Bloodworth, and John Sevier
Pennsylvania—Daniel Hiester, John Muhlenberg, and Thomas Scott
South Carolina—Aedanus Burke, Daniel Huger, Thomas Sumter, and

Thomas Tucker
Virginia—Theodoric Bland, John Brown, Isaac Coles, William Giles, Samuel
   Griffin, James Madison, Andrew Moore, John Page, and Josiah Parker

Second Congress, Pro-administration (40)

Connecticut—James Hillhouse, Amasa Learned, Jonathan Sturges, Jonathan
   Trumbull, and Jeremiah Wadsworth
Delaware—John Vining
Maryland—William Hindman, Philip Key, William Vans Murray, William
   Pinkney, and Joshua Seney
Massachusetts—Fisher Ames, Sheasabub Bourne, Benjamin Goodhue,
   George Leonard, Theodore Sedgwick, George Thacher, and Artemus
   Ward
New Hampshire—Nicholas Gilman and Jeremiah Smith
New Jersey—Elias Boudinot, Jonathan Dayton, and Aaron Kitchell
New York—Egbert Benson, James Gordon, John Laurance, and Peter
   Silvester
North Carolina—William Grove, John Steele, and Hugh Williamson
Pennsylvania—Thomas Fitzsimons, Thomas Hartley, Israel Jacobs, and
   John Kittera
Rhode Island—Benjamin Bourn
South Carolina—Robert Barnwell and William Smith
Virginia—Richard Lee, Josiah Parker, and Alexander White

Second Congress, Anti-administration (32)

Georgia—Abraham Baldwin, John Milledge, Anthony Wayne, and Francis
   Willis
Kentucky—Christopher Greenup and Alexander Orr
Maryland—John Mercer, Upton Sheridine, and Samuel Sterett
Massachusetts—Elbridge Gerry
New Hampshire—Samuel Livermore
New Jersey—Abraham Clark
New York—Cornelius Schoonmaker and Thomas Tredwell
North Carolina—John Ashe and Nathaniel Macon
Pennsylvania—William Findley, Andrew Gregg, Daniel Hiester, and Fred-
   erick Muhlenberg
South Carolina—Daniel Huger, Thomas Sumter, and Thomas Tucker
Vermont—Nathaniel Niles and Israel Smith

Virginia–John Brown, William Giles, Samuel Griffin, James Madison, Andrew Moore, John Page, and Abraham Venable

Third Congress, Pro-administration (53)

Connecticut–Joshua Coit, James Hillhouse, Amasa Learned, Zephaniah Swift, Uriah Tracy, Jonathan Trumbull, and Jeremiah Wadsworth
Delaware–Henry Latimer
Maryland–George Dent, Benjamin Edwards, Uriah Forrest, William Hindman, and William Vans Murray
Massachusetts–Fisher Ames, Sheasabub Bourne, David Cobb, Peleg Coffin, Samuel Dexter, Dwight Foster, Benjamin Goodhue, Theodore Sedgwick, George Thacher, Peleg Wadsworth, and Artemus Ward
New Hampshire–Nicholas Gilman, Jeremiah Smith, and Paine Wingate
New Jersey–John Beatty, Elias Boudinot, Lambert Cadwallader, Jonathan Dayton, and Aaron Kitchell
New York–Ezekiel Gilbert, Henry Glen, James Gordon, Silas Talbot, John Van Alen, and John Watts
North Carolina–William Grove
Pennsylvania–James Armstrong, Thomas Fitzsimons, Thomas Hartley, William Irvine, and John Kittera
Rhode Island–Benjamin Bourn and Francis Malbone
South Carolina–Robert Harper and William Smith
Virginia–George Hancock, Richard Lee, John Page, Josiah Parker, and Robert Rutherford

Third Congress, Anti-administration (57)

Delaware–John Patten
Georgia–Abraham Baldwin and Thomas Carnes
Kentucky–Christopher Greenup and Alexander Orr
Maryland–Gabriel Christie, Gabriel Duvall, John Mercer, Samuel Smith, and Thomas Sprigg
Massachusetts–Henry Dearborn, Samuel Holton, and William Lyman
New Hampshire–John Sherburne
New Jersey–Abraham Clark
New York–Theodore Bailey, Thomas Tredwell, Philip Van Cortlandt, and Peter Van Gaasbeck

North Carolina–Thomas Blount, William Dawson, James Gillespie, Matthew Locke, Nathaniel Macon, Joseph McDowell, Alexander Mebane, Benjamin Williams, and Joseph Winston

Pennsylvania–William Findley, Andrew Gregg, Daniel Hiester, William Montgomery, Frederick Muhlenberg, John Muhlenberg, Thomas Scott, and John Smilie

South Carolina–Lemuel Benton, Alexander Gillon, John Hunter, Andrew Pickens, and Richard Winn

Vermont–Nathaniel Niles and Israel Smith

Virginia–Thomas Claiborne, Isaac Coles, William Giles, Samuel Griffin, Carter Harrison, John Heath, James Madison, Andrew Moore, Joseph Neville, Anthony New, John Nicholas, Francis Preston, Abraham Venable, and Francis Walker

Fourth Congress, Federalists (57)

Connecticut–Joshua Coit, Samuel Dana, James Davenport, Chauncey Goodrich, Roger Griswold, James Hillhouse, Nathaniel Smith, Zephaniah Swift, and Uriah Tracy

Maryland–Jeremiah Crabb, William Craik, George Dent, William Hindman, and William Vans Murray

Massachusetts–Fisher Ames, Theodore Bradbury, Dwight Foster, Nathaniel Freeman, Benjamin Goodhue, George Leonard, Samuel Lyman, John Reed, Theodore Sedgwick, Samuel Sewall, Thomas Skinner, George Thacher, and Peleg Wadsworth

New Hampshire–Abiel Foster, Nicholas Gilman, and Jeremiah Smith

New Jersey–Jonathan Dayton, Thomas Henderson, Aaron Kitchell, Isaac Smith, and Mark Thomson

New York–William Cooper, Ezekiel Gilbert, Henry Glen, John Van Alen, and John Williams

North Carolina–William Grove and William Strudwick

Pennsylvania–George Ege, Thomas Hartley, John Kittera, Samuel Sitgreaves, and Richard Thomas

Rhode Island–Benjamin Bourn, Francis Malbone, and Elisha Potter

South Carolina–Robert Harper and William Smith

Vermont–Daniel Buck

Virginia–George Hancock, John Page, Josiah Parker, and Robert Rutherford

Fourth Congress, Republicans (58)

Delaware—John Patten
Georgia—Abraham Baldwin and John Milledge
Kentucky—Christopher Greenup and Alexander Orr
Maryland—Gabriel Christie, Gabriel Duvall, Samuel Smith, Richard Sprigg,
    and Thomas Sprigg
Massachusetts—Henry Dearborn, William Lyman, and Joseph Varnum
New Hampshire—John Sherburne
New York—Theodore Bailey, John Hathorn, Jonathan Havens, Edward
    Livingston, and Philip Van Cortlandt
North Carolina—Thomas Blount, Nathan Bryan, Dempsey Burges, Jesse
    Franklin, James Gillespie, James Holland, Matthew Locke, Nathaniel
    Macon, and Absalom Tatom
Pennsylvania—David Bard, William Findley, Albert Gallatin, Andrew
    Gregg, Daniel Hiester, Samuel Maclay, Frederick Muhlenberg, John
    Richards, and John Swanwick
South Carolina—Lemuel Benton, Samuel Earle, Wade Hampton, and
    Richard Winn
Tennessee—Andrew Jackson
Vermont—Israel Smith
Virginia—Richard Brent, Samuel Cabell, Thomas Claiborne, John Clopton,
    Isaac Coles, William Giles, Carter Harrison, John Heath, George
    Jackson, James Madison, Andrew Moore, Anthony New, John
    Nicholas, Francis Preston, and Abraham Venable

Fifth Congress, Federalists (64)

Connecticut—John Allen, Jonathan Brace, Joshua Coit, Samuel Dana,
    James Davenport, William Edmond, Chauncey Goodrich, Roger
    Griswold, and Nathan Smith
Delaware—James Bayard
Maryland—George Baer, William Craik, John Dennis, George Dent, William
    Hindman, and William Matthews
Massachusetts—Bailey Bartlett, Theophilus Bradbury, Stephan Bullock,
    Dwight Foster, Samuel Lyman, Harrison Otis, Isaac Parker, John Reed,
    Samuel Sewall, William Shepard, George Thacher, and Peleg Wadsworth
New Hampshire—Abiel Foster, Jonathan Freeman, William Gordon,
    Jeremiah Smith, and Peleg Sprague

New Jersey—Jonathan Dayton, James Imlay, James Schureman, Thomas
  Sinnickson, and Mark Thomson
New York—David Brooks, James Cochran, Henry Glen, Hezekiel Hosmer,
  John Van Alen, and John Williams
North Carolina—William Grove and Richard Spaight
Pennsylvania—John Chapman, George Ege, Thomas Hartley, John Kittera,
  Samuel Sitgreaves, Richard Thomas, and Robert Waln
Rhode Island—Christopher Champlin and Elisha Potter
South Carolina—Robert Harper, Thomas Pinckney, John Rutledge, and
  William Smith of Charleston
Vermont—Lewis Morris
Virginia—Thomas Evans, James Machir, Daniel Morgan, and Josiah Parker

Fifth Congress, Republicans (53)

Georgia—Abraham Baldwin and John Milledge
Kentucky—Thomas Davis and John Fowler
Maryland—Samuel Smith and Richard Sprigg
Massachusetts—Nathaniel Freeman, Thomas Skinner, and Joseph Varnum
New York—Lucas Elmendorf, Jonathan Havens, Edward Livingston, and
  Philip Van Cortlandt
North Carolina—Thomas Blount, Nathan Bryan, Dempsey Burges, James
  Gillespie, Matthew Locke, Nathaniel Macon, Joseph McDowell,
  Richard Stanford, and Robert Williams
Pennsylvania—David Bard, Robert Brown, William Findley, Albert
  Gallatin, Andrew Gregg, John Hanna, Joseph Hiester, Blair McClena-
  chan, and John Swanwick
Rhode Island—Thomas Tillinghast
South Carolina—Lemuel Benton, William Smith of Pinckney, and Thomas
  Sumter
Tennessee—William Claiborne
Vermont—Matthew Lyon
Virginia—Richard Brent, Samuel Cabell, Thomas Claiborne, Matthew Clay,
  John Clopton, John Dawson, Joseph Eggleston, William Giles, Carter
  Harrison, David Holmes, Walter Jones, Anthony New, John Nicholas,
  Abraham Trigg, John Trigg, and Abraham Venable

Sixth Congress, Federalists (67)

Connecticut—Jonathan Brace, Samuel Dana, John Davenport, William
  Edmond, Chauncey Goodrich, Elizur Goodrich, Roger Griswold, and
  John Smith
Delaware—James Bayard
Georgia—James Jones and Benjamin Taliaferro
Maryland—George Baer, William Craik, John Dennis, George Dent, and
  John Thomas
Massachusetts—Bailey Bartlett, Dwight Foster, Silas Lee, Samuel Lyman,
  Ebenezer Mattoon, Harrison Otis, Nathan Read, John Reed, Theodore
  Sedgwick, Samuel Sewall, William Shepard, George Thacher, Peleg
  Wadsworth, and Lemuel Williams
New Hampshire—Abiel Foster, Jonathan Freeman, William Gordon, James
  Sheafe, and Samuel Tenney
New Jersey—Francis Davenport and James Imlay
New York—John Bird, William Cooper, Henry Glen, and Jonas Platt
North Carolina—Willis Alston, Joseph Dickson, William Grove, Archibald
  Henderson, and William Hill
Pennsylvania—Thomas Hartley, John Kittera, Richard Thomas, Robert
  Waln, and Henry Woods
Rhode Island—John Brown and Christopher Champlin
South Carolina—Robert Harper, Benjamin Huger, Abraham Nott, Thomas
  Pinckney, and John Rutledge
Vermont—Lewis Morris
Virginia—Thomas Evans, Samuel Goode, Edwin Gray, Henry Lee, John
  Marshall, Robert Page, Josiah Parker, and Levi Powell

Sixth Congress, Republicans (47)

Kentucky—Thomas Davis and John Fowler
Maryland—Gabriel Christie, Joseph Nicholson, and Samuel Smith
Massachusetts—Phanuel Bishop, Levi Lincoln, and Joseph Varnum
New Jersey—John Condit, Aaron Kitchell, and James Linn
New York—Theodore Bailey, Lucas Elmendorf, Jonathan Havens, Edward
  Livingston, John Smith, John Thompson, and Philip Van Cortlandt
North Carolina—Nathaniel Macon, Richard Spaight, Richard Stanford,
  David Stone, and Robert Williams
Pennsylvania—Robert Brown, Albert Gallatin, Andrew Gregg, John Hanna,

Joseph Hiester, Michael Leib, John Muhlenberg, John Smilie, and John
Stewart
South Carolina–Thomas Sumter
Tennessee–William Claiborne
Vermont–Matthew Lyon
Virginia–Samuel Cabell, Matthew Clay, John Dawson, Joseph Eggleston,
David Holmes, George Jackson, Anthony New, John Nicholas, John
Randolph, Littleton Tazewill, Abraham Trigg, and John Trigg

APPENDIX III :
STATISTICAL ANALYSES

The method of analysis and presentation employed throughout this study involved calculation of cohesion differences for pairs of voting blocs, division of these differences into ranges (usually 0 to 34 percent, 35 to 64 percent, and 65 to 100 percent), and discrimination of the differences among categories of roll calls (government power, foreign policy, the West, economic issues, partisan politics, and miscellaneous and personal). This procedure made possible detailed explanation of the process of inter-action between issue-oriented factions and office-seeking parties. More powerful techniques of statistical generalization provide parallel confirma-tion of the broad outlines of the conclusions reached in the main body of this study. This appendix begins with simple correlations and then builds from these a multiple regression equation. Finally, a factor analysis based on all roll calls during the period will be presented.

The data base consists of cohesion differences for each of fifty-four pairs of voting blocs analyzed for the years 1789 through 1801. These dif-ferences are separated, as in the entire study, into three ranges and a mean for each of six types of issue. When the "all roll calls" category is added to this, the data include 1,492 cohesion difference figures, each of which summarizes voting by 25 to 110 delegates on a series of roll calls.

Table 54 displays Pearson correlation coefficients that reveal strong lin-ear relationships among all variables measuring frequency of low cohesion or very high cohesion. The phenomenon of a strong inverse relationship between high and low cohesion differences denies a gradualistic interpreta-tion of developing polarization during the decade. That is, moderation was not characteristic of the years 1789 through 1801. For this reason, correla-tion analysis fails to elucidate occasions of moderate cohesion, providing only a clue to the pattern that moderateness on one type of issue was asso-ciated with moderateness on other issues as well.

The high levels of correlations on average cohesion differences assure that the structure of factional politics which this book sets forth, based partially on more traditional historical sources, provides as well a good mathematical solution. There are possible divisions into a larger number of categories of issues that would produce higher correlations, but such a procedure can be extended until each roll call is in its own category. In other words, the researcher chooses the number of roll call categories to be used knowing that more categories will produce higher correlations. Although no solution is optimum from a purely mathematical standpoint, the one chosen clearly produces strong linear relationships that are consistent over time.

Table 55 uses correlation analysis to demonstrate portions of common variance among different issues for similar cohesion levels. Again, moderation is most difficult to explain and least frequently associated across various issues, a fact that supports the hypothesis that voting blocs were issue-oriented in the 1790s. Variance in frequency of low cohesion levels shows greater communality, ranging as high as 59 percent on some government power issues. But common variance on low cohesion economic issues never exceeded 32 percent, and so we are often left with the major portion of voting behavior unexplained. Only when groups polarized sharply and frequently, mostly later in the decade, did unity consistently develop on different issues. These years, as demonstrated in Chapter 7, saw the triumph of party over faction. Finally, the data show how sharply averaging of cohesion differences and of issues changes the picture of legislative behavior. The bottom row of numbers in Table 55 (common variances between the mean cohesion difference for all roll calls and the respective means for each issue category) reveals the aggregate truth of high interdependence, even though common variance decreases radically at low and moderate cohesion levels. Clearly, researchers who wish to find only two legislative parties in the 1790s have a statistically average base for their conclusion, but the limits of such an hypothesis are equally evident.

Analysis of such highly correlated variables as these mean cohesion differences requires a sophisticated multivariate technique such as regression. Table 56 summarizes the expected high multiple r^2s produced using stepwise regression. Because all the variables are strongly related, the entry for a particular dependent variable in the table fluctuates greatly and the technique gives potentially misleading results. For example, if the regression procedure is controlled to force mean level of cohesion difference on foreign policy (F-A) as the first independent variable entered into the equation, it will "explain" 85 percent of the variance in mean cohesion difference for all roll calls (A-A), whereas Table 56 gives the correct (but potentially misleading) figure of 0 percent once other variables are in the equation.

Table 54. Correlations Among Categories of Roll Calls and Levels of Cohesion, 1789-1801

Range	Variable	Highest Six Correlations[a]					
Low (0 to 34 percent)							
Govt. power	(G-L)	G-A (-.89)	F-L (.77)	F-A (-.77)	A-L (-.77)	G-H (-.75)	W-A (-.75)
Foreign pol.	(F-L)	F-A (-.91)	A-L (.86)	A-A (-.82)	F-H (-.81)	G-A (-.80)	M-A (-.80)
Western	(W-L)	W-A (-.97)	W-H (-.86)	A-L (.84)	A-A (-.84)	G-A (-.81)	A-H (-.79)
Politics	(P-L)	P-A (-.92)	A-L (.89)	A-A (-.87)	A-H (-.79)	M-H (-.75)	W-L (.74)
Economic	(E-L)	P-H (-.93)	E-A (-.91)	P-A (-.83)	A-L (.71)	E-H (-.68)	A-A (-.67)
Misc.	(M-L)	M-A (-.92)	A-L (.83)	A-A (-.79)	F-A (-.77)	F-H (-.75)	W-H (-.73)
All issues	(A-L)	A-A (-.94)	P-A (-.89)	F-A (-.89)	P-L (.89)	F-L (.86)	W-L (.84)
Moderate (35 to 64 percent)							
Govt. power	(G-M)	A-M (.74)	G-H (-.66)	A-H (-.64)	E-H (-.58)	F-H (-.57)	P-H (-.55)
Foreign pol.	(F-M)	A-M (.58)	G-M (.45)	F-L (-.44)	P-M (.40)	G-L (-.37)	W-M (.32)
Western	(W-M)	A-M (.45)	W-L (-.40)	A-L (-.33)	P-M (.32)	F-M (.37)	P-L (.32)
Politics	(P-M)	A-M (.58)	M-M (.51)	P-H (-.44)	F-M (.40)	P-L (-.37)	E-L (.37)
Economic	(E-M)	A-M (.72)	W-H (-.55)	E-H (-.49)	G-H (-.48)	A-H (-.47)	G-A (-.46)
Misc.	(M-M)	A-M (.59)	P-M (.51)	P-H (-.48)	M-L (-.46)	E-M (.41)	G-M (.39)
All issues	(A-M)	G-M (.74)	E-M (.72)	E-H (-.61)	M-M (.58)	F-M (.58)	P-M (.58)
High (65 to 100 percent)							
Govt. power	(G-H)	G-A (.95)	A-H (.89)	A-A (.86)	F-A (.85)	F-H (.83)	W-A (.80)
Foreign pol.	(F-H)	F-A (.95)	A-H (.90)	A-A (.87)	M-A (.86)	M-H (.85)	G-H (.84)
Western	(W-H)	W-A (.94)	W-L (-.86)	A-H (.83)	M-A (.82)	A-A (.81)	G-H (.80)
Politics	(P-H)	E-A (.95)	E-L (-.93)	E-H (.94)	P-A (.90)	A-H (.87)	M-H (.84)
Economic	(E-H)	A-H (.93)	P-H (.92)	E-A (.91)	M-H (.89)	P-A (.87)	A-A (.87)
Misc.	(M-H)	A-H (.94)	A-A (.90)	E-H (.89)	M-A (.86)	F-H (.85)	P-H (.84)
All issues	(A-H)	M-H (.94)	A-A (.94)	G-H (.90)	G-H (.90)	F-H (.89)	M-A (.89)

Table 54. Correlations Among Categories of Roll Calls and Levels of Cohesion, 1789-1801 (Continued)

Range	Variable	Highest Six Correlations[a]					
Mean							
Govt. power	(G-A)	G-H (.95)	G-L (-.89)	A-A (.86)	F-A (.86)	A-H (.84)	W-A (.82)
Foreign pol.	(F-A)	F-H (.95)	A-A (.92)	F-L (-.91)	A-L (-.89)	A-H (.89)	G-A (.86)
Western	(W-A)	W-L (-.97)	W-H (.94)	A-A (.85)	M-A (.83)	A-H (.83)	G-A (.82)
Politics	(P-A)	A-A (.94)	A-H (.92)	P-L (-.92)	P-H (.90)	A-L (-.89)	E-A (.88)
Economic	(E-A)	P-H (.95)	E-L (-.91)	E-H (.91)	P-A (.88)	A-A (.85)	A-H (.84)
Misc.	(M-A)	A-A (.93)	A-L (-.90)	A-H (.90)	M-H (.86)	F-H (.86)	A-H (.86)
All issues	(A-A)	A-L (-.94)	A-H (.94)	P-A (.94)	M-A (.93)	F-A (.92)	M-H (.90)

[a]Coefficients greater than ±.29 are significant at the .01 level; coefficients greater than ±.43 are significant at the .001 level.

Table 55. Coefficients of Determination (r^2) for Categories of Roll Calls in Pairings of Equal Levels of Cohesion Difference (CD%), 1789–1801

Variable	CD%	Foreign Policy	West	Party	Economic	Misc & Personal	All
Government power	Low	.59	.54	.29	.07	.44	.59
	Moderate	.20	.01	.08	.19	.15	.55
	High	.71	.64	.54	.52	.62	.81
	Mean	.74	.67	.48	.30	.59	.74
Foreign policy	Low		.56	.44	.26	.53	.74
	Moderate		.10	.16	.03	.07	.34
	High		.56	.53	.56	.72	.81
	Mean		.64	.66	.49	.74	.85
Western issues	Low			.54	.13	.52	.70
	Moderate			.10	.05	.01	.20
	High			.36	.45	.54	.69
	Mean			.54	.31	.69	.72
Partisan politics	Low				.32	.45	.79
	Moderate				.00	.26	.34
	High				.84	.70	.76
	Mean				.77	.67	.88
Economic	Low					.30	.51
	Moderate					.17	.52
	High					.79	.86
	Mean					.57	.72
Misc. & Personal	Low						.69
	Moderate						.35
	High						.87
	Mean						.86
							Gov't. Power
ALL ROLL CALLS	MEAN	.85	.72	.88	.72	.86	.74

Table 56. Multiple Regression Analysis of Mean Cohesion Differences Among
Categories of Roll Calls, 1789-1801

Dependent Variable	R^2 Change For Independent Variables (From Table 54)						
	G-A	P-A	E-A	F-A	W-A	M-A	MULTIPLE R^2
A-A	.09	.87	0	0	0	.02	.98
G-A	–	.01	0	.74	.06	0	.81
P-A	0	–	.78	.01	.09	0	.88
E-A	0	.78	–	0	.02	.03	.83
F-A	.74	.02	0	–	0	.09	.85
W-A	.08	.03	0	.01	–	.68	.80
M-A	0	0	.04	.73	.06	–	.83

Table 57. Normalized Regression Coefficients Among Categories of Roll Calls,
1789-1801

Dependent Variable	Beta For Independent Variables (From Table 54)					
	G-A	P-A	E-A	F-A	W-A	M-A
A-A	.26	.31	.18	.09	.07	.10
G-A	–	-.15	0	.69	.46	-.09
P-A	-.11	–	.63	.27	.35	-.09
E-A	0	.89	–	-.06	-.40	.41
F-A	.53	.32	-.07	–	-.17	.37
W-A	.45	.54	-.44	-.21	–	.55
M-A	-.08	-.13	.38	.40	.46	–

A clearer understanding of the nature of interrelationships comes from
an examination of the normalized regression coefficients shown in Table
57. These beta or path coefficients summarize the complexities of legislative behavior analyzed in the present study. Variance in solidarity on party
roll calls explains more votes than any other category of issue (.31), a conclusion consistent with the tendency of partisan allegiance to diminish factional attachments. But government power (.26) and economic matters
(.18) also loom large in the decade as a whole. Moreover, variance in party
unity is itself explained in large measure by factionalism on economic
issues (.63) in a strong mutual relationship (.89 for party on economic).
The small negative coefficient for foreign policy on economic (-.06) and
the irrelevance of government power (.00) give powerful evidence that
congressmen in the 1790s voted in cohesive issue-oriented blocs until the
needs of party began to blur distinctions among different types of roll
calls. The deep ambiguity of delegates on the several facets of western poli-

cy is reflected in the close and conflicting pressures exerted by related matters (the coefficients being .55, .54, .45, -.44, and -.21). The mutual relationship between government power and foreign policy (.69, .53) suggests that they are part of an on-going process, aptly termed "securing the Revolution" by historian Richard Buel, that required establishment of strong central government at home and, after the Whiskey Rebellion, defense of this powerful state against the world community.

In sum, multiple regression techniques support the conclusions reached in the present study, though many of the nuances of legislative patterns must remain hidden using this telescopic procedure.

Factor analysis provides a particularly insightful statistical method to understand and explain human behavior. The technique begins by definition of a universe based on correlations among the data to be examined—in this case the twenty-eight variables listed in Table 54. Communality estimates give the researcher the clues needed to define the universe from which factors are to be extracted. The communalities, or portions of common variance, for W-M, F-M, G-M, and P-M are .32, .45, .56, and .61 respectively; again, moderation is most difficult to explain and is not a major part (in a statistical sense) of the universe of voting behavior in the 1790s. All the other twenty-four variables have communalities of at least .75, with eleven of these above .90. In sum, the universe rests equally upon high and low levels of unity, and upon cohesion differences for all categories of roll calls. The four most significant inferred factors extracted using a varimax rotation account for 88 percent of the total variance in the universe. The remaining 12 percent is not unimportant, for it reflects a low level of trivial roll calls, unanimous votes, log rolling, vote trading, and so forth. For the decade as a whole, however, the four factors shown in Table 58 explain voting behavior quite well.

The first factor alone explains nearly three of every five votes in the years 1789 through 1801. The loadings are consistently strongly negative on measures of low cohesion and strongly positive on measures of high cohesion. This factor, then, may be defined initially as the tendency toward unity. Further examination of loadings on categories of roll calls shows that the factor reflects primarily unity on the issues of government power, the West, and foreign policy. The second factor also reflects the trend toward unity, but its loadings are on economic matters and purely partisan roll calls. The third and fourth factors point to the underlying influence of moderation in legislative patterns. Although these two factors are less important in explaining votes, the separation of economic from other types of issues continues. These data support the conclusions (indicated also in

Table 58. Varimax Rotated Factor Matrix Among Categories of Roll Calls and Levels of Cohesion, 1789-1801

	Factor 1	Factor 2	Factor 3	Factor 4
Portion of Variance				
Explained	*59%*	*15%*	*9%*	*5%*
Variable (From				
Table 54)		*Factor Loadings*		
G–L (government power low)	–.82	–.03	–.27	–.08
G–M (government power moderate)	–.39	–.26	.47	.32
G–H (government power high)	.89	.19	–.13	–.16
G–A (government power mean)	.91	.13	.05	–.17
W–L (frontier low)	–.89	–.15	–.18	.07
W–M (frontier moderate)	.09	.12	.54	–.03
W–H (frontier high)	.92	.09	–.18	–.03
W–A (frontier mean)	.91	.14	.04	–.09
P–L (partisan politics low)	–.69	–.45	–.31	.16
P–M (partisan politics moderate)	.21	–.42	.61	.10
P–H (partisan politics high)	.47	.83	–.22	–.23
P–A (partisan politics mean)	.68	.66	.07	–.22
E–L (economic low)	–.23	–.90	–.03	–.15
E–M (economic moderate)	–.50	.26	.33	.58
E–H (economic high)	.63	.60	–.25	–.31
E–A (economic mean)	.48	.83	–.08	–.08
F–L (foreign policy low)	–.79	–.30	–.23	–.05
F–M (foreign policy moderate)	.11	–.07	.65	.07
F–H (foreign policy high)	.80	.40	–.20	.02
F–A (foreign policy mean)	.86	.36	.01	.01
M–L (miscellaneous low)	–.78	–.32	–.01	–.50
M–M (miscellaneous moderate)	.12	–.30	.28	.83
M–H (miscellaneous high)	.72	.53	–.22	–.16
M–A (miscellaneous mean)	.84	.45	–.05	.21
A–L (all roll calls low)	–.79	–.53	–.36	–.08
A–M (all roll calls moderate)	–.29	–.03	.94	.44
A–H (all roll calls high)	.83	.48	–.15	–.18
A–A (all roll calls mean)	.85	.51	.11	–.09

the regression analysis summarized in Table 57) that (1) government power and foreign policy issues were closely related; (2) economic matters involved a separate and distinct dimension of voting behavior; (3) strong partisanship (.83 for P-H on factor 2) ultimately triumphed over issue-oriented attitudes on economic issues (-.90 for E-L on factor 2); and (4) moderation is not merely less of high unity but a distinct phenomenon.

NOTES

Chapter 1: Introduction

1. Jacob E. Cooke, ed., *The Federalist* (Middletown, Connecticut: Wesleyan University Press, 1961), p. 346.

2. Ibid., p. 64.

3. Richard Buel, Jr., *Securing the Revolution: Ideology in American Politics, 1789–1815* (Ithaca: Cornell University Press, 1972). Buel's work addresses these questions, and provides rich and detailed analysis of the respective ideologies of Federalists and Republicans. Although I had the benefit of hearing portions of Buel's work while it was in progress, the finished book appeared too late for me to make full use of it in my own work. For the most part, Buel's concern is with the thinking of the two parties, whereas mine is with the voting of many of the same individuals. The two phenomena are not always the same.

4. The organization of every major successful American political party along community rather than ideological or class lines is a crucial factor in any comparison between America's two-party system and the multi-party systems of many Western European democracies.

5. William Chambers, "Party Development and the American Mainstream," in *The American Party Systems: Stages of Political Development,* ed. by Chambers and Walter Burnham (New York: Oxford University Press, 1967), pp. 44–51.

6. Theodore Lowi, "Party, Policy, and Constitution in America," in *The American Party Systems,* p. 239.

7. The method used herein begins with that set forth by Stuart Rice, *Quantitative Methods in Politics* (New York: Russell and Russell, 1969; 1st ed., 1928), pp. 207–238. The difficulty with Rice's method is that, because it imposes no classification system on the roll calls, it provides few clues for defining issue-oriented and short-range voting blocs. However, using a computer to do the dreary calculations, the researcher can formulate various grouping systems and adjust their inclusiveness in terms of roll calls and of individuals until an acceptable solution is reached, from both a mathematical and a historical perspective. The equations used are based

on the same principle that underlies factor analysis: beneath a measurable reality (votes on roll calls) there lie several factors that "account for" or explain the given reality. Thus, the present study reduces hundreds of roll calls to four major issues. At the inclusiveness level (the number of members and the number of roll calls involved) of each group analyzed in this study, no other cluster of delegates and roll calls would provide a more cohesive voting pattern. I hope, also, to demonstrate that these mathematically optimum combinations make sense within a historical framework.

Several recent studies of legislative behavior make extensive use of "scaling" techniques to solve the problem of defining and measuring the strength of voting blocs. Two notable examples are Joel Silbey, *The Shrine of Party: Congressional Voting Behavior, 1841–1852* (Pittsburgh: University of Pittsburgh Press, 1967) and Thomas Alexander, *Sectional Stress and Party Strength: A Study of Roll-Call Voting Patterns in the United States House of Representatives, 1836–1860* (Nashville: University of Tennessee Press, 1967). In my judgment the application of Guttman scales to study legislative behavior necessitates several unacceptable assumptions. Guttman scales *must* be unidimensional and cumulative; that is, they measure behavior (legislative or other) as distance in a single direction through a single point. Any nonconforming behavior is deemed an error and too many "errors" indicate a need to construct some other scale, which however must also have one point of reference and one dimension. Moreover, a survey of their use by researchers and interpretation by general readers reveals additional pitfalls: positions held by fewest numbers are deemed "extreme" or radical; positions held by greatest numbers inevitably become "middle" or moderate; differences between scores, say the difference between +3 and +4 and the difference between +2 and +3, are judged equal. Such errors of interpretation, while understandable, are incorrect from a theoretical standpoint and fatal from a historical perspective. Leaving aside the philosophical questions raised by equating number of supporters with extremeness of a position, Guttman scaling cannot effectively deal with several vital aspects of legislative behavior—vote trading, compromise, shifting external pressures, failure to understand what is being voted upon, and, most important, conflicting attachments or principles.

Use of different scales for different issues only complicates the problem by failure to deal with interrelationships among "different" issues. Although attractive for its apparent ability to focus sharply on a unidimensional problem (such as strength of sectionalism, the effectiveness of party discipline, the degree of loyalty to a leader, or the rise of support for a particular bill), the distortion of reality that accompanies the answer provided by Guttman scaling is too great when applied to legislative behavior.

Another important study is Mary P. Ryan, "Party Formation in the

United States Congress, 1789 to 1796: A Quantitative Analysis," *William and Mary Quarterly*, 3d Ser., 28 (October 1971), pp. 523–542. Ryan introduces the "mu score," a measure that makes a significant methodological advance by adjusting for random chance in the agreement levels of pairs of delegates. Unfortunately, the author eliminates, without explanation, all negative mu scores (which indicate lack of agreement) from the analysis and then reaches the conclusion that, "The fundamental discovery of this study was the emergence in the first session of the United States Congress of two voting blocs which remained remarkably stable in the eight sessions that followed." Moreover, Ryan states that "agreement ratios were calculated from party votes only," certainly a procedure that casts doubt on conclusions about party strength. The author's division of congressmen into two blocs is self-defining and ignores significant mu score differences among delegates within a bloc. Yet another difficulty with the study is the calculation of "only" 24 alterations of bloc alignments "among hundreds of representatives." Given the flow of legislative business from one session of Congress to another, shifts within a Congress are very unlikely. Since only re-elected representatives have the possibility of shifting bloc alignments, the accurate figure for the House would be 24 of 152. Even this figure gives no indication of within-bloc shifts and counts delegates each time they are re-elected.

The result of Ryan's methodological decisions is an overestimate of the strength of legislative parties, especially in the First and Second Congresses. Nevertheless, she demonstrates overwhelmingly that early voting behavior was not completely random and that polarized legislative activity preceded the Jay Treaty controversy.

8. Walter Burnham, "Party Systems and the Political Process," in *The American Party Systems*, pp. 277–280.

Chapter 2: Politics and Sectionalism

1. Election returns reveal a similar absence of deep conflict over issues. For the entire New England region for the years 1790 through 1798, only the following contests produced new representatives whose views differed substantially from those of their predecessors: in 1790 pro-Hamilton Artemus Ward replaced Jonathan Grout in Massachusetts; in 1794 consistently pro-administration Daniel Buck replaced Nathaniel Niles in Vermont and staunch Republican Joseph Varnum defeated Artemus Ward; in 1796 Federalists replaced anti-Adams men in two districts in central Massachusetts and one in New Hampshire; in 1798 two lukewarm Federalists gave way to more ardent and consistent men of the same party, Theodore Sedgwick in western Massachusetts and John Brown in Rhode Island.

2. Richard Purcell, *Connecticut in Transition* (Middletown, Connecticut: Wesleyan University Press, 1963; 1st ed., 1930), pp. 7–64.

3. Paul Goodman, *The Democratic Republicans of Massachusetts: Politics in a Young Republic* (Cambridge: Harvard University Press, 1964), pp. 70–127. James Banner, Jr., *To The Hartford Convention: The Federalists and the Origins of Party Politics in Massachusetts, 1789-1815* (New York: Alfred Knopf, 1970), pp. 168–215.

4. David Ludlum, *Social Ferment in Vermont, 1791-1850* (New York: Columbia University Press, 1939), pp. 17–61.

5. Peter Coleman, *The Transformation of Rhode Island, 1790-1860* (Providence: Brown University Press, 1963), pp. 26–70 and 218–294. Irwin Polishook, *Rhode Island and the Union, 1774-1795* (Evanston: Northwestern University Press, 1969), pp. 21–52 and 221–241.

6. Douglass North, *The Economic Growth of the United States, 1790-1860* (New York: W. W. Norton, 1966), pp. 36–53 and 249. Curtis P. Nettles, *The Emergence of a National Economy, 1775-1818* (New York: Harper and Row, 1969), pp. 230–242.

7. The represented revealed a similarly deeper tendency toward divisiveness in the biannual contests for House seats. For the seven southern states, the following elections produced new representatives whose views differed substantially from those of their predecessors: in 1790 and in mid-session elections before 1792, John Mercer, Upton Sheridine, and Samuel Sterett broke the previously unanimous commitment of Maryland's six-man delegation to the administration and administration opponent Aedanus Burke of South Carolina gave way to Robert Barnwell; in 1792, when districts were radically redrawn on the basis of the first federal census, anti-administration strength increased in the delegations of Maryland, North Carolina, South Carolina, and Virginia by 13, 30, 11, and 14 percent, respectively; in 1794 and in mid-session elections before 1796, Republicans gained one seat in Maryland and one in Virginia (by Richard Brent in a fierce contest over the Jay Treaty against Richard Lee), but the party lost one seat in North Carolina and one in South Carolina; in 1796 the administration gained new seats, or at least moderate support for its policy positions, through the victories of Robert Williams in North Carolina, John Rutledge, Jr., in South Carolina, Thomas Evans and James Machir in Virginia, and William Matthews and George Baer, Jr., in Maryland; in 1798 Federalists lost one seat in Maryland, but gained two each in Georgia and South Carolina and four each in North Carolina and Virginia.

8. Charles Sydnor, *American Revolutionaries in the Making: Political Practices in Washington's Virginia* (New York: The Free Press, 1965), pp. 107–118.

9. Manning Dauer, *The Adams Federalists* (Baltimore: The Johns Hopkins Press, 1953), pp. 20–22.

10. The relationship between geographic characteristics and politics is treated extensively in the following studies: Harry Ammon, "The Formation of the Republican Party in Virginia, 1789-1796," *Journal of Southern History* 19 (1953), pp. 283-310; Delbert Gilpatrick, *Jeffersonian Democracy in North Carolina* (New York: Columbia University Press, 1931), pp. 11-81; Gilbert Lycan, "Alexander Hamilton and the North Carolina Federalists," *North Carolina Historical Review* 25 (1948), pp. 442-465; Ulrich Phillips, "The South Carolina Federalists," *American Historical Review* 14 (1909), pp. 529-543 and 731-743; Lucien Roberts, "Sectional Problems in Georgia During the Formative Period, 1776-1798," *Georgia Historical Quarterly* 18 (1934), pp. 207-227; Thomas Scharf, *History of Maryland from the Earliest Period to the Present Day* (Hatboro, Pennsylvania; 1967 reprint of 1869 ed.), 2, pp. 551-605; and John Wolfe, *Jeffersonian Democracy in South Carolina* (Chapel Hill: University of North Carolina Press, 1940), pp. 1-13 and 54-165.

11. Lisle Rose, *Prologue to Democracy: The Federalists in the South, 1789-1800* (Lexington: University of Kentucky Press, 1968), pp. 61-64 and 90-99.

12. A single exception that is of consequence but does not invalidate this generalization is the voting of William Cooper of New York on the Land Act of 1796.

13. Includes Georgia, Kentucky, Maryland, North Carolina, South Carolina, Tennessee, and Virginia.

14. Alfred Young, *The Democratic Republicans of New York: The Origins, 1763-1797* (Chapel Hill: University of North Carolina Press, 1967), pp. 257-276, 468-517, and 546-565.

15. Carl Prince, *New Jersey's Jeffersonian Republicans: The Genius of Early Party Machinery, 1789-1817* (Chapel Hill: University of North Carolina Press, 1967), pp. 3-68.

16. Harry Tinkcom, *The Republicans and Federalists in Pennsylvania, 1790-1801* (Harrisburg: Pennsylvania Historical and Museum Commission, 1950), pp. 269-270.

17. As in New England and the South, cohesion levels and frequency of significant electoral changes were closely correlated. Low cohesion among Middle Atlantic delegates paralleled the large number of elections in the region that produced new representatives whose views differed substantially from those of their predecessors. In 1790 the independent-minded Abraham Clark, Aaron Kitchell, and Jonathan Dayton replaced three solid administration supporters in New Jersey, while three changes in New York produced the opposite result and four in Pennsylvania began the delegation on its increasingly anti-administration course; in 1792 Delaware elected its first administration opponent, New Jersey returned a pro-Washington delegation, New York sent nine new representatives, and administra-

tion opponents swept Pennsylvania's expanded delegation; in 1794 independent Abraham Clark gave way to a staunch Federalist in New Jersey, while in New York William Cooper and Edward Livingston unseated incumbents of very different persuasion, and in Pennsylvania administration opponents gained from the addition of such notables as David Bard, Samuel Maclay, and Albert Gallatin; in 1796 James Bayard returned Delaware to the Federalist column, while the party gained two seats in New York at the expense of Theodore Bailey and John Hathorn and two more seats in Pennsylvania with the additions of John Chapman and Robert Waln; in 1798 four of five incumbents failed to return in New Jersey and a delegation that had unanimously supported the administration was replaced with a pro-Jefferson majority; Republicans also gained one seat in Pennsylvania and two in New York.

18. The effort to form national parties did not achieve success until the second party system, but legislative behavior reflecting an absence of sectional attachment long preceded (and I believe was partially responsible for) successful national parties.

Chapter 3: The Limits of Power

1. Seymour Lipset, *The First New Nation* (New York: Basic Books, 1963), pp. 17–68. Lipset believes that the crisis over legitimacy continued well beyond 1787. However, his analysis merges the problem of continued existence with that of establishing the limits of government authority.

2. *Annals of Congress,* 1st Cong., 1st sess., pp. 703–763. Among the amendments dropped were: limiting the president to two terms, a representative to six years in eight, yearly election of United States senators, and the prohibition of all foreign titles to United States citizens.

3. Ibid., p. 777. August 22, 1789.

4. Ibid., p. 759. August 18, 1789.

5. Ibid., p. 768. August 21, 1789. Support was as follows: Georgia 1, Maryland 1, Massachusetts 4, New Hampshire 1, New York 3, South Carolina 4, and Virginia 3.

6. Ibid., p. 772. August 21, 1789. Support was as follows: Georgia 2, Maryland 2, Massachusetts 4, New Hampshire 1, New York 4, Pennsylvania 1, South Carolina 4, and Virginia 4.

7. Ibid., p. 913. September 24, 1789. Opposition was as follows: Georgia 2, Massachusetts 2, New Hampshire 1, New York 3, South Carolina 3, and Virginia 3.

8. Internal splits in Massachusetts, New York, and Virginia eliminate a large state versus small state division. The wide difference in district characteristics among the nine hard core proponents of limiting amendments

eliminates a self-sufficient versus dependent division. The spread of this hard core from New Hampshire to South Carolina denies a region versus region analysis.

9. The state affiliations of the twenty-eight nationalists were as follows: Connecticut 4, Delaware 1, Maryland 3, Massachusetts 3, New Hampshire 2, New Jersey 4, New York 2, Pennsylvania 6, and Virginia 3.

10. The twenty-eight delegates classified as nationalists were: Connecticut—Roger Sherman, Jonathan Sturges, Jonathan Trumbull, and Jeremiah Wadsworth; Delaware—John Vining; Maryland—Daniel Carroll, George Gale, and William Smith; Massachusetts—Fisher Ames, Benjamin Goodhue, and Theodore Sedgwick; New Hampshire—Abiel Foster and Nicholas Gilman; New Jersey—Elias Boudinot, Lambert Cadwallader, James Schureman, and Thomas Sinnickson; New York—Egbert Benson and John Laurance; Pennsylvania—George Clymer, Thomas Fitzsimons, Thomas Hartley, John Muhlenberg, Thomas Scott, and Henry Wynkoop; and Virginia—John Brown, Richard Lee, and James Madison.

11. *Annals of Congress,* 1st Cong., 1st sess., pp. 580–591. June 24, 1789. Anti-nationalists were 82 percent against allowing removal by the president alone, 91 percent against dropping the issue because the Constitution handled it, and 85 percent against passage of the bill itself. Nationalists were 87 percent for allowing removal by the president alone, 48 percent for dropping the issue because the Constitution handled it, and 88 percent for final passage.

12. The single exception, a cohesion difference of 67 percent on a vote to appropriate money for Indian treaties, will be considered as part of a discussion of factionalism on frontier issues. It may be noted at this point, however, that anti-nationalists tended to oppose appropriations that might expand the role of government. See *Annals of Congress,* 1st Cong., 2d sess., p. 1646. June 22, 1790.

13. Other delegates classified as nationalists who joined Madison in opposing Hamiltonian plans for expanding government power were: William Smith of Maryland; Nicholas Gilman of New Hampshire; Thomas Hartley, John Muhlenberg, and Thomas Scott of Pennsylvania; and John Brown of Virginia. All, however, supported various other proposals to expand national power.

14. *Annals of Congress,* 1st Cong., 1st sess., p. 927. September 28, 1789.

15. Ibid., p. 928. September 28, 1789. The states voted as follows: Connecticut 3–0, Georgia 0–3, Maryland 3–2, Massachusetts 2–3, New Hampshire 2–1, New Jersey 0–4, New York 3–2, Pennsylvania 1–3, South Carolina 0–3, and Virginia 2–4.

16. Ibid., 1st Cong., 2d sess., p. 1620. May 27, 1790. The states voted as follows: Connecticut 2–1, Delaware 1–0, Georgia 0–3, Maryland 2–3, Massachusetts 3–5, New Hampshire 0–3, New Jersey 0–3, New York 1–5,

North Carolina 0-3, Pennsylvania 3-3, South Carolina 1-4, and Virginia 3-6.

17. Merrill Jensen, *The New Nation: A History of the United States During the Confederation, 1781-1789* (New York: Alfred Knopf, 1950), pp. 55 and 399.

18. *Annals of Congress*, 2d Cong., 1st sess., pp. 191 and 208. November 15, 1791 and November 23, 1791. This determination is made by dividing the House figure into 120 and the Senate assignment into 105. For example, Delaware's votes would constitute less than 1 percent (1 of 105) under the Senate plan and nearly 2 percent (2 of 120) under the House version; Pennsylvania's strength would decrease under the House plan from 12 to 11 percent.

19. Ibid., p. 260. December 19, 1791.

20. Ibid., p. 179. November 14, 1791.

21. Ibid., p. 270. December 19, 1791.

22. Ibid., pp. 208, 251, 274, and 548. November 23, 1791; December 14, 1791; December 19, 1791; and April 9, 1792.

23. Ibid., pp. 191 and 208. November 11, 1791 and November 23, 1791.

24. Ibid., pp. 191, 208, 210, 251, 274, 335, 336, 415, 416, 418, 473, 482, 541, and 548. *Journal of Congress*, 2d Cong., 1st sess., pp. 473 and 508. In the lists that follow, the percentage after each name gives the consistency with which each delegate adhered to the voting bloc in which he is included for this series of eighteen roll calls. The thirty proponents of radically increasing the size of the House were: Georgia—Abraham Baldwin 100%, Anthony Wayne 100%, and Francis Willis 95%; Maryland—Philip Key 78%, William Vans Murray 100%, Joshua Seney 82%, Upton Sheridine 90%, and Samuel Sterett 100%; New York—John Laurance 75% and Thomas Tredwell 72%; North Carolina—John Ashe 88%, William Grove 82%, Nathaniel Macon 89%, and Hugh Williamson 100%; Pennsylvania—William Findley 100%, Daniel Hiester 70%, and John Muhlenberg 94%; South Carolina—Daniel Huger 82%, Thomas Sumter 100%, and Thomas Tucker 78%; and Virginia—John Brown 100%, William Giles 100%, Samuel Griffin 100%, Richard Lee 100%, James Madison 94%, Andrew Moore 89%, John Page 87%, Josiah Parker 100%, Abraham Venable 100%, and Alexander White 95%. The twenty opponents of radically increasing the size of the House were: Connecticut—James Hillhouse 69%, Jonathan Sturges 72%, and Jeremiah Wadsworth 73%; Massachusetts—Fisher Ames 86%, Sheashabub Bourne 95%, Benjamin Goodhue 95%, Amasa Learned 80%, Theodore Sedgwick 92%, George Thacher 100%, and Artemus Ward 83%; New Hampshire—Nicholas Gilman 95%, Samuel Livermore 100%, and Jeremiah Smith 94%; New Jersey—Elias Boudinot 100%, Abraham Clark 94%, Jonathan Dayton 100%, Aaron Kitchell 87%; Rhode Island—Benjamin Bourn 89%; and Vermont—Nathaniel Niles 100% and Israel Smith 95%.

25. *Annals of Congress,* 2d Cong., 1st sess., pp. 251 and 274. December 14, 1791 and December 19, 1791.

26. Ibid., pp. 418 and 541. February 21, 1792 and April 6, 1792.

27. *Journal of Congress,* 2d Cong., 1st sess., p. 508. February 14, 1792.

28. *Annals of Congress,* 2d Cong., 1st sess., p. 484. March 24, 1792.

29. Ibid., p. 485. March 25, 1792. The states voted as follows: Connecticut 0–4, Georgia 2–0, Maryland 3–0, Massachusetts 0–5, New Hampshire 1–2, New Jersey 2–1, New York 2–3, North Carolina 2–0, Pennsylvania 4–2, Rhode Island 0–1, South Carolina 2–3, Vermont 1–0, and Virginia 7–1.

30. Voting affirmatively were John Laurance and Thomas Tredwell of New York and Thomas Fitzsimons, Andrew Gregg, Daniel Hiester, and John Kittera of Pennsylvania. Voting negatively were Egbert Benson, Cornelius Schoonmaker, and Peter Silvester of New York and Thomas Hartley and Israel Jacobs of Pennsylvania. Abraham Clark and Aaron Kitchell of New Jersey voted affirmatively while Elias Boudinot voted in the negative. Economic issues will be discussed in detail in Chapter 5.

31. *Annals of Congress,* 2d Cong., 1st sess., p. 489. March 26, 1792. The states voted as follows: Connecticut 4–0, Delaware 0–1, Georgia 0–1, Maryland 0–4, Massachusetts 7–0, New Hampshire 2–1, New Jersey 1–2, New York, 2–2, North Carolina 0–5, Pennsylvania 4–2, South Carolina 3–2, Vermont 0–2, and Virginia 0–10.

32. *Annals of Congress,* 1st Cong., 1st sess., p. 927. September 28, 1789. New England favored the measure by seven to four while the rest of the country opposed it by a ratio of more than two to one.

33. *Annals of Congress,* 2d Cong., 1st sess., p. 552. April 12, 1792.

34. Negative votes were cast by Abraham Baldwin and Francis Willis of Georgia, John Steele of North Carolina, Nathaniel Niles and Israel Smith of Vermont, and John Brown, Andrew Moore, John Page, and Josiah Parker of Virginia.

35. The notable exception was William Findley of western Pennsylvania, who voted affirmatively, thereby breaking his normal pattern.

36. *Annals of Congress,* 2d Cong., 1st sess., p. 555. April 12, 1792. The states voted as follows: Connecticut 3–1, Delaware 1–0, Georgia 0–2, Maryland 1–5, Massachusetts 5–1, New Hampshire 2–1, New Jersey 0–3, New York 4–2, North Carolina 0–5, Pennsylvania 5–2, Rhode Island 1–0, South Carolina 2–3, Vermont 0–2, and Virginia 0–10.

37. James Richardson, ed., *Messages and Papers of the Presidents, 1789–1897* (Washington: Government Printing Office, 1896), 1, p. 166. Sixth State of the Union Message, November 19, 1794. For the most thorough analysis of the government's response to the Whiskey Rebellion, see Richard H. Kohn, "The Washington Administration's Decision to Crush the

Whiskey Rebellion," *The Journal of American History,* 59 (December 1972), pp. 567–584. Kohn's intensive analysis of the series of decisions involved in the government's reactions to the rebellion shows that Washington gave great weight to questions of tactics and public image, but that he never entertained serious consideration of the possibility that force *could* not be used.

38. Ibid.

39. Ibid., p. 169. Senate's Reply to the President, November 22, 1794.

40. *Annals of Congress,* 3d Cong., 2d sess., pp. 900–913. November 25, 1794.

41. Ibid., p. 943. November 27, 1794. The states voted as follows: Connecticut 6–0, Delaware 1–0, Georgia 0–2, Kentucky 0–2, Maryland 3–3, Massachusetts 12–2, New Hampshire 4–0, New Jersey 4–0, New York 6–3, North Carolina 2–7, Pennsylvania 5–6, Rhode Island 2–0, South Carolina 0–2, Vermont 0–2, and Virginia 2–16.

42. These issues will be considered in detail in Chapters 4 and 5.

43. *Annals of Congress,* 3d Cong., 2d sess., p. 920. November 26, 1794.

44. Ibid., p. 944. November 27, 1794. Changes were: Smith of Maryland, who had voted to condemn, abstained; Dawson of North Carolina, who had voted to condemn, voted to limit; F. Muhlenberg of Pennsylvania, who as Speaker had abstained, voted to limit; and Smith of South Carolina, who had abstained, voted to condemn all societies.

45. Ibid. Changes were: Gilman and Sherburne of New Hampshire, who had voted to condemn all societies, voted against this amendment; F. Muhlenberg, who had voted to limit, abstained; Grove of North Carolina, who had voted to condemn all societies, voted against this amendment as did Griffin of Virginia.

46. Joseph Charles, *The Origins of the American Party System: Three Essays* (Williamsburg: Institute of Early American History and Culture, 1956), p. 94. William Chambers, *Political Parties in A New Nation: The American Experience, 1776–1809* (New York: Oxford University Press, 1963), p. 90, accepts Charles' figures. Noble Cunningham, *The Jeffersonian Republicans: The Formation of Party Organization, 1789–1801* (Chapel Hill: University of North Carolina Press, 1957), pp. 70–72. Cunningham asserts that "The roll calls of the Third Congress (1793–1795) indicate that no party regularity was shown in the voting records of nearly half of the members." For an opposite conclusion, see Mary P. Ryan, "Party Formation in the United States Congress, 1789 to 1796: A Quantitative Analysis," *William and Mary Quarterly,* 3d Ser., 28 (October 1971), pp. 531 and 541.

47. Richardson, *Messages,* p. 170. House's Reply to the President, November 28, 1794.

48. The strongest case for the conclusion which I am questioning at this

point is found in Cunningham, *Jeffersonian Republicans,* especially pp. 50–88 and 270–272. Also see Charles, *Origins of the American Party System,* pp. 91–103.

49. *Annals of Congress,* 4th Cong., 1st sess., p. 759. March 24, 1796.

50. Ibid.

51. Cunningham, *Jeffersonian Republicans,* p. 83, cites Madison to Jefferson, April 4, 1796 in Hunt ed., *Madison Writings,* VI, p. 265.

52. *Annals of Congress,* 4th Cong., 1st sess., p. 782. April 7, 1796. The states voted as follows: Connecticut 0–7, Delaware 1–0, Georgia 2–0, Kentucky 1–0, Maryland 5–2, Massachusetts 3–9, New Hampshire 2–2, New Jersey 0–2, New York 5–5, North Carolina 8–0, Pennsylvania 9–3, Rhode Island 0–2, South Carolina 4–2, Vermont 1–1, and Virginia 16–0.

53. Ibid., p. 783. April 7, 1796.

54. Cunningham, *Jeffersonian Republicans,* p. 83. The author accepts Madison's excuse for failure that the votes melted away. For further analysis of voting on the Jay Treaty, see the present study, pp. 146–150.

55. Ibid., pp. 78–85.

56. *Annals of Congress,* 4th Cong., 1st sess., p. 1289. April 30, 1796. The states voted as follows: Connecticut 0–7, Georgia 2–0, Kentucky 2–0, Maryland 1–6, Massachusetts 3–10, New Hampshire 0–3, New Jersey 0–4, New York 5–5, North Carolina 9–1, Pennsylvania 7–5, Rhode Island 0–2, South Carolina 4–2, Vermont 1–1, and Virginia 15–4.

57. *The Statutes at Large of the United States, 1789–1873* (Boston, 1845–1873), I, pp. 596–597.

58. Zechariah Chafee, Jr., *Free Speech in the United States* (Cambridge: Harvard University Press, 1941), pp. 20–24. James Morton Smith, *Freedom's Fetters: The Alien and Sedition Laws and American Civil Liberties* (Ithaca: Cornell University Press, 1956), p. 431. Smith concludes his study with the following statement, one that I believe is contradicted by much of his own evidence. "The Alien and Sedition Laws played a prominent role in shaping the American tradition of civil liberties. Based on the concept that the government was master, these laws provoked a public response which clearly demonstrated that the people occupied that position."

59. Leonard Levy, *Legacy of Suppression* (Cambridge: Harvard University Press, 1960), p. 307. For a more extended but less balanced treatment of Jeffersonian thought and action in the area of civil liberties, see Levy's *Jefferson and Civil Liberties: The Darker Side* (Cambridge: Harvard University Press, 1963).

60. Smith, *Freedom's Fetters,* pp. 94–155.

61. This is not to say that old policies were not pursued with vigor. See Manning Dauer, *The Adams Federalists* (Baltimore: The Johns Hopkins Press, 1953), pp. 198–211, for a perceptive account of continuing efforts to establish a powerful central government by eroding sources of external

restraint.

62. *Annals of Congress,* 6th Cong., 1st sess., p. 419. January 23, 1800.

63. Ibid., p. 423. January 23, 1800.

64. Ibid., p. 425. January 23, 1800.

65. *Annals of Congress,* 6th Cong., 2d sess., pp. 975, 1038, and 1049. January 23, 1801; February 19, 1801; and February 21, 1801.

66. Levy, *Legacy of Suppression,* pp. 299-307.

67. Smith, *Freedom's Fetters,* p. 35. Italics added.

68. *Annals of Congress,* 5th Cong., 2d sess., p. 1454. April 19, 1798.

69. Ibid., p. 2035. June 25, 1798.

70. Smith, *Freedom's Fetters,* p. 48.

71. *The Statutes at Large of the United States,* I, pp. 577-578. Italics added.

72. Smith, *Freedom's Fetters,* p. 161.

73. *Annals of Congress,* 5th Cong., 3d sess., pp. 2545, 2590, 2599, 2648, 2676, 2679, 2680, 2681, and 2721. December 28, 1798; January 9, 11, 15, 16, and 17, 1799. Final passage was by the substantial margin of 58 to 36.

74. John Miller, *The Federalist Era, 1789-1801* (New York: Harper & Brothers, 1960), pp. 28-29.

75. Dauer, *Adams Federalists,* pp. 202-203.

76. Richardson, *Messages,* pp. 289-290.

77. *Annals of Congress,* 6th Cong., 1st sess., pp. 644 and 648. March 25, 1800 and March 28, 1800.

Chapter 4: Politics and Abundant Land

1. Frederick Jackson Turner, "The Significance of the Frontier in American History," in *The Frontier in American History* (New York: Henry Hold & Co., 1920), p. 24.

2. Ibid., p. 8.

3. Thomas McCormick, "American Expansion in China," *American Historical Review* 75 (June 1970), p. 1394.

4. David Potter, *People of Plenty: Economic Abundance and the American Character* (Chicago: University of Chicago Press, 1954), pp. 142-165.

5. *Annals of Congress,* 1st Cong., 1st sess., p. 703. August 12, 1789.

6. Ibid., 1st Cong., 2d sess., p. 1646. June 21, 1790.

7. The fourteen were: Connecticut—Roger Sherman and Jonathan Sturges; Maryland—Joshua Seney; Massachusetts—Elbridge Gerry, George Leonard, and Theodore Sedgwick; New Hampshire—Samuel Livermore; New Jersey—James Schureman; New York—William Floyd, John Hathorn, and Jeremiah Van Rensselaer; Pennsylvania—Daniel Hiester; South Carolina—Thomas Sumter; and Virginia—Josiah Parker.

8. The nineteen were: Connecticut—Jonathan Trumbull and Jeremiah Wadsworth; Georgia—Abraham Baldwin and George Matthews; Maryland—George Gale; New Jersey—Lambert Cadwallader; New York—Egbert Benson and John Laurance; North Carolina—John Steele; Pennsylvania—Thomas Fitzsimons, Thomas Hartley, John Muhlenberg, and Thomas Scott; South Carolina—William Smith; and Virginia—John Brown, Samuel Griffin, Richard Lee, James Madison, and John Page.

9. The ten were: Benson, Cadwallader, Fitzsimons, Gale, Hartley, Laurance, Lee, Madison, Trumbull, and Wadsworth.

10. *Annals of Congress,* 1st Cong., 1st sess., pp. 927–928. September 28, 1789. The vote was 25 to 16 against the Senate amendment.

11. Samuel Flagg Bemis, *Jay's Treaty: A Study in Commerce and Diplomacy* (New Haven: Yale University Press, 1962; rev. ed.), p. 153.

12. *Annals of Congress,* 2d Cong., 1st sess., p. 493. March 27, 1792. Giles' effort to have the president conduct the investigation met defeat by a vote of 21 to 35, after which the House established its own investigating committee by a vote of 44 to 10.

13. *Annals of Congress,* 3d Cong., 1st sess., p. 711. May 21, 1794. Broadus Mitchell, *Alexander Hamilton: The National Adventure, 1788-1804* (New York: Macmillan, 1962), pp. 245–247. John C. Miller, *Alexander Hamilton: Portrait in Paradox* (New York: Harper & Row, 1959), pp. 326–327.

14. *Annals of Congress,* 2d Cong., 1st sess., p. 354. January 30, 1792. The votes of North Carolina's delegates and of Josiah Parker, Thomas Sumter, and Francis Willis of Virginia, South Carolina, and Georgia, respectively, in favor of adding three regiments of regular infantry to federal forces on the frontier (defeated by 18 to 34) but against the frontier protection bill demonstrate this position clearly.

15. Ibid., p. 355. February 1, 1792. Against the bill from New England were: Connecticut, 1 of 3; Massachusetts, 4 of 5; New Hampshire, 2 of 2; Rhode Island, 1 of 1; and Vermont, 2 of 2.

16. Ibid., p. 569. April 21, 1792.

17. Ibid., p. 572. April 21, 1792. The states voted as follows: Connecticut 4–0, Delaware 1–0, Georgia 0–2, Maryland 3–3, Massachusetts 6–0, New Hampshire 2–1, New Jersey 3–0, New York 4–2, Pennsylvania 5–0, Rhode Island 1–0, South Carolina 3–2, Vermont 1–1, and Virginia 3–5.

18. *Annals of Congress,* 2d Cong., 2d sess., p. 749. December 18, 1792. Western proponents of the measure were the entire Georgia delegation, Christopher Greenup of Kentucky, William Findley of Pennsylvania, and Andrew Moore, John Page, and Abraham Venable of Virginia.

19. *Annals of Congress,* 3d Cong., 1st sess., pp. 735–736. May 30, 1794.

20. Ibid., pp. 709 and 738. May 19 and 30, 1794.

21. Ibid., pp. 775–777. June 6, 1794.

22. Ibid., p. 779. June 6, 1794. Support for the amendment was as fol-

lows: Connecticut, 6 of 6; Delaware, 1 of 1; Maryland, 3 of 4; Massachusetts, 6 of 8; New Jersey, 1 of 2; New York, 6 of 9; Pennsylvania, 1 of 7; Rhode Island, 1 of 1; South Carolina, 1 of 3.

23. *Annals of Congress,* 3d Cong., 2d sess., p. 1256. February 27, 1795. The states voted as follows: Connecticut 1-4, Delaware 0-1, Georgia 2-0, Kentucky 2-0, Maryland 4-2, Massachusetts 1-11, New Hampshire 1-3 New Jersey 3-1, New York 3-5, North Carolina 7-0, Pennsylvania 4-6, Rhode Island 0-2. South Carolina 1-2, and Virginia 14-0.

24. Ibid. p. 1269. February 28, 1795.

25. *Annals of Congress,* 4th Cong., 1st sess., pp. 1410-1420. May 21, 1796.

26. *Journal of Congress,* 4th Cong., 1st sess., pp. 572-573. May 23, 1796. *Annals of Congress,* 4th Cong., 1st sess., 2d sess., pp 1422, 1981–1982, 2094, and 2332. May 21, 1796; January 24, 1797; February 7, 1797; and March 1, 1797.

27. The twenty-three were: Connecticut—Joshua Coit, Chauncey Goodrich, Roger Griswold, Nathaniel Smith and Uriah Tracy; Maryland—William Hindman and William Vans Murray; Massachusetts—Fisher Ames, Theodore Bradbury, Dwight Foster, Samuel Lyman, John Reed, and Peleg Wadsworth; New Jersey—Mark Thomson; New York—William Cooper, Ezekiel Gilbert, and Henry Glen; Pennsylvania—Thomas Hartley, John Kittera, and Samuel Sitgreaves; Rhode Island—Benjamin Bourn and Francis Malbone; and South Carolina—William L. Smith.

28. The twenty-six were: Connecticut—Zephaniah Swift; Kentucky—Christopher Greenup; Maryland—Richard Sprigg; New York—Theodore Bailey and John Hathorn; North Carolina—Thomas Blount, Nathan Bryan, Dempsey Burges, Jesse Franklin, William Grove, James Holland, and Nathaniel Macon; Pennsylvania—Albert Gallatin and Samuel Maclay; South Carolina—Wade Hampton and Richard Winn; Tennessee—Andrew Jackson; Vermont—Israel Smith; and Virginia—Samuel Cabell, Thomas Claiborne, Isaac Coles. Carter Harrison, George Jackson, Andrew Moore, Anthony New, and Abraham Venable.

29. *Annals of Congress,* 4th Cong., 2d sess., p. 1979. February 27, 1797.

30. William Appleman Williams, *The Contours of American History* (Chicago: Quadrangle, 1966; 1st ed., 1961), p. 135.

31. Payson Jackson Treat, *The National Land System 1785-1820* (New York: E. B. Treat & Co., 1910), pp. 66-77.

32. *Annals of Congress,* 4th Cong., 1st sess., p. 858. April 5, 1796.

33. *Journal of Congress,* 4th Cong., 1st sess., pp. 495-496. April 5, 1796. Later amendments and compromises with the Senate raised the minimum acreage requirement to 640 acres; therefore the discussion here involves attitudes rather than accomplished policy.

34. The forty were: Delaware–John Patten; Kentucky–Christopher Greenup and Alexander Orr; Maryland–Jeremiah Crabb; New York–Theodore Bailey, John Hathorn, Jonathan Havens, John Van Alen, Philip Van Cortlandt, and John Williams; North Carolina–Nathan Bryan, Dempsey Burges, Jesse Franklin, James Gillespie, William Grove, James Holland, and Matthew Locke; Pennsylvania–William Findley, Andrew Gregg, Daniel Hiester, John Richards, John Swanwick, and Richard Thomas; South Carolina–Lemuel Benton, Samuel Earle, Wade Hampton, and Richard Winn; and Virginia–Samuel Cabell, Thomas Claiborne, John Clopton, William Giles, George Hancock, Carter Harrison, George Jackson, Andrew Moore, Anthony New, John Page, Francis Preston, Robert Rutherford, and Abraham Venable.

35. The thirty-six were: Connecticut–Chauncey Goodrich, Roger Griswold, James Hillhouse, Nathaniel Smith, and Uriah Tracy; Georgia–Abraham Baldwin and John Milledge; Maryland–Gabriel Christie, William Hindman, William Vans Murray, and Thomas Sprigg; Massachusetts–Theodore Bradbury, Henry Dearborn, Dwight Foster, Benjamin Goodhue, Samuel Lyman, John Reed, Theodore Sedgwick, George Thacher, and Peleg Wadsworth; New Hampshire–Abiel Foster, John Sherburne, and Jeremiah Smith; New Jersey–Thomas Henderson and Aaron Kitchell; New York–William Cooper and Edward Livingston; North Carolina–Thomas Blount, Nathaniel Macon, and Absalom Tatom; Pennsylvania–Thomas Hartley; Rhode Island–Benjamin Bourn and Francis Malbone; South Carolina–William L. Smith; Vermont–Israel Smith; and Virginia–John Nicholas.

36. *Annals of Congress*, 4th Cong., 1st sess., p. 1473. May 28, 1796.

37. *Journal of Congress*, 4th Cong., 1st sess., p. 588. May 28, 1796.

38. Ibid., pp. 588–589. May 28, 1796. *Annals of Congress*, 4th Cong., 1st sess., pp. 1328 and 1473. May 6 and 28, 1796.

39. *Annals of Congress*, 6th Cong., 2d sess., pp. 837, 1376–1397. December 19, 1800.

40. Ibid., 1037-1038 and 1074. March 3, 1801. The recommendation to discontinue proceedings against Sargent lost by a vote of 38 to 40.

41. *Annals of Congress*, 6th Cong., 1st sess., pp. 632 and 682. March 18, 1800 and April 24, 1800. The roll calls occasioned respective votes of 54 to 37 and 49 to 42. The groups used in Table 25 consist of delegates who voted on either or both occasions.

Chapter 5: Money, Party, and Faction

1. Jacob E. Cooke, ed., *The Federalist*, p. 59.

2. The literature generated by Beard's analysis in *An Economic Interpretation of the Constitution of the United States* (New York: Macmillan,

1913), especially pp. 152-188, is immense, but on this particular point see Douglas Adair, "The Tenth Federalist Revisited," *William and Mary Quarterly*, 3rd Ser., 8 (January 1951), pp. 48-67.

3. Stuart Bruchey, *The Roots of American Economic Growth, 1607-1861* (New York: Harper & Row, 1968; 1st ed., 1965), pp. 96-98.

4. *Annals of Congress*, 1st Cong., 1st sess., pp. 102-366. April 8 through May 16, 1789.

5. William H. Michael and Pitman Pulsifer, *Tariff Acts Passed by the Congress of the United States from 1789 to 1895* (Washington: Government Printing Office, 1896), pp. 9-39. Sidney Ratner, *Taxation and Democracy in America* (New York: John Wiley & Sons, 1967; 1st ed., 1942), pp. 26-30.

6. Joseph Charles, *The Origins of the American Party System: Three Essays* (Williamsburg: Institute of Early American History and Culture, 1956), p. 21.

7. *Annals of Congress*, 1st Cong., 3d sess., p. 1870. January 17, 1791. The states voted as follows: Connecticut 0-4, Delaware 0-1, Georgia 3-0, Maryland 1-2, Massachusetts 0-7, New Hampshire 1-2, New Jersey 0-4, New York 0-5, North Carolina 4-0, Pennsylvania 3-3, South Carolina 2-1, and Virginia 3-5.

8. Ibid., p. 1884. January 27, 1791.

9. *Journal of Congress*, 1st Cong., 2d sess., p. 292. August 6, 1790.

10. Richard B. Morris, ed., *Alexander Hamilton and the Founding of the Nation* (New York: Dial Press, 1957), p. 360.

11. *Annals of Congress*, 2d Cong., 1st sess., p. 562. April 19, 1792.

12. The ten northerners were: Connecticut—Jonathan Sturges; New Hampshire—Jeremiah Smith; New York—Cornelius Schoonmaker and Thomas Tredwell; Pennsylvania—William Findley, Andrew Gregg, Daniel Hiester, and Israel Jacobs; and Vermont—Nathaniel Niles and Israel Smith. The five southerners were: Maryland—Philip Key and William Vans Murray; and South Carolina—Robert Barnwell, Daniel Huger, and William L. Smith.

13. *Annals of Congress*, 2d Cong., 1st sess., p. 588. April 30, 1792.

14. Delegates favoring the excise in 1791 and the eight cent rate in 1792 were: Connecticut—Jonathan Sturges and Jeremiah Wadsworth; Massachusetts—Fisher Ames, Elbridge Gerry, Benjamin Goodhue, and George Thacher; New Hampshire—Nicholas Gilman; New Jersey—Elias Boudinot; New York—Egbert Benson, John Laurance, and Peter Silvester; Pennsylvania—Thomas Fitzsimons; Rhode Island—Benjamin Bourn; South Carolina—William L. Smith; and Virginia—Richard Lee.

Delegates opposing the excise in 1791 and favoring a rate lower than eight cents in 1792 were: Georgia—Abraham Baldwin; Maryland—Joshua Seney; North Carolina—John Ashe, John Steele, and Hugh Williamson; Pennsylvania—Daniel Hiester; South Carolina—Thomas Tucker; and Virginia–John Brown, Andrew Moore, and Josiah Parker.

15. *Annals of Congress*, 3d Cong., 1st sess., p. 620. May 1, 1794.
16. Ibid., p. 617. May 1, 1794.
17. Ibid., p. 648. May 3, 1794.
18. Ibid., p. 656. May 7, 1794. On a motion to eliminate the carriage tax the states voted as follows: Connecticut 0–6, Delaware 0–1, Georgia 0–1, Kentucky 1–1, Maryland 4–1, Massachusetts 1–11, New Hampshire 0–3, New Jersey 1–4, New York 2–8, North Carolina 4–6, Pennsylvania 5–4, Rhode Island 0–2, South Carolina 2–3, Vermont 1–1, and Virginia 13–1.
19. Ibid., pp. 740–741. May 31, 1794. On liquor licenses and property sold at auction, the respective votes of the states were: Connecticut 5–1, 7–0; Delaware 0–0, 1–0; Georgia 1–0, 2–0; Kentucky 1–0, 1–0; Maryland 1–4, 3–2; Massachusetts 10–1, 10–1; New Hampshire 2–0, 2–0; New Jersey 2–0, 2–0; New York 7–3, 8–2; North Carolina 8–2, 3–6; Pennsylvania 5–3, 6–3; Rhode Island 0–2, 2–0; South Carolina 3–2, 3–2; Vermont 0–2, 0–1; and Virginia 8–3, 5–10.
20. Ibid., pp. 621 and 628. May 1 and 2, 1794.
21. Ibid., p. 667. May 8, 1794. The states voted as follows: Connecticut 0–7, Delaware 0–1, Georgia 0–1, Kentucky 2–0, Maryland 3–2, Massachusetts 2–10, New Hampshire 0–3, New Jersey 1–3, New York 4–5, North Carolina 5–5, Pennsylvania 7–2, Rhode Island 0–2, South Carolina 1–3, and Virginia 16–1.
22. Ibid., p. 666. May 8, 1794. The states voted as follows: Connecticut 0–7, Delaware 0–1, Georgia 0–1, Kentucky 1–1, Maryland 4–1, Massachusetts 1–11, New Hampshire 0–3, New Jersey 0–4, New York 2–8, North Carolina 7–3, Pennsylvania 5–5, Rhode Island 0–2, South Carolina 0–5, Vermont 2–0, and Virginia 14–4.
23. Ibid., p. 726. May 27, 1794. The states voted as follows: Connecticut 3–4, Delaware 1–0, Georgia 0–2, Kentucky 0–1, Maryland 3–2, Massachusetts 8–3, New Hampshire 0–2, New Jersey 3–1, New York 3–5, North Carolina 3–6, Pennsylvania 5–5, Rhode Island 0–2, South Carolina 3–1, Vermont 0–2, and Virginia 0–14.
24. Ibid., p. 670. May 9, 1794. The states voted as follows: Connecticut 5–1, Delaware 1–0, Georgia 0–1, Kentucky 0–2, Maryland 2–1, Massachusetts 12–0, New Hampshire 3–0, New Jersey 3–2, New York 7–2, North Carolina 3–7, Pennsylvania 3–6, Rhode Island 2–0, South Carolina 2–3, Vermont 0–2, and Virginia 7–10.
25. Ibid., p. 699. May 16, 1794. The states voted as follows: Connecticut 1–6, Georgia 2–0, Kentucky 1–1, Maryland 1–2, Massachusetts 1–10, New Hampshire 0–3, New Jersey 2–2, New York 5–3, North Carolina 8–1, Pennsylvania 4–4, Rhode Island 0–2, South Carolina 3–2, Vermont 2–0, and Virginia 9–9.

26. The eighteen were: Connecticut—James Hillhouse, Zephaniah Swift, and Uriah Tracy; Maryland—William Vans Murray; Massachusetts—David Cobb, Peleg Coffin, Dwight Foster, Benjamin Goodhue, Theodore Sedgwick, George Thacher, and Peleg Wadsworth; New York—Ezekiel Gilbert, Silas Talbot, John Van Alen, and Peter Van Gaasbeck; North Carolina—William Grove; and South Carolina—Andrew Pickens and William L. Smith.

27. The twenty-two were: Connecticut—Joshua Coit, Jonathan Trumbull, and Jeremiah Wadsworth; Delaware—Henry Latimer; Georgia—Abraham Baldwin; Massachusetts—Fisher Ames, Amasa Learned, and Artemus Ward; New Hampshire—Nicholas Gilman and Jeremiah Smith; New Jersey—Lambert Cadwallader and Jonathan Dayton; New York—Henry Glen and John Watts; North Carolina—William Dawson, Matthew Locke, Alexander Mebane, and Benjamin Williams; Pennsylvania—John Kittera and William Montgomery; Rhode Island—Francis Malbone; and Virginia—Richard Lee.

28. The eleven were: Maryland—Gabriel Christie; Massachusetts—William Lyman; North Carolina—Nathaniel Macon and Joseph McDowell; Pennsylvania—William Findley and Daniel Hiester; South Carolina—Alexander Gillon; and Virginia—James Madison, Anthony New, John Nicholas, and Francis Walker.

29. The nine were: Maryland—Thomas Sprigg; New York—Philip Van Cortlandt; North Carolina—Thomas Blount; Vermont—Nathaniel Niles and Israel Smith; and Virginia—Thomas Claiborne, Andrew Moore, Francis Preston, and Robert Rutherford.

30. *Annals of Congress*, 5th Cong., 1st sess., pp. 391, 431–433, 443, and 446. June 27, July 1, 3, 4, and 5, 1797.

31. Ibid., p. 430. July 1, 1797.

32. See Chapter 6 for the wider foreign policy context within which these roll calls were decided.

33. *Annals of Congress*, 6th Cong., 1st sess., 2d sess., pp. 667, 705, and 911. April 14 and May 7, 1800; and January 16, 1801.

34. *Annals of Congress*, 4th Cong., 2d sess., pp. 1891–1894. January 16, 1797.

35. Ibid., pp. 1933, 1941. January 20, 1797. The initial vote for a land tax was 48 to 39; the vote to include a tax on slaves was 68 to 23.

36. Ibid., pp. 1916–1917 and 1925.

37. On the land tax, see *Annals of Congress*, 5th Cong., 2d sess., pp. 1925 and 2066. June 13 and July 2, 1798. The votes were 69 to 19 and 62 to 18 for the land tax. Opponents are counted as those who opposed the bill on either occasion. On relative rates of tax on land and buildings, see ibid., p. 2060. June 29, 1798.

38. For a positive view of Confederation finance, see Merrill Jensen, *The New Nation: A History of the United States During the Confederation,*

1781-1789 (New York: Alfred Knopf, 1950), pp. 375-398. An outstanding example of the kind of study needed at the state level is James R. Morrill, *The Practice and Politics of Fiat Finance: North Carolina in the Confederation, 1783-1789* (Chapel Hill: University of North Carolina Press, 1969).

39. The widely reprinted report is readily available in Richard B. Morris, ed., *Alexander Hamilton and the Founding of the Nation* (New York: Harper & Row, 1957), pp. 289-303.

40. E. James Ferguson, *The Power of the Purse* (Chapel Hill: University of North Carolina Press, 1961), pp. 289-343.

41. *Annals of Congress*, 1st Cong., 2d sess., p. 1619. May 26, 1790.

42. Ibid. The amendment lost by a tally of 15 to 42.

43. The three South Carolinians in the group opposed New Englanders on the issue of location of the capital, but the cohesion level for the group as a whole nevertheless differed sharply from the position taken by "enemies" of the speculator.

44. *Annals of Congress*, 1st Cong., 2d sess., pp. 1716-1717. July 29, 1790. Indents were certificates for interest due on old securities during the Confederation years.

45. Ibid., 1715. July 29, 1790.

46. Ferguson, *Power of the Purse*, p. 301.

47. The seventeen were: Georgia—James Jackson and George Matthews; Maryland—Benjamin Contee, Joshua Seney, and William Smith; New Hampshire—Nicholas Gilman; New York—John Hathorn and Jeremiah Van Rensselaer; North Carolina—Timothy Bloodworth, John Sevier, and John Steele; South Carolina—Thomas Sumter; and Virginia—Isaac Coles, James Madison, Andrew Moore, John Page, and Josiah Parker.

48. The ten were: Connecticut—Jonathan Sturges and Jonathan Trumbull; Massachusetts—Fisher Ames and Elbridge Gerry; New Hampshire—Abiel Foster; New Jersey—James Schureman; New York—Egbert Benson, John Laurance, and Peter Silvester; and Virginia—Alexander White.

49. The twenty-one were: Connecticut—Benjamin Huntington and Roger Sherman; Delaware—John Vining; Maryland—Daniel Carroll and George Gale; Massachusetts—Benjamin Goodhue, Jonathan Grout, George Leonard, George Partridge, Theodore Sedgwick, and George Thacher; New Jersey—Lambert Cadwallader and Thomas Sinnickson; Pennsylvania—George Clymer, Thomas Fitzsimons, and Henry Wynkoop; South Carolina—Aedanus Burke, Daniel Huger, William L. Smith, and Thomas Tucker; and Virginia—Richard Lee.

50. The twelve were: Georgia—Abraham Baldwin; Maryland—Michael Stone; New Hampshire—Samuel Livermore; New York—William Floyd; North Carolina—John Ashe and Hugh Williamson; Pennsylvania—Daniel Hiester, Thomas Hartley, John Muhlenberg, and Thomas Scott; and Virginia—John Brown and Samuel Griffin.

51. Delaware, with only one delegate, is a necessary exception.

52. Ferguson, *Power of the Purse*, pp. 307-322, shows the importance of state interest in all but the middle states.

53. *Annals of Congress*, 1st Cong., 2d sess., p. 1710. July 24, 1790.

54. Ibid., p. 1712. July 26, 1790.

55. Jacob E. Cooke, "The Compromise of 1790," *William and Mary Quarterly*, 3rd Ser., 27 (October 1970), pp. 523-545.

56. Charles, *Origins of the American Party System*, p. 21.

57. *Annals of Congress*, 1st Cong., 1st sess., 3d sess., pp. 777, 928, and 1884. August 22 and September 28, 1789; and January 25, 1791.

58. Ibid., p. 618. July 1, 1789. Also see Chapter 6.

59. *Annals of Congress*, 2d Cong., 2d sess., p. 846. January 28, 1793.

60. Ibid., p. 842. January 25, 1793.

61. Ibid., pp. 843, 844, 850, and 851. January 24, 25, and 28, 1793.

62. *Annals of Congress*, 3d Cong., 1st sess., pp. 685, 1311-1312. December 4, 1793 and April 8, 1794.

63. Ibid., pp. 686-687 and 696. May 14 and 16, 1794.

64. *Annals of Congress*, 1st Cong., 3d sess., pp. 1894, 1902, and 1960. February 2, 3, and 8, 1791. *Journal of Congress*, 1st Cong., 3d sess., p. 240. February 8, 1791.

65. *Annals of Congress*, 2d Cong., 1st sess., p. 486. March 26, 1792. The vote for establishment of a national mint was 32 to 22. On the cotton duty question proponents and opponents polarized against each other on 85 percent of all roll calls involving economic issues but on less than half of all other roll calls.

66. *Journal of Congress*, 4th Cong., 1st sess., p. 577. May 25, 1796. The vote was 45 to 35 for selling government held shares of bank stock. *Annals of Congress*, 4th Cong., 1st sess., p. 1472. May 28, 1796. The vote was 45 to 35 for letting shares in government debt sell below par.

67. *Annals of Congress*, 6th Cong., 1st sess., 2d sess., pp. 508, 534, and 1061. January 31 and February 21, 1800; and February 27, 1801.

Chapter 6: The Search for Security, Wealth, and Peace

1. The standard sources are: Samuel Flagg Bemis, *Jay's Treaty: A Study in Commerce and Diplomacy* (New Haven: Yale University Press, 1962; rev. ed.); Alfred Burt, *The United States, Great Britain, and British North America from the Revolution to the Establishment of Peace after the War of 1812* (New Haven: Yale University Press, 1940); Jerald A. Combs, *The Jay Treaty: Political Battleground of the Founding Fathers* (Berkeley: University of California Press, 1970); Alexander DeConde, *Entangling Alliance: Politics and Diplomacy under George Washington* (Durham: Duke University Press, 1958) and *The Quasi-War: The Politics and Diplo-*

macy of the Undeclared War with France 1797-1801 (New York: Charles Scribner's Sons, 1966); and Bradford Perkins, *The First Rapproachement: England and the United States, 1795-1805* (Philadelphia: University of Pennsylvania Press, 1955).

2. *Annals of Congress,* 1st Cong., 1st sess., pp. 102-366, especially pp. 201-206, for Madison on tariff discrimination.

3. Ibid., pp. 615-618, for speeches by John Vining and John Page on this point.

4. Ibid., p. 618. July 1, 1789. The states voted as follows: Connecticut 4-1, Georgia 3-0, Delaware 0-1, Maryland 2-3, Massachusetts 6-1, New Hampshire 2-0, New Jersey 2-1, New York 4-1, Pennsylvania 2-4, South Carolina 3-1, and Virginia 3-6.

5. DeConde, *Entangling Alliance,* p. 75.

6. Combs, *The Jay Treaty,* p. 33.

7. *Annals of Congress,* 1st Cong., 2d sess., pp. 1570-1573, 1653-1656. May 13, June 25, 28, and 30, 1790. The initial margin for discrimination was 32 to 19. The final vote against discrimination was not recorded, but the debate implies that southerners again defected.

8. Ibid., p. 1657.

9. *Annals of Congress,* 1st Cong., 3d sess., pp. 1962 and 1969. Madison himself was on the committee, but his only supporter was John Vining of Delaware. The other members—Benjamin Goodhue, Thomas Fitzsimons, Benjamin Bourn, John Laurance, and William L. Smith—strongly opposed commercial retaliation. Combs, *The Jay Treaty,* p. 58, implies more support for Madison's position at this time, but the evidence he cites leads to the opposite conclusion.

10. *Annals of Congress,* 2d Cong., 1st sess., pp. 456-457. March 10, 1792.

11. The fullest account is Charles Thomas, *American Neutrality in 1793: A Study in Cabinet Government* (New York: Columbia University Press, 1931).

12. *Annals of Congress,* 3d Cong., 1st sess., p. 154. January 2, 1794.

13. Ibid., pp. 174-430. January 3 through February 5, 1794.

14. Ibid., pp. 529-530. March 22 and 25, 1794. Combs, *The Jay Treaty,* pp. 120-122, recognizes that the embargo applied to all ships; nevertheless, he places the measure within a broad fabric of anti-British actions. The critical point here is whether there ever existed a majority willing to fundamentally alter Anglo-American trade patterns. Combs accepts Madison's statement that such a majority existed.

15. *Annals of Congress,* 3d Cong., 1st sess., pp. 556-557. March 31, 1794.

16. Ibid., pp. 596, 600, 602, and 604-605. April 15, 18, and 21, 1794. For Senate rejection, see ibid., pp. 89-90. April 25, 1794.

17. For continued willingness to talk, see ibid., p. 716. May 23, 1794. For refusals to act, see ibid., pp. 672, 682, and 683. May 10 and 12, 1794.

18. The forty-one were: Georgia—Abraham Baldwin and Thomas Carnes; Kentucky—Christopher Greenup and Alexander Orr; Maryland—Gabriel Christie; Massachusetts—William Lyman; New Jersey—Abraham Clark; New York—Theodore Bailey and Thomas Tredwell; North Carolina—Thomas Blount, James Gillespie, William Grove, Matthew Locke, Nathaniel Macon, Alexander Mebane, Benjamin Williams, and Joseph Winston; Pennsylvania—William Findley, Andrew Gregg, William Irvine, William Montgomery, and John Smilie; South Carolina—John Hunter and Andrew Pickens; Vermont—Israel Smith; and Virginia—Isaac Coles, William Giles, George Hancock, Carter Harrison, John Heath, James Madison, Andrew Moore, Joseph Neville, Anthony New, John Nicholas, John Page, Josiah Parker, Francis Preston, Robert Rutherford, Abraham Venable, and Francis Parker.

19. The thirty-three were: Connecticut—Joshua Coit, James Hillhouse, Amasa Learned, Zephaniah Swift, Uriah Tracy, Jonathan Trumbull, and Peleg Wadsworth; Maryland—Uriah Forrest and William Hindman; Massachusetts—Fisher Ames, Sheasabub Bourne, David Cobb, Peleg Coffin, Samuel Dexter, Dwight Foster, Benjamin Goodhue, Samuel Holton, Theodore Sedgwick, George Thacher, Jeremiah Wadsworth, and Artemus Ward; New Jersey—Elias Boudinot; New York—Ezekiel Gilbert, Henry Glen, James Gordon, Silas Talbot, John Van Alen, and John Watts; Pennsylvania—John Kittera; Rhode Island—Benjamin Bourn and Francis Malbone; South Carolina—William L. Smith; and Virginia—Richard Lee.

20. There were sixteen moderately pro-Jefferson delegates: Maryland—George Dent, Samuel Smith, and Thomas Sprigg; Massachusetts—Henry Dearborn; New Hampshire—Nicholas Gilman and John Sherburne; New Jersey—John Beatty; New York—Philip Van Cortlandt; North Carolina—William Dawson and Joseph McDowell; Pennsylvania—James Armstrong, John Muhlenberg, and Thomas Scott; South Carolina—Richard Winn; and Virginia—Thomas Claiborne and Samuel Griffin.

There were ten moderately pro-administration delegates: Delaware—Henry Latimer; Maryland—William Vans Murray; New Hampshire—Jeremiah Smith and Paine Wingate; New Jersey—Lambert Cadwallader and Jonathan Dayton; New York—Peter Van Gaasbeck; and Pennsylvania—Thomas Fitzsimons, Thomas Hartley, and Daniel Hiester.

21. Combs, *The Jay Treaty,* p. 158.

22. See Chapter 3 on this point.

23. Stephen Kurtz, *The Presidency of John Adams* (Philadelphia: University of Pennsylvania Press, 1957), pp. 55 and 67. For another view, see Combs, *The Jay Treaty,* p. 172. He contends that "The idea that Madison and the Republicans in the House were not determined to overthrow the

treaty arose from a gross misunderstanding of Republican tactics in the congressional debates. A close examination of the House fight will demonstrate that Madison and the Republicans were dead serious in their attempt to destroy the treaty."

24. *Annals of Congress,* 4th Cong., 1st sess., p. 1157. April 22, 1796.

25. The twenty-nine and the areas they represented were: Connecticut—Samuel Dana of Middlesex, James Davenport of Fairfield, and Chauncey Goodrich of Hartford; Maryland—William Craik of Frederick, George Dent of Charles, William Hindman of Talbot, William Vans Murray of Dorchester, and Samuel Smith of Baltimore; Massachusetts—Theodore Bradbury of Essex, Dwight Foster of Worcester, Samuel Sewall of Suffolk, and George Thacher of Maine; New Hampshire—Abiel Foster of Rockingham and Nicholas Gilman of Rockingham; New Jersey—Mark Thomson of Sussex; New York—William Cooper of Otsego, Ezekiel Gilbert of Columbia, Henry Glen of Albany, Edward Livingston of New York City, and John Van Alen of Rensselaer; North Carolina—Dempsey Burges of Camden; Pennsylvania—Thomas Hartley of York, Samuel Sitgreaves of Northampton, John Swanwick of Philadelphia, and Richard Thomas of Chester; Rhode Island—Francis Malbone of Providence; South Carolina—Robert Harper and William L. Smith of Charleston; and Virginia—Josiah Parker of Isle of Wight.

26. *Annals of Congress,* 4th Cong., 1st sess., 2d sess., pp. 886, 891, 893, 2148-2150, 2208, and 2351. April 8 and 9, 1796; February 11 and 18 and March 2, 1797.

27. The seventeen and the areas they represented were: Connecticut—Joshua Coit of New London; Maryland—Gabriel Christie of Baltimore; Massachusetts—William Lyman of Worcester; New York—Theodore Bailey of Dutchess, Jonathan Havens of Suffolk, and John Williams of Washington; North Carolina—Nathan Bryan of Jones and James Holland of Rutherford; Pennsylvania—Albert Gallatin of Fayette and Samuel Maclay of Franklin; South Carolina—Wade Hampton of Richland; Vermont—Israel Smith of Rutland; and Virginia—John Clopton of New Kent, Isaac Coles of Halifax, William Giles of Amelia, George Jackson of Wood, and Anthony New of Glocester.

28. *Annals of Congress,* 4th Cong., 1st sess., 2d sess., pp. 886, 891, 893, and 2149-2150. April 8 and 9, 1796 and February 11, 1797.

29. John Williams voted against the Livingston Resolution and for the Jay Treaty.

30. *Annals of Congress,* 5th Cong., 1st sess., pp. 267, 297, 324, 347, 385, 391, 392, 430, 443, and 446. June 8, 10, 16, 20, 24, 27 and July 1, 4, and 5, 1797.

31. The ten groups are the result of applying the highest possible test of cohesiveness; that is, each of the groups voted in the same way more often

than any other combination of delegates. If one delegate were to be moved from one group to another, cohesion levels would be lower.

32. The twenty-seven were: Connecticut—John Allen, Samuel Dana, James Davenport, Chauncey Goodrich, and Nathaniel Smith; Delaware—James Bayard; Maryland—John Dennis, William Hindman, and William Matthews; Massachusetts—Theodore Bradbury, Dwight Foster, Samuel Sewall, William Shepard, George Thacher, and Peleg Wadsworth; New Hampshire—Abiel Foster, William Gordon, and Jeremiah Smith; New Jersey—James Imlay, James Schureman, Thomas Sinnickson, and Mark Thomson; New York—Hezekiel Hosmer; Pennsylvania—Samuel Sitgreaves; Rhode Island—Christopher Champlin; and South Carolina—John Rutledge and William L. Smith.

33. Two types of evidence lead to this conclusion. One is that there are obvious differences in the economic characteristics of these three states. The second, and more significant, is that these states had not exhibited cohesive voting patterns in earlier Congresses (see, in particular, votes on taxation in the Third Congress, discussed in the preceding chapter).

34. The "revival" of 1798, led by establishment clergy such as Timothy Dwight, Jedidiah Morse, and Josiah Strong, injected religion sharply into the political process.

35. The eight were: Maryland—George Baer and William Craik; Massachusetts—Harrison Gray Otis and John Reed; Pennsylvania—Thomas Hartley; South Carolina—Robert Harper; and Virginia—Thomas Evans and James Machir.

36. The six were: Massachusetts—Samuel Lyman; New York—John Williams; Pennsylvania—John Kittera and Richard Thomas; Rhode Island—Elisha Potter; and Virginia—Daniel Morgan.

37. The seventeen were: Georgia—John Milledge; Kentucky—Thomas Davis and John Fowler; Maryland—George Dent and Samuel Smith; New York—Lucas Elmendorf; North Carolina—Dempsey Burges, James Gillespie, William Grove, and Robert Williams; Pennsylvania—John Hanna and John Swanwick; and Virginia—Carter Harrison, David Holmes, John Nicholas, Josiah Parker, and John Trigg.

38. The seven were: Maryland—Richard Sprigg; Massachusetts—Nathaniel Freeman; North Carolina—Nathan Bryan and Richard Stanford; South Carolina—William Smith (Pinckney District); Vermont—Matthew Lyon; and Virginia—Walter Jones.

39. The seven were: Connecticut—Joshua Coit; Massachusetts—Joseph Varnum; North Carolina—John Dawson; Pennsylvania—John Chapman and Andrew Gregg; South Carolina—Thomas Sumter; and Virginia—John Dawson.

40. Manning Dauer, *The Adams Federalists* (Baltimore: The Johns Hopkins Press, 1953), pp. 132 and 268.

41. The ten were: New York—Jonathan Havens; North Carolina—

Matthew Locke, Nathaniel Macon, and Joseph McDowell; Pennsylvania—David Bard; and Virginia—Richard Brent, Thomas Claiborne, William Giles, Anthony New, and Abraham Venable.

42. The votes of the ten on key roll calls in earlier Congresses were as follows: Livingston Resolution, 9–0; implementing the Jay Treaty, 0–9; surveying 160-acre tracts in the West, 7–1; reducing the military establishment, 7–0; and condemning Democratic Societies on the Whiskey Rebellion, 0–7.

43. The six were: Connecticut—Roger Griswold; New York—Edward Livingston and Philip Van Cortlandt; Pennsylvania—George Ege; and Virginia—Matthew Clay and Abraham Trigg.

44. The nine were Bayard, Bradbury, D. Foster, Goodrich, Gordon, Schureman, Sewall, N. Smith, and Thomson.

45. The eleven were Dennis, D. Foster, Matthews, Rutledge, Schureman, Sewall, Shepard, Sinnickson, J. Smith, N. Smith, and Thomson.

46. The eight were Bayard, Champlin, A. Foster, D. Foster, Hosmer, Sitgreaves, N. Smith, and W. L. Smith.

47. The apparent breaks on roll calls 28 and 29 are caused by the assumption made at the outset that the majority of Group 1 represented the administration position. In fact, on these two roll calls to eliminate exemptions from the stamp tax, the position of the majority of Group 10 and of Group 1 were the same; both opposed exemptions for bank notes and military lands. The factions that operated on roll calls 28 and 29 were motivated by their commitment to banking and to speculation in western lands and they are, therefore, outside the framework of this entire analysis, which is based on positions with regard to war against France. These two roll calls, the only ones recorded during the session that brought monetary interests to the foreground, are insignificant compared with the main issue of the session. It is of note, however, that factions which appeared indestructible on certain issues melted away on others.

48. The five were Bard, Giles, Macon, McDowell, and Venable.

49. The three were Locke, Macon, and Venable.

50. The four were Giles, Locke, Macon, and McDowell.

51. Dauer, *The Adams Federalists*, pp. 171 and 269.

52. Matthew Clay, William Findley, Edward Livingston, and Abraham Trigg generally opposed the administration. Jonathan Dayton, who did not vote because of his position as Speaker, Lewis Morris, Thomas Pinckney, and Peleg Sprague all supported the Adams program.

53. The eleven were Bartlett, Dana, Imlay, Hosmer, Matthews, Rutledge, Sewall, Schureman, Shepard, Sinnickson, and N. Smith.

54. *Journal of Congress*, 5th Cong., 2d sess., pp. 297–298 and 338. May 17 and June 15, 1798.

55. The nine were D. Foster, Goodrich, Griswold, Hindman, Imlay, Morris, I. Parker, Sitgreaves, and Thacher.

56. Dauer, *The Adams Federalists*, pp. 141–142. DeConde, *The Quasi-War*, pp. 71–72. DeConde's appraisal is partially based upon and agrees with Dauer.

57. Supporters of restricting naval combat were Bartlett, Hosmer, Matthews, and Rutledge. They were joined at least once in voting for army restrictions by Allen, Bayard, Dennis, and Wadsworth.

58. The exceptions were: Claiborne's vote to suspend trade with France (roll call 78), Bard's vote to allow capture of unarmed French vessels (roll call 97), and Venable's vote against authorizing Gerry to continue negotiations (roll call 98).

59. *Annals of Congress*, 5th Cong., 3d sess., pp. 2790–2791 and 2822. January 25 and 28 and February 7, 1799.

60. Ibid., pp. 2953, 3018, and 3042. February 20 and 26 and March 1, 1799.

61. The ten factions isolated during the 1797 session are continued, with the following additions: Jonathan Brace to Group 1 (replaced Joshua Coit); Robert Brown to Group 5 (replaced Samuel Sitgreaves); Stephen Bullock to Group 1 (previously unclassifiable); Matthew Clay to Group 5 (previously absent frequently); Joseph Eggleston to Group 10 (replaced William Giles); William Findley to Group 10 (previously absent frequently); Edward Livingston to Group 10 (previously absent frequently); Lewis Morris to Group 1 (previously absent frequently); Thomas Pinckney to Group 1 (previously absent frequently); Richard Spaight to Group 2 (replaced Nathan Bryan); Peleg Sprague to Group 2 (previously absent frequently); Thomas Tillinghast to Group 1 (previously unclassifiable); Abraham Trigg to Group 10 (previously absent frequently); and Robert Waln to Group 1 (replaced John Swanwick). Additions are based on voting during the third session of the Fifth Congress.

62. There were no occasions on which both blocs divided internally on the same roll call.

63. See Chapter 3 for a detailed analysis of these roll calls.

64. *Annals of Congress*, 6th Cong., 1st sess., p. 531. February 20, 1800.

65. The twenty-eight were: Kentucky—John Fowler; Maryland—Gabriel Christie; Massachusetts—Joseph Varnum; New York—Theodore Bailey, Lucas Elmendorf, Edward Livingston, and Philip Van Cortlandt; North Carolina—Nathaniel Macon, David Stone, and Robert Williams; Pennsylvania—Robert Brown, Andrew Gregg, John Hanna, Michael Leib, and John Muhlenberg; South Carolina—Thomas Sumter; Vermont—Matthew Lyon; and Virginia—Samuel Cabell, Matthew Clay, John Dawson, Joseph Eggleston, David Holmes, George Jackson, Anthony New, John Nicholas, John Randolph, Abraham Trigg, and John Trigg.

66. The seventeen were: Georgia—James Jones; Kentucky—Thomas Davis; Maryland—Joseph Nicholson and Samuel Smith; Massachusetts—

Phaneul Bishop; New Jersey—Aaron Kitchell and James Linn; New York—
John Condit, John Smith, and John Thompson; North Carolina—Willis
Alston and Richard Stanford; Pennsylvania—Albert Gallatin, Joseph
Hiester, and John Smilie; South Carolina—Abraham Nott; and Tennessee—
William Claiborne.

   67. *Annals of Congress,* 6th Cong., 1st sess., p. 714. May 10, 1800.
   68. Ibid., 6th Cong., 2d sess., pp. 1058 and 1061. February 26 and 27,
1801.
   69. The thirty-one were: Connecticut—Roger Griswold; Delaware—
James Bayard; Georgia—Benjamin Taliaferro; Maryland—George Baer,
William Craik, John Dennis, George Dent, and John Thomas; Massachu-
setts—Bailey Bartlett, Silas Lee, Levi Lincoln, Ebenezer Mattoon, Nathan
Read, John Reed, William Shepard, George Thacher, and Lemuel Williams;
New Hampshire—Samuel Tenney; North Carolina—William Grove, Archi-
bald Henderson, William Hill, and Richard Spaight; Pennsylvania—John
Kittera, John Stewart, and Robert Waln; Rhode Island—John Brown;
South Carolina—Robert Harper; Vermont—Lewis Morris; and Virginia—
Thomas Evans, Levi Powell, and Littleton Tazewell.
   70. The thirty-six were: Connecticut—Jonathan Brace, Samuel Dana,
John Davenport, William Edmond, Chauncey Goodrich, Elizur Goodrich,
and John Smith; Massachusetts—Dwight Foster, Samuel Lyman, Harrison
Gray Otis, Theodore Sedgwick, Samuel Sewall, and Peleg Wadsworth; New
Hampshire—Abiel Foster, William Gordon, and James Sheafe; New Jersey—
Francis Davenport and James Imlay; New York—John Bird, William
Cooper, Henry Glen, and Jonathan Platt; North Carolina—Joseph Dickson;
Pennsylvania—Thomas Hartley, Richard Thomas, and Henry Woods;
Rhode Island—Christopher Champlin; South Carolina—Benjamin Huger,
Thomas Pinckney, and John Rutledge; and Virginia—Samuel Goode, Ed-
win Gray, Henry Lee, John Marshall, Robert Page, and Josiah Parker.

Chapter 7: The Triumph of Party

   1. Richard P. McCormick, *The Second American Party System: Party
Formation in the Jacksonian Era* (Chapel Hill: University of North Carolina Press, 1966). See p. 26 for the author's application of this thesis to
the first party system.
   2. William N. Chambers, *Political Parties in A New Nation: The American Experience, 1776–1809* (New York: Oxford University Press, 1963),
p. 39.
   3. The error receives well-deserved attention from David H. Fischer,
Historians' Fallacies: Toward A Logic of Historical Thought (New York:
Harper & Row, 1970), pp. 167–169. Contrary to the impression left by

Fischer, in addition to simple correlation analysis, the statistician has the techniques of partial correlation and multiple regression available to aid in the dismissal of spurious or casual relationships. See Appendix III.

NOTE ON SOURCES

The standard source for congressional proceedings for this period, cited as *Annals of Congress*, is U.S. Congress, *The Debates and Proceedings in the Congress of the United States, 1789–1824* (Washington: Gales and Seaton, 1834–1856). For additional roll calls and to correct an error rate of nearly 2 percent in the *Annals*, this should be supplemented by U.S. House of Representatives, *Journal of the House of Representatives of the United States, 1789–1815* (Washington: Gales and Seaton, 1826).

Voting blocs were selected by starting with the two groups defined by affirmative and negative votes on each roll call and, for each pair, adding roll calls on which the two groups polarized above a level set by the researcher. Scores for each individual on these related sets of roll calls were examined and, where appropriate, polarity was calculated for *n* groups set apart by cohesion level. Additional blocs were formed for personal characteristics, geographic location, election pattern, and party affiliation. The computer programs for the procedure are available at the Rutgers University Computation Center.

Any study of American politics at the national level must begin with an understanding of state and local politics. The most important works for the early national years are: on New England, James Truslow Adams, *New England in the Republic, 1776–1850* (Boston: Little and Brown, 1926); James M. Banner, Jr., *To The Hartford Convention* (New York: Alfred A. Knopf, 1969); Paul Goodman, *The Democratic Republicans of Massachusetts: Politics in A Young Republic* (Cambridge: Harvard University Press, 1964); Van Beck Hall, *Politics Without Parties: Massachusetts, 1780–1791* (Pittsburgh: University of Pittsburgh Press, 1972); David Ludlum, *Social Ferment in Vermont, 1791–1850* (New York: Columbia University Press, 1939); Anson E. Morse, *The Federalist Party in Massachusetts to the Year 1800* (Princeton: University Library, 1909); Irwin Polishook, *Rhode Island and the Union, 1774–1795* (Evanston: Northwestern University Press, 1969); Richard J. Purcell, *Connecticut in Transition, 1775–1818* (Middletown: Wesleyan University Press, 1963); on the middle states, Walter R. Fee, *The Transition from Aristocracy to Democracy in New Jersey, 1789–1829* (Somerville: Somerset Press, 1933); Russell Ferguson, *Early Western*

Pennsylvania Politics (Pittsburgh: University of Pittsburgh Press, 1938); Dixon Ryan Fox, *The Decline of Aristocracy in the Politics of New York, 1801–1840* (New York: Longmans, Green and Co., 1919); John A. Munroe, *Federalist Delaware, 1775–1815* (New Brunswick: Rutgers University Press, 1954); Carl Prince, *New Jersey's Jeffersonian Republicans: The Genius of Early Party Machinery, 1789–1817* (Chapel Hill: University of North Carolina Press, 1967); Earl B. Thomas, *Political Tendencies in Pennsylvania, 1783–1794* (Philadelphia: Temple University Press, 1939); Harry M. Tinkcom, *The Republicans and Federalists in Pennsylvania, 1790–1801: A Study in National Stimulus and Local Response* (Harrisburg: Pennsylvania Historical Museum Commission, 1950); Alfred F. Young, "The Mechanics and the Jeffersonians: New York, 1789–1801," *Labor History* (1964), 247–276; Alfred Young, *The Democratic Republicans of New York: The Origins, 1763–1797* (Chapel Hill: University of North Carolina Press, 1967); on the southern states, Charles H. Ambler, *Sectionalism in Virginia from 1776–1851* (Chicago: University of Chicago Press, 1910); Harry Ammon, "The Formation of the Republican Party in Virginia, 1789–1796," *Journal of Southern History* 19 (1953), 283–310 and "The Jeffersonian Republicans in Virginia: An Interpretation," *Virginia Magazine of History and Biography* 71 (1963), 153–167; Delbert Gilpatrick, *Jeffersonian Democracy in North Carolina* (New York: Columbia University Press, 1931); Gilbert Lycan, "Alexander Hamilton and the North Carolina Federalists," *North Carolina Historical Review* 25 (1948), 442–465; Ulrich B. Phillips, "The South Carolina Federalists," *American Historical Review* 14 (1909), 529–543 and 731–743; J. R. Pole, "Constitutional Reform and Election Statistics in Maryland, 1790–1812," *Maryland Historical Magazine* 55 (1960), 275–292; Lucien E. Roberts, "Sectional Problems in Georgia During the Formative Period, 1776–1798," *Georgia Historical Quarterly* 18 (1934), 207–227; Lisle A. Rose, *Prologue to Democracy: The Federalists in the South, 1789–1800* (Lexington: University of Kentucky Press, 1968); John H. Wolfe, *Jeffersonian Democracy in South Carolina* (Chapel Hill: University of North Carolina Press, 1940).

Biographical material on congressmen is painstakingly collected in B. B. Lightfoot, "The State Delegations in The Congress of the United States, 1789–1801" (PhD thesis in 2 vols., University of Texas, 1958). In the last decade scholars have given considerable attention to "second-line" figures, and in the process they have added great depth to the meaning of party attachment, especially for Federalists. Examples of these recent works are Winfred Bernhard, *Fisher Ames, Federalist and Statesman, 1758–1808* (Chapel Hill: University of North Carolina Press, 1965); Morton Borden, *The Federalism of James A. Bayard* (New York: Columbia University Press, 1955); Chester M. Destler, *Joshua Coit, American Federalist, 1758–1798* (Middletown: Wesleyan University Press, 1962); Robert Ernst, *Rufus*

King, American Federalist (Chapel Hill: University of North Carolina Press, 1968); Donald Higginbotham, *Daniel Morgan, Revolutionary Rifleman* (Chapel Hill: University of North Carolina Press, 1961); George C. Rogers, Jr., *William Loughton Smith of Charleston: Evolution of A Federalist, 1758-1812* (Columbia: University of South Carolina Press, 1962); Richard E. Welch, Jr., *Theodore Sedgwick, Federalist: A Political Portrait* (Middletown: Wesleyan University Press, 1964); Marvin Zahniser, *Charles Cotesworth Pinckney: Founding Father* (Chapel Hill: University of North Carolina Press, 1967).

Politics in the 1790s has received extensive treatment in Sidney H. Aronson, *Status and Kinship in the Higher Civil Service: Standards of Selection in the Administrations of John Adams, Thomas Jefferson, and Andrew Jackson* (Cambridge: Harvard University Press, 1964); John S. Bassett, *The Federalist System, 1789-1801* (New York: Harper and Brothers, 1906); Charles A. Beard, *Economic Origins of Jeffersonian Democracy* (New York: Macmillan, 1915); Richard Buel, Jr., *Securing the Revolution: Ideology in American Politics, 1789-1815* (Ithaca: Cornell University Press, 1972); William N. Chambers, *Political Parties in a New Nation: The American Experience, 1776-1809* (New York: Oxford University Press, 1963); Joseph Charles, *The Origins of the American Party System: Three Essays* (Williamsburg: Institute of Early American History and Culture, 1956); Noble E. Cunningham, *The Jeffersonian Republicans: The Formation of Party Organization, 1789-1801* (Chapel Hill: University of North Carolina Press, 1957); Manning Dauer, *The Adams Federalists* (Baltimore: The Johns Hopkins Press, 1953); Bernard Fay, "Early Party Machinery in the United States in the Election of 1796," *Pennsylvania Magazine of History and Biography* 60 (1936), 375–390; David H. Fischer, *The Revolution of American Conservatism: The Federalist Party in the Era of Jeffersonian Democracy* (New York: Harper and Row, 1965); Linda K. Kerber, *Federalists in Dissent: Imagery and Ideology in Jeffersonian America* (Ithaca: Cornell University Press, 1970); Richard Hofstadter, *The Idea of A Party System: The Rise of Legitimate Opposition in the United States, 1780-1840* (Berkeley: University of California Press, 1969); Stephen G. Kurtz, *The Presidency of John Adams: The Collapse of Federalism, 1795-1800* (New York: A. S. Barnes, 1961); Orin G. Libby, "Political Factions in Washington's Administration," *Quarterly Journal of the University of North Dakota* 3 (1912), 293–318; Donald H. Stewart, *The Opposition Press of the Federalist Period* (Albany: State University of New York Press, 1969).

INDEX